ENGAGING CULTURE, RACE AND SPIRITUALITY

Studies in the
Postmodern Theory of Education

Shirley R. Steinberg
General Editor

Vol. 454

The Counterpoints series is part of the Peter Lang Education list.
Every volume is peer reviewed and meets
the highest quality standards for content and production.

PETER LANG
New York • Washington, D.C./Baltimore • Bern
Frankfurt • Berlin • Brussels • Vienna • Oxford

Engaging Culture, Race and Spirituality

New Visions

Edited by Cynthia B. Dillard and Chinwe L. Ezueh Okpalaoka

PETER LANG
New York • Washington, D.C./Baltimore • Bern
Frankfurt • Berlin • Brussels • Vienna • Oxford

Library of Congress Cataloging-in-Publication Data

Engaging culture, race and spirituality: new visions /
edited by Cynthia B. Dillard, Chinwe L. Ezueh Okpalaoka.
pages cm. — (Counterpoints: studies in the postmodern theory of education; vol. 454)
Includes bibliographical references.
1. African American women—Education (Higher)
2. Feminism and education—United States.
3. Discrimination in higher education—United States. 4. Blacks—Race identity.
5. Spiritual life—United States. I. Dillard, Cynthia B.
LC2781.E58   378.1'98296073—dc23   2013008618
ISBN 978-1-4331-2328-3 (hardcover)
ISBN 978-1-4331-2327-6 (paperback)
ISBN 978-1-4539-1121-1 (e-book)
ISSN 1058-1634

Bibliographic information published by **Die Deutsche Nationalbibliothek**.
Die Deutsche Nationalbibliothek lists this publication in the "Deutsche
Nationalbibliografie"; detailed bibliographic data is available
on the Internet at http://dnb.d-nb.de/.

The paper in this book meets the guidelines for permanence and durability
of the Committee on Production Guidelines for Book Longevity
of the Council of Library Resources.

This book is dedicated to brilliant writer, activist,
wise woman, and muse,
Alice Walker,
who reminds us,
"We are the ones we've been waiting for."

Contents

Acknowledgments

The work reflected in these pages could not have been accomplished without the support of family, friends, and colleagues who have shared in the labor of love that goes into the birth of any book.

First, to the Creator, who continues by the gift of breath to remind us that we have work to do on this earthly journey and supports us in getting it done;

To the chapter contributors—Tami Augustine, Eyatta Fischer, Brooke Harris Garad, Gilbert Kaburu, Chris Landauer, Angela Lynskey, Ashley Patterson, Erica Womack, and Deb Zurmehly—for boldly embracing the challenge of difficult dialogues and not being afraid to creatively tackle the topics of culture, race, and spirituality: The proof is evidenced in your diverse and insightful contributions in this volume;

To other members of the Spirit, Race and Dialogue seminar: David To, Heather Hill, Seunghye Kim, Colby Hirn, and Umi Retnaningsih. Your contributions were not unnoticed: They are echoed here in *every* page;

To Dr. Barbara Seidl, whose honest dialogues about culture, race, and spirituality served as inspiration for us throughout the process of this book-making and in our lives;

To the Visionaries: Robin Boylorn, Barbara Dray, Marcelle Haddix, Khosi Kubeka, Bettina Love, Samara Madrid, and Carmen Medina. Thank you for saying *yes*. Your beautifully crafted responses to these chapters have extended the dialogue around spirit and race and exemplify the harmony of the human spirit that really *can* transcend difference and;

To Chris Myers, Managing Director, and to Shirley Steinburg, Cultural Counterpoint Series Editor, at Peter Lang Publishing for their vision and support in pushing the critical dialogue around culture, race, and spirit.

Cynthia: I wish to acknowledge my husband, Henry Oppong: You are God's love personified. I am grateful to walk with you in all things, including this birth of our third book!

Chinwe: And I wish to acknowledge Osita Okpalaoka, my husband and partner in life's journey, and our children, Ugonna, Chineze, Dubem, and Amara, who share the journey with us.

Cover Photo Acknowledgment

Cover art: Many thanks to Tami Augustine for sharing this image from her personal collection. The photograph was taken at Acadia National Park in Maine.

Foreword

H. Richard Milner, IV

In his speech, *A Talk to Teachers*, James Baldwin (1963) profoundly spoke to teachers about Black children and what was necessary for them to succeed in educational systems. The talk was bold and important, especially at that time, because he dared to shed light on perspectives, realities, experiences, ideas, and ideals that were laced with politically incorrect themes. One salient theme of the talk was race and how teachers and other educators failed to understand how sociological and psychological matters influenced Black people. The talk was especially illuminating because he spoke about Black students' reactions through their behaviors, albeit implicitly or unknowingly, to hegemonic structures and systems that attempted to socialize them but rarely if ever provided the kinds of learning environments that supported students to reach their full capacity to succeed. Even knowing that they were a tenacious group of people, Baldwin questioned how Black students in the United States could maintain their sanity and not become "schizophrenic" (p. 146) when indeed the educational system, as he knew it, was not designed for them. It was a miracle, he suggested, that Black students and Black people in the US were able to maintain their sanity in a system that did not even recognize them as whole human beings. A central point of Baldwin's speech was that Black students persisted and were resilient *in spite of* their schooling experiences not *because of* it.

But what happens when Black students' resilience wanes, and they begin to believe the untruths about themselves, their potential, their assets, and their overall contributions to humankind? What happens when students begin to believe they are as Baldwin questioned "less than human" (p. 150) because their lived experiences and views are inconsistent with and run precisely counter to the White majority? Similar questions, I argue, can be posed about those of us—especially Black academics—who engage and conduct educational research. What Baldwin challenged educators to think about is the salient role race plays in the educational experiences of Black people.

Key questions for scholarship are these: What happens to people when their worldviews, ontologies, and overall paradigms run counter to an established system of inquiry and knowledge construction that were not created for them or by them from the outset? Do they create their own space of reality, or do they falter to believe what others have decided for them in the name of adhering to a predetermined set of guidelines? What keeps us going, as educational researchers, when we are knocked down, knocked out, and not expected to get up and get back into the work we are supposed to do? Underlying these questions are questions of the spirit. In this volume, Dillard and Okpalaoka along with their scholar-colleagues engage these questions in provocative and important ways. Similar to Baldwin, they speak truth to power especially regarding the intersected nature of race and spirituality in ways that will surely advance what we know and need to know and understand about researching and teaching the self and others. And although Baldwin's speech was written many years ago, Dillard and Okpalaoka have answered his "call" to examine the ways in which race intersects with other important aspects of the human experience because the challenges Baldwin outlined remain very salient today. *Engaging Culture, Race and Spirituality in Education* brings together an all-star group of budding scholars and more seasoned responders to address important questions that will leave readers reexamining their own work in education in order to more deeply understand it. While questions about the nature of reality and knowledge construction are prevalent in the educational discourse, what this volume provides pushes beyond the more established themes related to race and culture. By placing spirituality at the center, this volume addresses tensions related to epistemology, ontology, axiology and worldview in new and provocative ways. Indeed, important questions explored in this volume include: Why do Black people persist in the midst of difficult situations? From where does their resilience come? How do we teach and research about the intersected nature of race and spirituality? And how do we engage in conversations within ourselves and with others to move us closer to emancipation but also closer to knowing more about the *human* condition? This is an important volume that inspires and teaches readers as it simultaneously convicts us—educational researchers, teachers, and theorists in particular—to action. It challenges readers to not only know more but to do more and to do better!

My grandmother and great-grandmother, who were born and raised in the racist and segregated Jim Crow South often talked about their persistence and survival through race, racism and other forms of discrimination unlike any I have encountered in my years on earth. Their resilience, they professed unwaveringly, came from God, from their spirituality. Although not rich in material possessions, from their description, they were "rich in faith." They relied on their spiritual connectedness to get them through difficult circumstances and realities. As I reflect on the stories they shared with me, it is clear that voice scholarship linking race and spirituality are understudied and grossly underreported in education. My point is not that race and spirituality are not currently as intricately connected as they were when my elders voiced their experiences. Rather, my point is that educational researchers, practitioners, policymakers, and theorists tend to shy away from these interrelated matters and especially spirituality because

- some are not aware of how to study them;
- some see an emphasis on spirituality as unscholarly;
- traditional educational research tools are not necessarily designed to focus on these matters of the "evidence of things unseen";

- instructional practices in classrooms tend to require working
  with people who have a range of different views and perceptions on topics of race and spirituality; and
- some fear institutional backlash for engaging the spirit.

But unlike the authors in this volume, what happens when we avoid discussions about spirituality because our pedagogical, epistemological,
ontological, institutional and overall paradigmatic frameworks and
toolkits do not allow us to adequately address the spirit? What gets
omitted from storylines (even when we embrace voice scholarship as a
useful space of inquiry and knowledge construction) when we do not
allow the spirit to emerge as a legitimate site of knowing and coming to
know? This question is essential both when we deductively search for
elements of knowledge construction that we seek to determine (quan-
titatively) as well as when we allow reality to emerge deductively from
the ground up (qualitatively). I have found reasons for underdevelop-
ment of scholarship and practice in education on the spirit are both
straightforward and complex. For instance, how do we study the spirit
when the tools we use are not designed to understand, nuance, measure,
or predict the nature of it? This volume demonstrates that just because
we do not know *how* to study the spirit does not mean it should not be
studied or that it is not present as essential sites of the people and places
we examine. How do we engage the spirit when traditional paradigms
in education research do not provide tools for such engagement? In
what ways might addressing the spirit (and especially studying spiritual encounters) require new or at best expansive tools? In important
ways, Dillard and Okpalaoka have provided a roadmap for tool development and the volume itself can be seen as a tool.

  Engaging Culture, Race and Spirituality in Education provides a counter-
rationale for engaging spirituality, race, and their intersection. Dillard
and Okpalaoka and the contributors of this volume challenge us to
push past the boundaries of established systems that suggest that focusing on the spirit, in particular, is unnecessary. Indeed, the breadth and
depth of topics explored in this volume are noteworthy: Teacher education, prekindergarten–12 instructional practices, global perspectives,
and (racial and gender) identity. I am particularly excited to read the

sophisticated and well-nuanced ways in which the authors engaged theory, drawing from both established theoretical frameworks and personal philosophies. Moreover, it is refreshing for me to witness myriad ways in which spirituality is taken up to expand our definitions, conceptions and lenses of the spirit and spirituality. In this volume, reflections of love, care, hope, and healing are all related to spirituality and expand the reference group of scholars who—and who *can*—engage the spirit in their work. For instance, scores of researchers have pointed to notions of care and love in their scholarly recommendations about how best to educate African Americans, just as President Barack Obama's platform of hope energized an entire country to venture into previously unseen territory. However, in the current definitions within the literature, such work may not be classified as spiritual. But researchers, theorists or practitioners interested in spirituality and/or the interrelated nature of spirituality and race will find this as an essential text in understanding and working through foundational perspectives on what *matters* in education, and more seasoned scholars will find that the volume pushes their perspectives beyond what they think they may know about the relevance of spirituality in education.

Boldly and timely, *Engaging Culture, Race and Spirituality in Education* speaks directly to the possibilities of important dialogues about spirituality and race. It tackles two distinctly contentious areas and examines their intersectionality (spirit and race), in ways that are not well established in the discourse. Like Baldwin's speech, this volume demonstrates how the dialogic can open up the realm of possibility and potential of what really matters (and should matter) in the work we do as educational researchers, theorists, and practitioners. In critically important ways, this volume addresses the power of studying, naming, critiquing, and understanding what spirituality means and could mean to engage the limits and possibilities related to culture and race in education. This book has the potential to make us better educational researchers and practitioners.

Reference

Baldwin, J. (1963). A talk to teachers. Delivered October 16, 1963, as "The Negro Child—His Self-Image." Originally published in *The Saturday Review*, December 21, 1963.

Introduction

Culture, Race, and Dialogue

Toward a Spiritual Praxis in Education

Cynthia Dillard & Chinwe L. Ezueh Okpalaoka

If there is one issue that our current social and political climates have brought to the fore, it is that race is a permanent part of our daily lives (Bell, 1992; Omi & Winant, 1994; West, 1993). In public settings, such as school classrooms and social media, and in our private lives, there is always an ongoing conversation that we have with ourselves about race. In our observations and experience, as Black women educators, what seems to be lacking in these conversations is a kind of persistence: A tacit agreement to stay until the conversation ends, even if staying creates some discomfort, renders us vulnerable (Behar, 1996). And too often, even when space has been made to engage in what seem to be difficult conversations about race, culture, and diversity, a typical outcome is a sense of futility, frustration, and hopelessness. Particularly in the academy, teachers and facilitators of discussions about race and culture often encounter a proverbial wall when, across the multitude of differences we embody, conversations about the ways we have *all* been affected by racial discourses and racism arise. The result? Too often, our conversations are mostly superficial and often solely "politically correct," as we tip-toe around but rarely address the substantive issues of race and racism that really *matter*. Sometimes the conversations even stop because we do not know how to "be" within these discourses without feeling guilty, shamed, distrustful, and angry.

The voices gathered in this volume suggest that a missing piece in our conversations about race, culture, and diversity is the need for a concomitant focus on spirituality, on how engaging the inner life might be a radical intervention in our talk about how race matters (Dillard, 2006). This is no small task, as the foundations of the academy were established to educate the mind (hooks, 1994; Palmer, 1993): The idea that the human spirit might need to be equally developed is a radical departure from these material foundations of education. Today, as in centuries before, when teachers and students enter the doors of the Western academy, there is an implicit understanding that spiritual thoughts and talk should be checked at the door (Dillard, Tyson, & Abdur-Rashid, 2000; hooks, 1994; Palmer, 1993; 2007; Tisdell, 2003). A number of scholars have attempted to understand this material versus spiritual split in the academy, expounding on the origin of the bifurcation of the material and the spiritual in Western thought (Ani, 1994; Dillard & Okpalaoka, 2011; hooks, 1994; King, 2005; Palmer, 1993; Paris, 1995; Reason, 1993). By tracing the origin of European epistemology to Platonic theory, Ani (1994) argues that European thought laid a foundation that denied "cosmic, intuitive knowledge" by advocating for a "materialization of the universe" (p. 30). The separation of the human into two distinct parts of reason and appetite (or reason and emotion) is attributed to Plato, who accorded reason a higher ranking and role than its counterpart, emotion (Boler, 1999). Ani (1994) further explains that such conceptualizations have led to "one of the most problematical dichotomies in European thought and behavior" (p. 32): a splitting of the human whole or a separation of the spirit from the matter. Miller et al. (2005) state that "our present culture is not interested in educating the *whole* person" (p. 1; emphasis ours). Dillard (2006) posits another possibility for the dearth of conversations about race and culture through discourses of spirituality: that there is still a risk to individuals who embrace an overtly spiritual paradigm in the academy. Thus, in a radical shift from normative practices in the academy where the spiritual is silenced or treated as a part of our lives that we pick up when we step outside the academy, scholars such as Dillard (2006) advocate a worldview that "is conceived as a unified spiritual whole...[where] one's self-hood is understood and constituted as body, mind, *and* spirit and affirmed in relationship to both one's group and to one's creator" (p. 32).

Spirit, Race, and Dialogue: The Course That Led to This Book

In the fall of 2011, the editors co-taught a doctoral seminar titled Spirit, Race, and Dialogue (SRD). It was a course designed to provide a space for dialogue and explorations about the pervasive individual, epistemological, structural, systemic, and institutional dimensions and complexities of race and identity from a spiritual perspective. The premise of the course was simple: While race often arose as topics within our courses in teacher education (with varying degrees of success in its unpacking), talk of spirituality was missing. So our underlying assumption in developing the course was to "talk back" to racial and cultural discourses by posing a different set of questions that addressed both our inner lives *and* the outward structures in education and society that continue to distort humanity and to support oppressive race and racial discourses and cultural knowledge. The SRD seminar was an attempt to develop new responses to old struggles with race, culture, and identities in both our everyday conversations and in the reading and conduct of research, creating new sites of possibilities, new discourses, and new understandings about race and the human condition that are informed by the foundations and theories of spirituality.

Four central questions framed this course:

1. Why are we here?
2. Why do so many feel a sense of angst and limit, especially in our dialogues around race in our work of teaching and research?
3. Is it possible to heal ourselves, our work, our understandings of each other, and our research, particularly around race?
4. How do we make a space in our academic lives to do that?

To address these questions, the required reading list (see Appendix) drew on scholars both within and outside the fields of education who anchored their work in epistemologies and discourses of various spiritualities and articulated critical relationships between race, culture, education, and the spiritual lives of human beings. These authors included bell hooks, Alice Walker, M. Jacqui Alexander, Parker Palmer, Peter Paris, and Njoki Wane, to name a few. They were selected to help us answer the questions that guided the course, not only making knowledge and discourses of spirituality *explicit*, but also by modeling ways that spirituality can be marshaled, theorized, and practiced in our schools and in the academy.

Students in the SRD seminar were assigned individual readings to prepare and present every week with the objective to create a context where we could assist one another in understanding what we knew about race, culture, and spirituality (however much or little), and how these understandings influenced our teaching, research, community work, and activism. Additionally, through these class presentations and weekly journal writings, space emerged for explicit examinations of race and culture and the ways that spirituality might serve as a catalyst for a different kind of dialogue. The readings, weekly responses, and classroom dialogue culminated in a final paper where students theoretically and epistemologically "talked back" to their prospective fields of study using race, culture, and spirituality as their interventions. In reading the final student papers, we realized that both the topics and the manner in which the students had begun to engage new relationships with race, culture, and spirituality in education (creating new knowledge for themselves and with education more generally) was worthy of a wider audience. Thus, we began this edited volume.

As we started conceptualizing this book (and in the course of our previous scholarship around spirituality and endarkened feminist thought), we also began to meet a number of emerging young scholars whose thinking and research (albeit usually in an *implicit* manner) embodied theories of spirituality as intervention in discourses about culture and race. To support and encourage them as new scholars, we invited their voices here as *visionaries* for each chapter, as scholars who might be able to point a way for educators and educational researchers to see more clearly the usefulness of spiritualities as articulated by each of the chapter authors. Their voices—deeply political, sometimes humorous, always insightful, and thoughtfully provocative—are the visionary responses that follow each chapter.

In Chapter 1, Tami A. Augustine and Deborah Justice Zurmehly's "Conversations about Race: How Embracing Spirituality Opens Space for Dialogue in Teacher Education" uses spirituality as the lens through which they position their teaching, allowing for honest and meaningful dialogue with their students and themselves about race. This chapter is a demonstration of the authors' modeling critical spirituality and the ways that it can facilitate dialogue about race among teacher educators and their students. In her Visionary Response, Barbara Dray draws from her own experience with preparing teachers to work in urban and diverse communities in "With Mindfulness as a Guide: Engaging Conversations in Teacher Education." She makes the connection between her work and the work of this chapter by illustrating the ways enacting critical spirituality in her teaching provides a way to invite dialogue about race identity formation and politics in education for teacher education students.

In Chapter 2, "Writing and Telling: Healing the Pain of Disconnection," Eyatta Fischer discusses the importance of building a culture of community in the classroom through the use of narrative and reflective writing. Using Parker Palmer's notion of the pain of disconnection, she builds a counternarrative that marries a culture of community alongside a cosmology of respect. A cosmology of respect challenges the energy of violence found in our language and illuminates the importance of respecting the humanity of another being simply because he or she is human. Robin M. Boylorn's Visionary Response, "On Teaching and Telling: Two Sides of a Teaching (Cassette) Tape," uses the metaphor of a cassette to enact the ways that our active participation in dialogue can lead to mutual teaching and learning, the cosmology of respect that is inherent in storytelling. Like Fischer, she highlights the intentionality of communication, of listening deeply to hear what is and is not being said not only in the classroom but also in our daily conversations.

In Chapter 3, "Spiritually Centered Caring: An Approach for Teaching and Reaching Black Students in Suburbia," Brooke Harris Garad's discussion on caring in education takes up the existence of culturally different ways of caring. She presents the notion of spiritually centered caring as an approach that builds upon culturally relevant caring approaches to teaching and learning. Samara D. Madrid's Visionary Response, "Care as a Racialized, Critical, and Spiritual Emotion," invites a conversation with Harris Garad's work about how care can be viewed as a site of racialized and political existence, a site of tension and transformation in critical consciousness, and a site that recognizes our collective divinity and spirituality.

Gilbert Kaburu and Chris Landauer, in Chapter 4, speak to "Less Religion, More Spirituality: Spiritually Relevant Pedagogy in the Global Era." They cogently argue that the current state of education globally seems to ignore the role of spirituality in the intellectual development of students. They assert that spiritualities are plural and are ever-present spaces that can open windows for personal and intellectual fulfillment that empower students and teachers while creating an environment in which students have agency in pursuit of their personal and community goals. In her Visionary Response, "Infusing Identity Enactment as a Component of Spiritually Relevant Pedagogy," Khosi Kubeka echoes in principle the holistic education forwarded in Kaburu and Landauer's chapter. At the same time, she extends the dialogue by making a case for an infusion of the notion of identity and the strategic centering of rich indigenous knowledge and heritage, especially within the context of education in post-Apartheid South Africa.

In Chapter 5, Angela Cartwright Lynskey's "Occupy Classrooms: Teaching from a Spiritual Paradigm" describes how a high school class used Dillard's (2006) spiritual paradigm, Palmer's (1993) conceptions of communal truth and education as transcendence, and hooks's (1989) ideas on dialogue to critically investigate the World Trade Organization and Occupy Movement. Carmen L. Medina takes up the notion of occupation as a global response to injustice everywhere in her Visionary Response, "Spiritual Occupations: Reflections on Pedagogies and Everyday Stories of Globalization," insightfully drawing from a personal story to illustrate global interconnectedness and solidarity in the human experience with social injustice. She argues that it is within the *local* response to everyday oppressions that we must turn our vision to understand political movements that occur on a global scale.

In Chapter 6, Ashley N. Patterson's "Can One Ever Be Wholly Whole? Fostering Biracial Identity Founded in Spirit" highlights the ways that U.S. society thrives on racial categorization and the expectation that a person choose only *one* racial identity. Contrarily, in this chapter she examines the ways that biracial persons mediate and navigate questions of their multiple identities and provides suggestions for teachers to affirm them in that process. With vision and clarity in "Biracial Identity, Spiritual Wholeness, and Black Girlhood," Bettina L. Love argues powerfully the necessity of Patterson's work in the growing scholarship on Black girlhood, as the need for wholeness is imperative not only for Black girls but for their communities and for those who educate them as well. Making the connection to her own work with hip-hop feminisms, Love concurs that the biracial identity of young Black girls complicates the already complex multilayered space of Black girlhood and hip-hop feminisms.

In Chapter 7, Erica Womack's "Lessons in Love, Literacy, and Listening: Reflections on Learning with and from Black Female Youth" emphasizes the role of listening in a research-based discussion group of Black adolescent females. Womack reframes traditional notions of mentoring from telling and teaching to being fundamentally about listening and learning, with implications for those working closely with Black female youth. Responding to Womack's chapter in "Listening Face-to-Face and Eye-to-Eye: Seeing and Believing Black Girls and Women in Educational Practice and Research," Marcelle M. Haddix reflects on her work with Black female preservice teachers and the importance of Black scholars taking up the task to accurately represent the lives of Black people. Like Womack, Haddix takes up the notion of listening and extends it to include listening to *our own hearts* as researchers as well.

Finally, the cover photograph is worth mentioning here: It is a perfect artistic demonstration of the kind of vision—keen, powerful, and with *soft* eyes—that is necessary in the engagement of dialogues about race and culture through a spiritual lens. Taken by Tami Augustine (one of the contributors to this book) at Acadia National Park in Maine, the gnarled roots of this tree appeared to look like hands, each eagerly reaching to embrace the other. This image profoundly captures the spirit of this text: the always complicated yet beautiful work of reaching across our differences toward the spirit of us *all*. And while we do not claim that spirituality is the magic solution to all of the challenges that our racial and cultural identities and knowledge bring to the educational endeavor, we do hope that readers might consider the possibilities of a new vision *with* spirit in education.

References

Alexander, M. J. (2005). *Pedagogies of crossing: Meditations on feminism, sexual politics, memory, and the sacred.* Durham, NC: Duke University Press.

Ani, M. (1994). *Yurugu: An African-centered critique of European cultural thought.* New Jersey: Africa World Press.

Behar, R. (1996). *The vulnerable observer: Anthropology that breaks your heart.* Boston: Beacon.

Bell, D. (1992). *Faces at the bottom of the well: The permanence of racism.* New York: Basic Books.

Boler, M. (1999). *Feeling power: Emotions and education.* London: Taylor & Francis.

Dillard, C. B. (2006). *On spiritual strivings: Transforming an African American woman's academic life.* New York: SUNY.

Dillard, C. B., & Okpalaoka, C. L. (2011). The sacred and spiritual nature of transnational Black feminist praxis in qualitative research. In N. K. Denzin & Y. S. Lincoln (Eds.), *The Sage handbook of qualitative research* (4th ed., pp. 147–162). Los Angeles: Sage.

Dillard, C. B., Tyson, C. A., & Abdur-Rashid, D. (2000). My soul is a witness: Affirming pedagogies of the spirit. *International Journal of Qualitative Studies in Education, 13,* 447–462.

hooks, b. (1989). *Talking back: Thinking feminist, thinking Black.* Cambridge, MA: South End Press.

hooks, b. (1994). *Teaching to transgress.* New York: Routledge.

hooks, b. (2000). *All about love: New visions.* New York: William Morrow.

King, J. E. (2005). *Black education: A transformative research and action agenda for the new century.* Washington, DC: American Educational Research Association.

Miller, J. P., Karsten, S., Denton, D., Orr, D., & Kates, I. C. (Eds.). (2005). *Holistic learning and spirituality in education.* Albany, NY: SUNY.

Omi, M., & Winant, H. (1994). *Racial formation in the United States from the 1960s to the 1990s.* New York: Routledge.

Palmer, P. (2007). *The courage to teach: Exploring the inner landscape of a teacher's life.* San Francisco: Jossey-Bass.

Palmer, P. (1993). *To know as we are known: Education as a spiritual journey.* New York: HarperCollins.

Paris, P. (1995). *The spirituality of African peoples: The search for a common moral discourse.* Minneapolis: Augsburg Fortress Press.

Reason, P. (1993). Sacred experience and sacred sciences. *Journal of Management Inquiry*, 2, 10–27.

Tisdell, E. J. (2003). *Exploring spirituality and culture in adult and higher education*. San Francisco: Jossey-Bass.

Walker, A. (2006). *We are the ones we have been waiting for: Inner light in a time of darkness*. New York: New Press.

Wane, N., Manyimo, E., & Ritskes, E. (Eds.). (2011). *Spirituality, education and society: An integrated approach*. The Netherlands: Sense Publishers.

West, C. (1993). *Race matters*. Boston: Beacon Press.

Chapter 1

Conversations about Race

How Embracing Spirituality Opens Space for Dialogues in Teacher Education

Tami A. Augustine & Deborah Justice Zurmehly

Introduction: Race (and Spirit) Matters

We were not taught how to have conversations around race in our own schooling. So a fundamental question, as teacher educators, becomes: How do we engage students who believe race is no longer an issue in American society, who believe a post-racial society has arrived? As the demographic divide between students and preservice teachers increases, we cannot deny the importance of having meaningful conversations about race and identity. In this chapter we propose that in using spirituality as the lens through which we position our teaching, we allow for honest and meaningful dialogue around race and identity. For this chapter, spirituality is not a lens through which we deny difference to see only a unifying humanity. Rather, we offer a critical spirituality that invites us to see the importance of, to acknowledge, and to embrace difference. It is this difference, however, that permits us to distinguish various aspects of humanity and does not serve as an agent of separation (Sloan, 2005).

Spirituality as methodology is a broad and sometimes overwhelming concept to address in a single work. However, considering it as a framework to examine how dialogue on race may be facilitated and demonstrated in classroom and school practices is a beginning. We will explore the concept of spirituality as method through our lived experience as two White scholars and educators with teaching experiences with children and preservice teachers in Early Childhood and Middle Childhood teacher education programs. We are driven in this examination by a passion for transformation in the thinking and actions of teachers regarding race and difference in and outside of their classroom. Further, we will explore the importance of and the struggles inherent to having conversations around race within a classroom setting, beginning with a brief autobiography and narrative of each author from the perspective of the other. Second, we will define what spirituality is and is not. We will then present the theoretical framework and positionality of the authors and discuss why this work is important at this time and in this context. Within the discussion of the importance of the work of teaching teachers and ourselves about race, the struggles and obstacles to open and honest conversations will be explored. We will present how spirituality can be used as the lens through which to address some of the challenges in teacher education programs and how it might lead to transformative work. Finally, the authors will engage in a dialogue about their own experiences in the classroom with Early Childhood and Middle Childhood preservice educators, focusing on what each of us believe to have been both the joys and tensions in our attempts to begin the conversation around race with our preservice teachers.

Within this chapter, we do not claim to speak for all teacher educators. It is our fervent belief that these challenging, difficult conversations are critical if we are to reach a level of respect in relating to one another across lines of difference. Based on our experience in explicitly acknowledging spirituality as serving a key function in our teaching, we believe that fostering conversations about race and identity in a manner that seeks healing brings numerous challenges within teacher education classrooms, given the current demographic of teachers in the United States. We cannot claim to relate to the struggles of our African American colleagues, but we know the importance of having knowledge relevant to the heritage and identity of African Americans and other people of color. These are the struggles: Having open, honest dialogues around race in teacher education still does not happen enough as race remains a taboo topic of conversation. How do we help people from different backgrounds connect and respect differences? How do we move preservice teachers to a place of acknowledging privilege and seeing the important role race has played in our society? How do we help ourselves as teacher educators engage in such conversations? We believe spirituality is one answer to these questions. And we start with ourselves.

We Teach Who We Are: Our Positionalities

Tami A. Augustine

Positioning myself in this chapter is an important aspect of this work. As a White, middle-class woman I am a person who comes from a place of race, class, and educational privilege. While I was born in Brooklyn, New York, and grew up in an Italian Catholic family, I now practice Buddhism. This shift has played an important role in my perspectives on spirituality. I say this to acknowledge not only my perspective as a member of White, middle-class American society but also to note that due to my gender, sexual orientation, and spiritual traditions, I am also a member of marginalized groups in America. The violence that accompanies marginalization—verbal, physical, emotional, and spiritual—is high, the impact of which cannot be underestimated in the role it plays in our internal world.

Easy is not a word I would use to describe work in equity and diversity. Talking about race itself is rife with controversy and difficulties. Adding a spiritual component to a setting such as education merely adds to the controversy. The push back, however, gives me confidence that we are onto something here. Dyer (2004) quotes Aldous Huxley, stating, "The spiritual journey does not consist in arriving at a new destination where a person gains what he did not have, or becomes what he is not....The finding of God is a coming to one self" (p. 18). This is what I hope education can offer more students in educating preservice teachers within a spiritual lens.

It is a privilege to work with my coauthor, Deb, on this chapter. I have had the honor of getting to know Deb over the last 18 months or so. Connections between our work became apparent soon after meeting, and our mutual longing to bring spirituality into education helped me become more open and move past my fears. Our passion for education and making a difference in the field is apparent. I see us both struggle, as White women, with issues of race and our place within that conversation. I see us both work to figure out how spirituality can fit into the world of academia. Most of all, though, I see Deb's humanity: her heart, her struggle, her caring, and her passion. Deb is a warm, kind, dedicated person who seeks to learn, discover, and change. Who Deb is as a spiritual being and how that plays out in her work is something I admire. This is the role spirituality can play in this work for me. It is a place of *connection*, not separation. It has been an honor to walk this walk with her.

Deborah Justice-Zurmehly

I recognize the importance of situating myself as a scholar in this research, and I admit it is what I struggle with most. My personal history is filled with privilege and power, much of which was personally unrecognized until well into my adult life. I am a White female, a member of the demographic groups holding much power in this country: heterosexual, middle-class, and Christian. I have come to acknowledge how this has offered endless opportunity for safety, comfort, pursuit of education, and advancement in a profession I love. While my life has been riddled with personal tragedy, the issues of poverty, marginalization, and oppression did not complicate these obstacles. The strength of my Christian faith has grown through the trials I have faced, and I embrace my own faith while recognizing the importance of spirituality in creating a climate of acceptance and true fellowship. This personal journey magnified my desire to place the spotlight on injustices and oppression of groups of people based on a societal definition of what is acceptable, and my desire to pursue this both personally and professionally grew deeper.

I am deeply inspired by the scholarly work of Cynthia Dillard and Parker Palmer as they integrate spirituality into education. Their validation and scholarly acknowledgment of the importance of this work provides the positive energy to continue this work I feel I was created to do.

After an initial encounter in a course approximately 18 months ago, I took away an impression of Tami as a very insightful scholar who shared my passion for examining spirituality in education. In spite of any differences in our individual life journeys, we were immediately connected in our quest for change. We both sought to highlight spirituality as a paradigmatic framework from which human connections and depth of caring would emanate. As we engaged in further dialogue she confirmed my perception through the depth of her inquiry and the urgency in her voice whenever the topic was raised of pushing back against the hegemonic discourse that dominates the field of education. The depth of her listening and engagement with the ideas shared by others spoke of the integrity of her work, which translates into how she lives her life. She genuinely considers the contributions of others and remains focused on the main objective of her work: improving the lives of students who have been marginalized or labeled in any manner. I have never heard Tami take on the voice of a victim. Instead, her commitment to advocacy is what resonates with anyone whom she encounters. Tami mirrors her beliefs in all aspects of her life. We have important work to do, *together*. And part of that work is explicitly defining and theorizing within paradigms that explicitly open a way for spirituality in our teaching and research.

Defining Spirituality

In the United States, people often equate spirituality with religion and therefore dismiss the inclusion of spirituality in public education as a violation of the First Amendment (Moffett, 1994). Merging the two as interchangeable privileges the notion of religion in the minds of many and promotes potential marginalization based on religious practice (for example, see Kabaru & Landauer, Chapter 4 in this volume). Within a religious framework, elements such as institutional beliefs and rituals become highly significant. Cole (2011) notes how religion can become oppressive if its adherence to codes of conduct and claims of holding a "monopoly on the truth" dominate (p. 5). We propose that bringing spirituality into the public education setting does not violate the U.S.

Constitution, as spirituality and religion are not the same thing. Religion may include spirituality; spirituality does not necessarily include religion (Dillard, Abdur-Rashid, & Tyson, 2000; Tisdell, 2006). Defining spirituality is a bit like walking through a minefield. Many authors and researchers in the field of education have chosen to avoid using the word because it can mean many things to many people and is emotionally charged. We encourage the use of the word *spirituality*, acknowledging that it can be messy, complicated, and not neatly defined. We also encourage using the word *spirituality* in our teaching in order to be up front about what can make a difference in the lives of students.

Authors from across many disciplines have offered various definitions of spirituality. There are multiple themes found in the literature, but we will focus on two. The first theme regards spirituality as *a connection to a life force, Source, or higher power* (Cutri, 2009; Dillard, Abdur-Rashid, & Tyson, 2000; Jones, 2005; Miller, 2006; Norton, 2008; Tisdell, 2006). A second theme focuses on spirituality as a *connection to self and to others* (Cutri, 2009; Dei, 2002; Dillard, Abdur-Rashid, & Tyson, 2000; Joldersma, 2009; Jones, 2005; Tisdell, 2000. Abdi (2011) reminds us of the complex nature of limiting spirituality by offering a narrow, fixed definition. Therefore, for the purposes of this chapter, we embrace Parker Palmer's rather open definition of spirituality as *"the eternal human yearning to be connected with something larger than our egos"* (Palmer, 2003, p. 377).

Specifically building upon this foundation, we also embrace Dillard's (2006) notion that spirituality is a *conscious* choice toward relationships with a higher being and engagement with others signifies the importance of our interactions with others. Both Dillard's (2006, 2012) and Motha's (2005) description of spirituality involves action as "liberating, not promoting fear, complacency or hatred" (Motha, 2005, p. 54). Taken as a whole, our definition of spirituality includes *the innate need and conscious choice to seek connections including relationships with a higher being as well as with others*. This relationship calls us into action in the face of injustice or hatred. Certainly this definition does not include everything that may be considered spiritual, but it serves as a place to help us remain open to what spirituality can be rather than providing a narrowly defined box in which it would be impossible to fit all that is spiritual. The alignment between our definition of spirituality and our scholarly work is emerging; however, the notion of spirituality within the field of education remains underexplored. The following is an attempt to locate the definition that guides our work into the larger discussion of paradigms of research and teaching.

Locating the Work of Teacher Education: A Spiritual Paradigm

In consideration of the paradigm within which our work lies, our stance is a fluid one. While we embrace tenets of several aspects from the Big Four paradigms (articulated by Denzin & Lincoln, 1994), we simultaneously are moving toward a spiritual paradigm. In reflection on what shapes this paradigm, culture dictates much of what we embrace as our paradigmatic worldview. As Palmer (1983) suggests, culture is what is valued and where the origin of truth lies. We recognize, for ourselves and those we teach, the profound impact of lived experiences within unique communities, the influence of the beliefs of those around us, and, most importantly, "what those who are perceived as legitimate and powerful in our eyes tell us of the nature of the world" (Dillard, 2006, p. 34). What we realized in this examination of spirituality, race, and dialogue in teacher education is that legitimacy and power often originate from an external and hegemonic source within our profession. We acknowledge the limitations and negativity often associated with the existing hegemonic power structure, and we seek a different lens through which to view the world and our work.

A spiritual paradigm embraces an epistemological stance that reconciles what Palmer (1983) describes as the pain of disconnection (see Fischer, Chapter 2 in this volume). The disconnection involves the struggle between what we have been socialized to believe and do and what the heart of a teacher seeks as truth. For us to view teaching with a depth that innately seeks connection, healing, and relationships that counter marginalization, hatred, bias, and intolerance, reflection on the beliefs about knowledge, specifically the knower, and the known must occur. Unfortunately, we are socialized to view ourselves as the knower with the implication that knowledge is a possession and the knower is separate and dominant over the known. According to Palmer (1983), this understanding shapes more than just our body of knowledge; it impacts our self-understanding and view of the world. He states: "The scope of the world became identical with the scope of my knowledge of it; my knowledge of the world became the world itself" (p. 21).

From a spiritual paradigm, Palmer (1983) suggests, as do the authors, that our view of the world and the work in teacher education must embody "the diverse ways we answer the heart's longing to be connected with the largeness of life" (p. 5). In other words, the spiritual connection to our inner self is the source for shaping our worldview, our epistemology, our paradigms as teachers and teacher educators. In terms of our actions as teachers, we lean on Dillard's (2006) Methodology of Surrender described as both "intimately meditative and faith filled" (p. 77). Operationally, this methodology includes deep listening and attention to our connection to a higher being in contemplation of the wisdom and courage of those we seek to understand and learn from. And as we seek to prepare students for their work as teachers who critically recognize and embrace race, identity, and difference, our version of a spiritual paradigm honors Freire's (1970) work, which tells us the oppressor as well as the oppressed must be freed for transformation to truly occur and obstacles to authentic relationships and understanding to be removed.

Thus, our spiritual paradigm holds that teacher education be pursued for the sake of healing rather than mere reconstruction or identification with the traditional Big Four paradigms (Denzin & Lincoln, 1994). Moving beyond either a critical or constructivist paradigmatic stance, a spiritual paradigm seeks to humanize the voice of the participants, honoring them as co-constructors of knowledge and revisiting the obstacles to healing in hopes of acknowledgment and movement away from the injurious. A spiritual approach also goes beyond just recognition of the presence of hegemony, but addresses the oppressor in power as well as the oppressed in a manner seeking healing through the acts and practices of teaching and learning. A closer examination of the teaching pipeline and the subsequent obstacles this creates reveals the need for racial understanding and equity.

Spirituality, Race, and
Demographic Divide in Schools

Schools in the United States are experiencing a significant increase in the diversity of the K–12 student population, while teacher education programs are filled with candidates who are largely White, middle-class, monolingual, female students (Davis, Ramahlo, Beyerbach, & London, 2008; Howard, 2010; Ladson-Billings, 2001; Taylor, 2010). While *Brown v. Board of Education of Topeka, Kansas* remains a hallmark in the civil rights movement, we must also examine the impact the implementation of desegregation had on African American educators. The closing of African American schools after the *Brown* decision meant the removal of African American teachers and administrators and began a history of African American students being taught by White educators (Ladson-Billings & Tate, 1995). The impact of the removal of African American educators continues to be felt today. In 2006, the Census reported that one in every three U.S. citizens were people of color (U.S. Census Bureau, 2007). Over the last century, the percentage of Whites has decreased from 88% to 65%, with the greatest increase in the percentage of Latinos and Asians (U.S. Census Bureau, 2007). Demographics will continue to shift as projections show that by 2050, almost one in five Americans will be immigrants (Taylor, 2010). The United States will experience its greatest influx of immigrants since the early 1900s. Additionally, projections indicate that by 2035 students of color will comprise the majority of the student population in the United States (Howard, 2010).

Statistical evidence suggests an increasing number of students will be taught by teachers who have different racial, cultural, and socioeconomic status than they have. In 2000, 75% of teachers in public schools were female, 88% were White, and almost all were middle-class (Ladson-Billings, 200). As the United States experiences an increase in immigration and students of color in school, in conjunction with a homogeneous largely White and female teaching population, teachers must learn how to successfully teach students who are different from themselves. Howard (2010) states, "Teacher educators must conceptualize the manner in which new teachers are prepared, and provide them with the skills and knowledge that will be best suited for effectively educating today's diverse student population" (p. 1). While differences in demographics play an important role in the cultural divide between teachers and students, the experiences and attitudes of preservice teachers present additional challenges for teacher education programs in preparing this currently homogeneous preservice teaching population to work with a diverse student body.

Critically examining the impact of race on American society and in American schools is an essential component of a successful teacher education program. Teacher education programs are charged with educating young, White, middle-class, primarily female teachers on how to successfully teach students that represent diversity of culture, perspectives, and experiences. Many preservice teachers acknowledge they have had limited interaction with people from cultures different than their own (Ladson-Billings, 2001). Preservice teachers, who are members of the dominant culture in the United States, have little experience with understanding what it means to be a member of a minority group in an educational environment that accepts White, middle-class values as the norm (Irvine, 2003; Ladson-Billings, 2001; Taylor, 2010). Without teacher educators including the often-difficult conversation about race in the classroom, how can preservice teachers be prepared to teach in diverse educational settings?

Embracing spirituality in teaching can address the destructive nature of racism as Orr (2005) describes how the whole individual must be addressed in an anti-oppressive pedagogy that teaches the acceptance of difference (p. 88). Ladson-Billings and Tate (1995) discuss culturally relevant pedagogy as including the criteria for students to develop a critical consciousness "through which they challenge the status quo of the current social order" (p. 160). And it is through trusting, authentic relationships that educators can begin having these dialogues with students. As noted by Cole (2011), "As educators move away from unilateral, rigid thinking, they open themselves up to the possibility of creating meaningful relationships with children. Relationships rooted in honesty and compassion honor the children's spirituality" (p. 11).

We suggest it is in this circumstance that spirituality can help to promote dialogue about race. The teacher educator, embracing a spiritual paradigm, recognizes the nature of knowledge as collaborative and dialogic. The teacher educators promote connections among themselves, their preservice teachers, and knowledge in relationships demonstrative of trust, respect, care, nurturance, and acceptance. The teacher educator addresses the status quo regarding race based on the innate desire to challenge oppression and hatred. This, we claim, creates an environment rich with potential for meaningful, transformative dialogue around race in education and society.

How Spirituality Appears in Our Teaching: An Example of Dialogues about Race and Identity

Dialogue and reflection about our teaching practice have been an essential part of our work. Here, we want to share some of the conversations we had while writing this chapter about our teaching, to illustrate some of our practices and ongoing struggles of embracing spirituality in our classrooms as a way to promote conversations about race. Both authors share similar teaching experiences with preservice educators in the same state with similar demographics, (White, middle-class, females from similar geographic regions). Over the span of several months and many cups of coffee, we spent hours reflecting on our memories, frustrations, successes, and hopes. We now share highlights from this ongoing dialogue, hoping that it reflects some of the challenges of addressing race from a spiritual paradigm in our work. In this section we reveal many unanswered questions, laying bare the areas where we both feel we need to develop as educators as illustrative of the challenges that race presents in teaching preservice teachers, particularly given the racial homogeneity of those currently in the teacher education pipeline.

The power of dialogue is an important part of the process of reflecting on our teaching. It provides an opportunity to hear each other, to deeply listen, to contemplate and identify where our struggles lie in a manner not offered through isolated study or individual writing. The relationship we built through our shared experiences and conversations created a safe space that models what we had not been taught, how to honestly talk about race and identity. But having conversations about race involves emotion. It is an emotionally invested topic that, in our experience, White, middle-class, female students fear for a couple of reasons. First, they fear being called a racist, which renders them silent about race. They fear that to talk about race means abandoning ties to their familial culture, a culture that may ignore or sometimes embrace privilege aligned with their race. Both of these fears are major obstacles that *can* be addressed within an environment in which we, as instructors, lay the spiritual groundwork that opens a safe space to explore, feel, struggle with, and hopefully embrace difficult conversations and acknowledge the fact that racism exists, can be addressed honestly, and ultimately will enlarge one's own identity. Our own investments with locating spirituality in our teaching about race and identity emerged as a vital factor in our teaching in the following dialogue.

Dialogue: Considering Spirituality in Teachings about Race

Tami: The fact that we both talk about our own identities to open dialogues with our students is key.

Deb: That is very powerful. It says *I'm willing to be vulnerable with all of you.* I'm bearing my soul in a lot of ways.

Tami: Did you share a lot of your own experiences with your students?

Deb: Absolutely and very painful ones. I framed it that way. I told them: "This is not as academic a course as it is a personal journey."

Tami: We cannot *intellectualize* the experiences of privilege or the experiences of racism. As a teacher, I have to *feel* them, because other people feel them. The emotional piece is such an important part.

Deb: Palmer and Wane talk about this. You cannot segregate emotions from the act of teaching and the act of learning.

Tami: But what makes those things "spiritual" and not just good teaching?

Deb: Because I go back to the source, the eternal source from the spiritual.

Tami: I agree. It feels like also with the spiritual component there is this place of acceptance. What we do is not just what we do, it is part of a greater whole. That drives a lot of the teaching. This notion that this thing [race and racism] is bigger than me. But it is not just bigger in terms of racism around the world but it means I have to connect to something beyond this world.

Deb: It also has to do with what the professor stressed in the Spirit, Race, and Dialogue course: that the goal is to be holistic. Who we are outside of the classroom? Bring that into the classroom instead of acting totally differently outside of the classroom.

Tami: Some of the spirituality piece that is in here for me is the interconnectedness. That doesn't mean we are the same: It is not universality. Interconnectedness means my behavior effects your behavior. If we can get to that community up front in our classes that impacts how we embrace and can talk about race.

Dialogue: Critical Thinking and Race

In our conversations, we found a major quandary in approaching the topic of race in teacher education. Do we present, up front, the fact that *racism exists, period. Now let's talk*? Or do we take the more emotionally charged path of *let me help you see that racism exists*? In discussing our own experiences, we arrived at the position that both have value. But as Wane, Manyimo, and Ritskes (2011) and Palmer (1998) note, both are not as much intellectual positions as emotional ones. As Tami shared: "We need to get people out of their heads and into their hearts. We cannot intellectualize this, I have to feel it." From our perspectives, regardless of the path, the most important element is reaching the point of critical thinking about race. And while some students may perceive such teaching as an assault or as an emotionally draining journey, it must be encounters like these that move them to think critically about race and identity:

Tami: The students did a bunch of reflections online. It really ran the gamut between thinking very thoughtfully and critically about race and not. They had to comment on each other's posts as well. I just don't know. This is one of those struggles. How much do you talk about race before they start to reflect about it? Or do you have them reflect about it first and then talk about it? In one class, we had the beginning of the conversation and then the students reflected. Their responses really showed where they started, where their starting point is.

Deb: I think that's an important question that you raise, the sequence or order of reflection versus just beginning the discussion about race and identity. I presented the *White Privilege* piece by Peggy McIntosh in class and we discussed it. So it was more immediate. And I think that you giving them work to do at the end of the class period to reflect on until next class period may have been more valuable. And giving them that anonymity that online reflection offers, you may have gotten more deep responses instead of the gut responses.

Tami: One of my professors has talked about that in her own research. She finds you can get much more in-depth responses when you are online because people feel safer. Even though they know each other they don't have to "look" at each other. But, then in a sense, maybe it contradicts what we try to do with spirituality in building connections?

Deb: I'm not quite sure. Maybe...?

Tami: We then started talking about why race matters. I introduced the demographics, like let's look at this classroom, here's who you're going to be teaching. The likelihood that you are going to be teaching in schools that have populations of students of color is pretty high. We started talking about Tyrone Howard's work. He offers a lot of stats, so I can paint this picture for them. So that's what I really modeled it after, the steps: Here's the situation. You think this isn't real? Let me show you this is real. Because I don't want to debate with you whether this is real or not!

Deb: Numbers don't lie in these cases.

Tami: Right. Now there was evidence of some deficit thinking in my students. So we engaged in this conversation about why certain groups of people are overrepresented in the picture I painted for them. And that conversation was hard, because I want them to get it, that it's not accidental or based on merit. And they don't. Most don't.

Deb: Then what do you think students took away from that class session? And are their other things that you thought or reflected,
"Wow. I wish I had . . ." (fill in the blank)?

Tami: Again, the struggle for me was how to engage more voices in the
class. And not just the two students of color, as I said before, but
more voices in general.

Deb: But do you think some students' learning style is more to just
kind of reflect on what is being said vs. speaking out? I think
there is value in that, too.

Tami: Another one of my professors just presented information about
race and identity and racism on the first day of our class, "Racism
exists," she said. "OK, let's move on." When I was in school,
that's just not how things were presented. Things were presented as "let me help you see that racism exists." So I had these two
different experiences. Now, I really liked how this professor did
it because the reality is racism exists. Why are we still having the
conversation as to whether it does or doesn't? I approach it much
more by using the stats that Howard gives us and some other
authors: "This is the reality. This is a problem. Racism still exists.
Now let's talk." I think it was a little shocking to them. I don't
know if it shut them down but they left quiet.

Deb: My sense is for some of these students, such new information that
has either been repressed, or ignored, especially a lot of it around
this notion of privilege. The typical response of the White student
is guilt and feelings of responsibility. I think that is a big part of
it. It is just a lot to consider and especially when they are realiz-
ing, "I'm tied to this history." I know that personally I went
through this in my graduate school, sitting in an African
American History course. I'm the only White student in there.
The African American professor was presenting date after date
of all these horrific things that had happened to Black people. I
am sitting there feeling the load of my entire race and guilt was
my response. I wanted to apologize to *everyone*. I think for a lot
of the students that we work with, they are at that point, because
they haven't acknowledged race, let alone racism. So to respond
to that is almost more than they can do. So maybe, as teacher educators, we should be thinking about ways to help them express

what they are feeling. I think writing is a tool that has worked really well. Giving them the initial tool of writing what they are thinking, maybe shared only between the instructor and the student, might give them that initial way of internalizing the fact that they too have a race and identity, that racism exists? Maybe that would give them a place to start processing and becoming more critical and being able to think, "OK, now what?"

Tami: The students did do more reflections for that week as well, focused on an article by Geneva Gay on culturally responsive teaching. And their reflections that week did focus more on how ill-prepared they felt.

Deb: I'm intrigued by their reflections. But you had them reflecting each time online, right? It's a public forum. Did you do any kinds of writing where it was more private?

Tami: Not until winter quarter. But I would want to do what Dr. X did, have them exchange with each other as well, because then they can't just hear my responses. I think that is the hard part. Would you have them do both [teacher-student exchange and student-student exchange of writing]?

Deb: Yes, I think there is value in both. But it may depend on group dynamics. Sometimes giving that space allows them to spew emotional vomit, given the safe space. I think the safe space is an important element, a space to push and challenge. And then moving them to a more public discussion of what they are comfortable sharing. Yes: While we want to encourage, we also must push.

Tami: For some of these students they come to us with these beliefs of what the whole world has looked like. What we are asking them now to do is rip the rug out from underneath that world for a minute. Getting them to that place, through the pain to say, "OK. It doesn't mean that everyone or everything in my life is terrible—or that I am terrible." In the process of writing this chapter, you and I have both experienced that on a personal level. But we have also learned how we can say "these are your beliefs, but I still love you and you're still a part of my family."

The Challenge of Seeing Race and Identity

There is no doubt in our minds and hearts that the work is difficult and, often, messy. We have not been exposed to or discovered for ourselves one way that makes this work "successful." We struggle with wanting students to understand, but we also must honor their process. It is difficult for us both to walk away from a classroom knowing that perhaps we have not affected how students think about race in American society and around the world. With over 85% of our students being White and middle-class, we were faced with challenging White privilege, deficit thinking, and belief in a colorblind society, all to be responded to and challenged within the framework of a 10-week quarter! However, the most pernicious challenge for both of us was in helping our students to see themselves as having a race, having a cultural identity:

Tami:	What I really wanted them to get out of this portion of the class was that they have culture. Even if you are White and middle-class, you have race, you have culture.
Deb:	Did you find that that is one of the most difficult concepts for White students to grasp?
Tami:	Yes.
Deb:	Exactly. I had the same experience.
Tami:	Some get so offended!
Deb:	And defensive!
Tami:	Yes, defensive is a good word. They also go to the colorblind place.
Deb:	Oh yeah. "Color doesn't matter. I see my students all the same. I love my students all the same." I get that 'cause they are teaching little ones.
Tami:	Right. I just need to "love" them.
Deb:	Yeah. Huge disconnect between who I am as a cultured, socialized individual and a racialized individual and how that can possibly matter in teaching.

Tami: Right. My students often ask [about culturally relevant peda-gogy]: "Isn't this just good teaching?" And I reply: "If this is just good teaching, then why aren't we seeing more of it?" That's the thing. White [people] in my experience, we just don't talk about race. African American people I have worked with talk about race regularly because it exists and it *matters*.

Deb: Yes, yes! You just hit the nail on the head!

Tami: My high school students used to say to me, "Man, you are so White-white." And I would think: "What is White-white?" But then when I would say: "Aw, you know, I'm just too White-white," they would get uncomfortable because in their experience White people don't talk about race.

Deb: That is huge! You are right.

Tami: That is just my experience.

Deb: But you are right! These are my experiences, too!

Tami: I'm comfortable talking about race for the most part, but I don't know necessarily how to engage anybody else. We are not taught how to do that. And who is modeling that for me? Where are we learning how to do this?

Deb: And time constraints with our preservice teachers are a reality regardless of the setting. There is so much that you want to cover. Do I cover it all at this level? Or do I choose or select things to go more in depth? That is the pedagogical decision we are always faced with. I don't know that this conversation about identity ever feels satisfying with them, like far enough or deep enough, or taken as far as I wanted them to go. I think there will always be still more to talk about. I think it is so important that there be multiple opportunities, in all of their classes and internships.

Tami: That's what I mean though. Do the courses that we offer reflect the fact that we see race and identity as important? Because we talk about it for three weeks and then we gotta move on. Even if it is integrated throughout the curriculum, I needed more time.

Deb: This is so foundational to who we are as teacher educators, to who our preservice teachers might eventually be. I think the syllabus we created as an introductory, foundational course regardless of the licensure should be one of the first classes you take. Then race and identity need to be revisited through multiple courses.

Conclusion

When we look back on our dialogue, we notice three main pedagogical practices: (1) the dialogic presentation of race; (2) the importance of journaling or writing as a way to encourage dialogue; and (3) the recognition of race and culture. We do not have an answer for the best way to begin talking to a largely White, middle-class, female preservice teaching population about race or the *best* way to help these preservice teachers acknowledge their own race and culture. We do agree, however, that to have such conversations we must first create an open space in classrooms in which these conversations can take place. Both Dillard (2006) and Palmer (1998) indicate that classroom spaces should be open, hospitable, balance the individual and the community, encourage dialogue, and give opportunities for reflection. When creating open classroom spaces, dialogue that encourages many viewpoints is emphasized for discussion of controversial issues and topics to be embraced and encouraged.

Thich Nhat Hanh (1976) reminds educators to embrace the kind of compassion that honors diverse viewpoints, as well as pushing them to acknowledge the conditions in our society that create suffering. hooks (2003) states: "The teacher who can ask of students, 'What do you need in order to learn?' or 'How can I serve?' brings to the work of educating a spirit of service that honors the students' *will to learn*" (p. 92). It is in these spaces that the potential for transformation can take place, as the discussion and study of race can lead to "awareness, resistance, solidarity, and revolutionary transformation" (Hatch, 2002, p. 17). This truly captures the kind of classroom setting that serves to open space for dialogue in teacher education.

Writing about spiritual approaches to teaching and their impact on talking about race leads to many questions, the biggest of which is: How can you know that spirituality is there or that it makes a difference? We are reminded that using spirituality as a lens through which to teach about race "lifts the veil of presumed absolute authority from conceptions of scholarly truth typically taught in schools. It helps students realize that no single version of 'truth' is total and permanent. Nor should it be allowed to exist uncontested" (Gay, 2010, p. 38). Teaching from a spiritual lens encourages preservice teachers to permit their students to express who they are and demonstrates that differences are not deficits, but strength in classrooms and communities. As Moffett (1994) states: "In keeping with a long American tradition of pragmatism, why not assume that the spiritual view is true? People who do so tend to feel better, treat others better, and fare better in their endeavors" (p. 31). If, as we are positing in this chapter, spirituality can enhance teacher education and can help educators create more caring, compassionate relationships with students (even as they engage the difficult impact that race and racism has had and continues to have on schools and schooling for so many), what do we have to lose?

References

Abdi, A. A. (2011). Foreword. In N. N. Wane, E. L. Manyimo, & E. J. Ritskes (Eds.), *Spirituality, Education & Society: An Integrated Approach* (pp. xi-xiii). Rotterdam, The Netherlands: Sense Publishers.

Cole, S. (2011). Situating children in the discourse of spirituality. In N. N. Wane, E. L. Manyimo, & E. J. Ritskes (Eds.), *Spirituality, education, & society: An integrated approach* (pp. 1–14). Rotterdam, Netherlands: Sense Publishers.

Cutri, R. M. (2009). Race through religious eyes: Focusing teacher reflectivity on race, culture, and spiritual beliefs. *Religion & Education, 36*(1), 56–71.

Davis, R. D., Ramahlo, T., Beyerbach, B., & London, A. P. (2008). A culturally relevant teaching course: Reflecting pre-service teachers' thinking. *Teaching Education, 19*(3), 223–234.

Dei, G. J. S. (2002). Learning culture, spirituality, and local knowledge: Implications for African schooling. *International Review of Education, 48*(5), 335–360.

Denzin, N. K., & Lincoln, Y. S. (Eds.). (1994). *Handbook of qualitative research.* Thousand Oaks: Sage.

Dillard, C. B. (2012). *Learning to (re)member the things we've learned to forget: Endarkened feminisms, spirituality and the sacred nature of research and teaching.* New York: Peter Lang.

Dillard, C. B. (2006). *On spiritual strivings: Transforming an African American woman's academic life.* Albany, NY: SUNY Press.

Dillard, C., Abdur-Rashid, D., & Tyson, C. (2000). My soul is a witness: Affirming pedagogies of the spirit. *Qualitative Studies in Education, 13*(5), 447–462.

Dyer, W. (2004). *The power of intention: Change the ways you look at things and the things that you look at will change.* Carlsbad, CA: Hay House, Inc.

Freire, P. (1970). *Pedagogy of the oppressed.* New York: Continuum.

Gay, G. (2010). *Culturally responsive teaching: Theory, research, and practice.* New York: Teachers College Press.

Hanh, T. N. (1976). *The miracle of mindfulness! A manual on meditation.* Boston, MA: Beacon Press.

Hatch, J. A. (2002). *Doing qualitative research in education settings.* Albany, NY: State University Press.

hooks, b. (2003). *Teaching community: A pedagogy of hope.* New York: Routledge.

Howard, T. C. (2010). *Why race and culture matter in schools: Closing the achievement gap in America's classrooms.* New York: Teachers College Press.

Irvine, J. J. (2003). *Educating teachers for diversity: Seeing with a cultural eye.* New York: Teachers College Press.

Joldersma, C. (2009). A spirituality of the desert for education: The call of justice beyond the individual or community. *Studies of Philosophy of Education, 28,* 193–208.

Jones, L. (2005). What does spirituality in education mean? Stumbling toward wholeness. *Journal of College & Character, 6*(7), 1–7.

Ladson-Billings, G. J. (2001). *Crossing over to Canaan: The journey of new teachers in diverse classrooms.* San Francisco, CA: Jossey-Bass.

Ladson-Billings, G. J., & Tate, W. F. (1995). Toward a critical race theory of education. *Teachers College Record, 97*(1), 47–68.

Miller, J. (2006). Reflecting on spirituality in education. *Encounter, 19*(2), 1–4.

Miller, J. P., Karsten, S., Denton, D., Orr, D., & Kates, I. C. (Eds.). (2005). *Holistic learning and spirituality in education: Breaking new ground.* Albany, NY: SUNY.

Moffett, J. (1994). *The universal schoolhouse: A spiritual awakening through education.* San Francisco, CA: Jossey-Bass.

Motha, J. (2011). Spirituality and its relevance for the contemplative educator. In N. N. Wane, E. L. Manyimo, & E. J. Ritskes (Eds.), *Spirituality, Education & Society: An Integrated Approach* (pp. 49–66). Rotterdam, The Netherlands: Sense Publishers.

Norton, N. E. L. (2008). Singing in the spirit: Spiritual practices inside public school classrooms. *Education & Urban Society, 40*(3), 342–360.

Orr, D. (2005). Minding the soul in education: Conceptualizing and teaching the whole person. In Miller, J. P., Karsten, S., Denton, D., Orr, D., & Kates, I. C. (Eds.). (2005). *Holistic learning and spirituality in education: Breaking new ground* (pp. 87–100). Albany, NY: SUNY.

Palmer, P. J. (1983). *To know as we are known: Education as a spiritual journey.* San Francisco, CA: Harper.

Palmer, P. J. (1998). *The courage to teach: Exploring the inner landscape of a teacher's life.* San Francisco, CA: Jossey-Bass.

Palmer, P. J. (2003). Teaching with heart and soul: Reflections on spirituality in teacher education. *Journal of Teacher Education, 54*(5), 376–385.

Sloan, D. (2005). Education and the modern assault on being human: Nurturing body, soul, and spirit. In J. P. Miller, S. Karsten, D. Denton, D. Orr, & I. C. Kates (Eds.), *Holistic learning and spirituality in education*. Albany, NY: SUNY.

Taylor, R. W. (2010). The role of teacher education programs in creating culturally competent teachers: A moral imperative for ensuring the academic success of diverse student populations. *Multicultural Education, 17*(3), 24–28.

Tisdell, E. J. (2006). Diversity and spirituality in secular higher education: The teaching paradox. *Religion & Education, 33*(1), 49–68.

Tisdell, E. J. (2000). Exploring spirituality and culture in adult and higher education. San Francisco: Jossey-Bass.

U.S. Census Bureau. (2007). *State & county Quickfacts: Allegany County, N.Y.* Retrieved from http://quickfacts.census.gov.

Wane, N. N., Manyimo, E. L., & Ritskes, E. J. (Eds.). (2011). *Spirituality, education & society: An integrated approach*. Rotterdam, Netherlands: Sense Publishers.

With Mindfulness as a Guide

Engaging Conversations in Teacher Education

Barbara Dray

As I sit and write this Visionary Response, it is Thanksgiving and I am reminded of all that I am thankful for and all that has brought me to this point in my career. To begin, I have the privilege and honor to write a piece about how spirituality informs my practice preparing teachers to work in urban and diverse communities, in particular, the ways I have come to enact critical spirituality in my teaching as a way to invite dialogue about race identity formation and politics in education. Further, I am grateful to have had the opportunity to examine how race and identity affect us as teachers both personally and professionally in U.S. schools with our children, their parents, our colleagues, and the communities in which our schools are situated. Here, I hope to illuminate the various ways my spirituality has guided my work with teachers, mainly supporting our collective journey toward developing a critical consciousness about race and identity formation and politics in education.

When I was invited to be a visionary for Augustine and Zurmehly's chapter, I thought to myself, *I don't practice religion in the traditional sense. What do I have to say?* And yet, at my core I have always considered myself a highly spiritual being. My work with teachers (White teachers in particular) has led me to use mindfulness as a core value to help frame how teachers make authentic connections with their students in understanding race and identity in the classroom align with teacher education pedagogy, but also in the ways I support teachers to develop more critical understandings of race and identity in U.S. schools.

There are two central questions that I drew from reading Augustine and Zurmehly's chapter: How does using spirituality as a lens to position our teaching in teacher education allow for "honest and meaningful dialogue around race and identity"? And in what ways does critical spirituality invite us "to see the importance of, to acknowledge, and to embrace difference?" I organize my response to their work around these central questions. First, I begin by articulating my spiritual lens. Then I will discuss the importance of being in touch with who we are as cultural beings and how these two aspects come together to promote dialogue about race and identity within a teacher preparation program.

My Spiritual Lens

> Do not force others, including children, by any means whatsoever, to adopt your views, whether by authority, threat, money, propaganda, or even education. However, through compassionate dialogue, help others renounce fanaticism and narrow-mindedness. (Third precept of *Engaged Buddhism*, Thich Nhat Hahn, 1993)

My spiritual lens as a teacher educator is situated within the notion of mindfulness. I first was introduced to this concept not in a spiritual context but within intercultural communication. Mindfulness is the process of moving away from automatic pilot or scripted/habitual responses based on our own cultural frames of reference toward conscious communication that seeks to understand our interactions with others (Gudykunst & Kim, 2003). Scripted behavior may serve us well in familiar contexts, but not in cross-cultural interactions. So the process of becoming a mindful educator involves a conscious choice to recognize our thoughts and refrain from reacting but rather to sit with the tension of our thoughts while seeking to understand another perspective (Dray

& Wisneski, 2011). Within this process we gain more information to help us learn to respond differently, more mindfully, or consciously.

More recently, I have been studying the teachings of Vietnamese Buddhist Monk Thich Nhat Hanh (1975) who suggests that mindfulness is the practice of being present. To be completely present, we must do so without judgment because our judgments can detract us from what we are experiencing. The practice of mindfulness or staying present in meditation entails noticing our thoughts without judgment but to let them pass by while noticing our reactions to them. In essence this practice is mindfulness of the mind. Thich Nhat Hanh believes the practice of mindfulness is a pathway to reduce suffering.

In Buddhist teachings, there is a conscious recognition for big mind and small mind. We all struggle with a critical, busy mind, which is affectionately referred to as the small mind or monkey mind, the mind that promotes suffering through delusion, impulses, or needs. Our big mind is the mind of the natural world, the calm, lucid, uncomplicated mind that is in touch with the bigger vision of life. This is the mind I am trying to help my students be in touch with, to turn down the small mind that is often full of insecurity and doubt and to tune into the big mind that can be in touch with the bigger picture of life to reduce personal suffering. Rather than judge ourselves for our life experiences and socialization, we can practice compassion toward ourselves by noticing the ways our identity (a result of experience and socialization) affects our relationships with others and learn to transform that suffering. How do we get there? We must know ourselves and have compassion toward ourselves *first*, which I will turn to in the next section.

In Buddhism there are three jewels that guide the practice. They are the Buddha, the Dharma, and the Sangha. The Buddha literally translates as the enlightened one; thus, it is believed that we all have the Buddha within us. We may not be aware or conscious of the Buddha, but the hope is to awaken the Buddha within and recognize that we are enlightened. To become enlightened, then, is to awaken. This relates to the idea that we already have the answers within us: If we can awaken to them, then we can work to end suffering. We all have the capacity to end suffering. The Dharma are our teachings. It is typical for Buddhists who follow the tradition of Thich Nhat Hanh to engage in dharma sharing, which means sharing of our teachings—sharing our experiences and how they have helped us gain insight. The final jewel is Sangha, which is community. The Sangha in Thich Nhat Hahn's tradition is strengthened through Dharma sharing and meditating together, as he believes that Dharma sharing can heal suffering. These three jewels come together to guide my teaching with teachers.

Thich Nhat Hahn was also a founder of the notion of Engaged Buddhism, which is our active involvement in ending suffering. The notion is that it is not enough to only meditate and develop insights for ourselves: We must also engage and apply our insights from meditation and Dharma sharing to real social, political, economic, and environmental injustices to reverse suffering. Engaged Buddhism with my teachers then becomes the act of self-reflection (meditation) and dialogic reflection (Dharma sharing) that occurs within my class as a pathway to engage with race and identity politics and to learn about power and privilege in education so we can work toward reducing and hopefully ending practices, conscious or unconscious, that perpetuate suffering in schools.

My Dharma Sharing

> To be mindful means to dwell deeply in the present moment, to be aware of what is going on within and around us. Practicing mindfulness cultivates understanding, love, compassion, and joy. This practice helps us to take care of and transform suffering in our lives and in our society. (Mindfulness Bell, 1999–2012)

I have learned through my journey with students in teacher education programs that many have not had the opportunity to think of themselves as racialized or cultured beings, particularly within the context of education. Thus, I begin my course by providing an opportunity for them to become conscious of their roots and their ancestry by creating a map of their ethnic and language history with particular attention toward when English became the dominant language of their lineage. As an example, I will share a brief snippet of my ethnic and language history so you have a sense of the practice.

I am a White woman with strong working-class roots (multigenerational) who was raised in the rust belt of Western New York. My maternal grandmother, Genevifka (Jean) Gac, was Polish; her parents emigrated to the United States from Poland prior to World War I. She had 11 siblings. My great-grandparents primarily spoke Polish and my great-grandfather spoke limited English because he was a soldier in World War I. Growing up, my grandmother Jean had a challenging school life, as she recounted stories to me of being punished by nuns for speaking in Polish and quickly became English dominant. Although her mother did not speak English, my grandmother maintained her ability to understand Polish but typically responded to her mother in English. Later in life, she expressed remorse over losing her Polish and not being bilingual. My mother remembers spending time at my great-grandparents' farm eating fresh pickles and sauerkraut from barrels in the barn and not always understanding her grandmother because she spoke English with a Polish accent. Growing up, my mother was raised working-class poor as my grandmother Jean was a single parent. Grandma Jean was a seamstress for wealthy families and used to cut patterns in such a way to ensure enough scrap fabric was left to make clothes for my mother and her three siblings. From her, I inherited a creative style, the ability to be resourceful, and my tenacity to be resilient.

My maternal grandfather, Sabastiano DeVito, was born in the United States. His parents immigrated to the United States from Italy in their early 20s. He was bilingual and code-switched a lot, sprinkling in Italian words even as he spoke English. He was absent for most of my mother's formative years, thus leaving my grandmother Jean to make due as a single parent with four young children. It was rumored that he was a card dealer for the Mafia and spent those years living underground. He later returned to Western New York State when my mother was an adult, and he owned a taxicab business. I remember staying with Grandpa Yano (short for Sabastiano) and his second wife Grandma Anna. Their home always smelled of fresh-cooked Italian food and was decorated with a traditional Italian flair with red velvet curtains and plastic-covered furniture in the living room; fresh fruit and bread always on the dining room table; and a host of barking Chihuahuas in the kitchen. When Grandpa Yano spoke, he would move back and forth between Italian and English while waving his chubby hands speckled with gold rings. He was round and stood just five feet tall. From him, I inherited a love of food and cooking as well as a deep connection with my Italian heritage.

The Teaching

This history is just a snapshot of my identity but one that often gets missed when viewed merely as White. Just as there is a legacy of essentializing people of color based on skin tone, language, or country of origin, Whites face the same phenomenon even as we are all complex cultural beings. So to promote dialogue about race and identity politics, one must first start with the self: Know thyself. This then becomes the gateway for understanding the other. When my students engage in the journey of mapping their ethnic and language history, I have witnessed many reactions from anger about the cultural amnesia of their family heritage to guilt for not maintaining language or cultural practices to pride for their heritage and recognition of their ancestors. Overwhelmingly it becomes an opportunity to connect with relatives whom they have not been in contact with for some time and most certainly a conversation they have not had before with their families. It is at this point that I am able to discuss the privilege of cultural amnesia: that being White affords them the opportunity to forget their ethnic/language history but when they remember, it can become a platform to make connections with the current experiences of students they serve, from the complexities of why they immigrate to the United States, to when language loss/maintenance occurs in a family, to recognition that African Americans who are descendants of those Africans who survived the horror of the slave trade have a much different history in becoming American.

Most importantly, in hearing each other's stories they become open to hearing stories of historically marginalized communities because they are in touch with the emotions of their heritage and can make the connection with suffering and the process of Americanization that has occurred in their own lineage and in our collective lineage. From this point I am then able to embark on the journey of talking about race, identity, and culture because we have unpacked our collective identities, which becomes a starting point to dialogue about identities of past and present. I intentionally use small group as a way to facilitate community building by getting to know each other more intimately. Because many students become emotional during the small-group share out, I have found this structure provides them more support and enables them to take more risks than if they had shared in whole group.

My Students' Dharma Sharing

You don't change people's minds, you change their hearts. (National Coalition Building Institute, ND)

When I first began to meet with my students in small groups after class, it was more for them to get to know me as a person and to see that I truly cared about their well-being and learning experience in my course. But I felt that my cultural interaction style (being from the East Coast and raised working-class) was being misinterpreted as rude or harsh. Given the already sensitive nature of the content, I knew I needed them to see me as human. Yet, over time these sessions became less and less about me and more about them being heard, being validated. It became a space for testimonials or sharing life stories/experiences. I was able to show empathy and connect with them on a personal level, which in turn promoted a deeper dialogue in class. When we did have challenging conversations about race and identity politics, I could connect with them personally by softening around the edges and see them as human, too. For example, one student was consistently late to class while always turning in high-quality work. I was feeling frustrated, a bit disrespected, and at times I casted her as a privileged White girl. Through meeting with her one on one she shared that she was enrolled in six graduate classes and just started her first part-time teaching position. She was feeling overwhelmed and disappointed in herself for not being able to make it to class on time and not handing in higher quality work. She pleaded that this was not typical of her and was struggling with what to do. It was obvious she was overcommitted. As I listened to her, I felt my assumptions/misinterpretations about her melt away and I became empathic. We worked through a solution together.

The Teaching

You might ask: What does this have to do with supporting dialogue about race and identity politics? During class we were discussing parent involvement and the misperception that certain families don't value or seem to care about their children's education because of a perceived lack of parent involvement. I was able to connect with this student's story of being overcommitted and how I began to seek to understand her further versus holding down my assumptions that she was enacting privilege and disrespect by coming to class late. Yet at the same time, we discussed how the system of privilege based on race made it "invisible" for her to be late, but if she were a student of color, she would more likely be noticed or, worse yet, negatively stereotyped because of it. We were then able to loop that back to assumptions and misinterpretations we make about families from various cultural backgrounds.

Closing

Be the change you want to see in the world. (Gandhi)

As a White woman who prepares predominantly White teachers to work in urban and diverse communities, providing a space to discuss power and privilege as they relate to race, identity, and inequity in education has become critical. It would be easy for me as a White educator to gloss over race and identity politics in education and focus only on traditional methods of teaching, yet through my own journey in becoming an educator, I have learned that omission only leads to more inequity. Equally important is the opportunity I have as a White educator, who is often perceived as an insider, to champion a dialogue about an often-silenced topic among Whites. I do not take this calling lightly; in fact, I embrace it as a badge of honor because if I do not, who will? And when I imagine the faces of my brother who is deaf and my former students, Ricardo (Isleta Pueblo Indian), Jesús (Mexican American), Gabriel (Mexican National), and Jesse (6th Street gang member of Mexican American, White Hispanic decent), I have no choice but to tell our stories together of fighting for equitable education.

If our goal is to truly develop critical educators for social change, then we must model the practices we want students to enact regardless of race, class, gender, socioeconomic status, etc. What I mean is that when I first began teaching, I had much more empathy for students who I perceived shared my identity as working-class or who came from historically marginalized communities. Now, however, I realize that everyone deserves the opportunity to experience that connection, to be heard. We are all suffering, and whether we want to believe it or not, suffering is part of the human condition. The teaching of Thich Nhat Hahn (1993) suggests that we must show compassion toward the oppressor as well as the oppressed for suffering to end. We cannot be selective about who we are compassionate toward; rather, we need to show compassion just as much to those who oppress, because within our compassion, there is possibility for healing and transformation.

In the chapter by Augustine and Zurmehly, they purport that spirituality allows "for honest and meaningful dialogue around race and identity." In my work I have asked the question, How do we evoke this honest and meaningful dialogue? Especially knowing that this journey of dialoguing about race, culture, and identity politics becomes emotional, it is essential that supports be provided to nurture this dialogue forward. Their dialogue and work points the way. I believe critical spirituality is the lens that can guide our intentions. For me, mindfulness and Buddhist teachings have become the lens from which I engage this important work with teachers. As the Buddha once said, "I teach on suffering and the way to end it." In my teaching, I also engage our suffering so that we may end the suffering of others.

References

Dray, B. J., & Wisneski, D. B. (2011). Mindful reflection as a process for developing Culturally Responsive Practices. *TEACHING Exceptional Children, 44*(1), 28–36.

Gudykunst, W. B., & Kim, Y. Y. (2003). *Communicating with strangers: An approach to intercultural communication* (4th ed.). New York: McGraw-Hill.

Hanh, T. N. (1975). *The miracle of mindfulness: An introduction to the practice of meditation* (M. Ho, Trans.). Boston: Beacon Press.

Hanh, T. N. (1993). *"Interbeing": Fourteen guidelines for Engaged Buddhism* (rev. ed.). Berkeley, CA: Parallax Press.

Harderwijk, R. (2012). A view of Buddhism: The three jewels. Retrieved from http://viewonbuddhism.org/

Unified Buddhist Church. (1999–2012). About the Mindfulness Bell Magazine. Retrieved from http://www.mindfulnessbell.org/magazine.php

Chapter 2

Writing and Telling

Healing the Pain of Disconnection

Eyatta Fischer

Introduction

There is a saying in Vietnamese: "It doesn't cost anything to have loving speech" (Hanh, 1998, p. 88). When was the last time you connected with a long-lost relative, friend, or neighbor? When was the last time you spent time alone, without technology or media, and used that time to connect with your spirit, thoughts, and feelings? When was the last time you had a conversation with a person or group of people, and gave them your undivided attention, without checking your email, answering a call, and/or text messaging?

Modern American culture is a disconnected culture, one that is increasingly becoming devoid of opportunities for the creation of tangible, human-to-human connection:

> Never in human history have we had so many means of communication—television, radio, telephone, fax, email, the Internet—yet we remain islands, with little real communication between family members, individuals in society, or nations. There are so many wars and conflicts. We have to find ways to open the doors of communication again. When we cannot communicate, we get sick, and we suffer and spill our suffering onto other people. We pay psychother-

apists to listen to us, but psychotherapists are just human beings who have problems also. (Hanh, 1998, p. 89)

Go to the movie theater, a restaurant, mall, church, classroom, etc., and it will not be uncommon to find people texting, checking emails, and engaging in social networking platforms—regardless of the fact that those people may be within the company of others.

Belonging and connecting are all integral aspects of being human and participating in human social constructs. Central to the core of belonging and connecting lies community. Humans connect to communities through shared experiences and stories. The process of telling one's story is both an informative and transformational act for both the storyteller and the listener (Butcher & Buckwalter, 2002). Jerome Bruner (1999), one of the creators of narrative psychology, states that telling stories is not just something we do, but rather it is the "very process in which we construct Self....No story, no self" (p. 8).

Over the course of history, many civilizations used storytelling as a means of entertainment, education, cultural preservation, and teaching moral values. Some of these cultures relied on bards, *scops, griots,* and others to create and maintain a community of culture. The process of telling one's story, via writing and verbal communication, is a process that allows the giver (storyteller) and the receiver (audience) to share an experience. Stories are relational; they build relationships, create bonding links between educators and learners, and complement analysis with more holistic views of experience. Sharing experiences can coalesce participants for mutual support, for stories offer an accessible venue for seeing others' perspectives (Pfahl & Wiessner, 2007, p. 12).

Stories remind us many realities can share one space. Stories have played an integral role, to the development and foundation of literacies, within post- and pre-literate societies (Pfahl & Wiessner, 2007). Within a classroom dynamic, these shared experiences can be used to build a community of practice that focuses on the conjunctive relationship between human connectivity, storytelling, and narrative writing. This connection is unrelated to educational level, thereby providing an accessible space for sharing variables of class, gender, race, culture, and age (Pfahl & Wiessner, 2007).

Does societal disconnection manifest itself in the classroom/educational politics? Since the inception of the No Child Left Behind (NCLB) Act of 2001, community making within the classroom has not been a widely accepted curricular practice because (in the eyes of the standards) it does not promote test-taking/passing skills. In this way, the American education system has fallen into a pattern of disconnection that mirrors the disconnection found outside of the classroom. Our culture of No Child Left Behind translates success into percentages, numbers, standards, and testing. Over the past 11 years, American education has moved toward an educational reform that promotes an ideology that the true mark of knowledge lies within a passing score, that a "good" teacher is one who follows the script by producing passing scores, that teaching/learning just enough to pass the test is all that is required, that intra/interpersonal communication has no room in the curriculum, that teaching students to view their curriculum through a critical lens is discouraged, along with teaching to the spirit of a student's identity.

In this chapter, I will examine the following questions: How can communities of practice, situated in narrative and reflective writing, assist participants in pushing past the notion of tolerance and into a cosmology of respect? How can narrative/reflective writing act as a vessel of inner-spiritual awakening? How can participation in a community of practice lead members to respect the identities of others and form more healthy intrapersonal identity perspectives? How does a Cosmology of Respect make space for connection, instead of data, within the classroom? I seek to use these questions as a sounding board to illustrate the range of challenges facing educators who do not want to follow the "drill and kill" methodology of standardized testing. In addition to this, I seek to illuminate the ways in which social and academic disconnection stem from a lack of nurture to the inner spirit. I will discuss how my participation in a graduate-level writing class for secondary English teachers provided a means for my inclusion into a community of writers and showed me that writing can be spiritually healing, as well as connective to the facets of myself that I had hidden away.

The Beginning

I started teaching Secondary English in August 2001, one school year before the implementation of the No Child Left Behind Act (NCLB). I had no prior educational training, save for the undergraduate degree I attained and the generational "coding" of educator passed on to me by my mother, grandparents, and aunts. I learned how to teach by emulating the Master Teachers, who were in abundance at my first school of my employment. The culture at that school conveyed the mentality of an education for knowledge's sake. Teachers were not teaching to fulfill the requirements of yearly grade-level and subject-specific tests, nor were teachers teaching to fulfill the requirements of a national report card that would announce a student (or teacher) as either a success or failure based on the numbers of the test, rather than the personal learning curve of the student.

Soon, the educational climate shifted and school administrators became more concerned with a teacher's classroom gain scores on state tests, the number of students who passed the national tests, and passing the domains of the Adequate Yearly Progress (AYP) report. During that time, the spirits of teachers and students were being broken, a hazing effect of these measures. My personal life was affected because I was always stressed—wondering if I had all of my essential questions, standards-based lesson plans, standards-based teaching charts, and verbiage placed in the correct places within my classroom. There was always a looming fear of "the county office" or "the state office" coming into your classroom and deeming you inefficient, incompetent, and dispensable.

It was not until June 2006, during my first semester as a graduate student in a teacher education program, that I was introduced to the concept of education for the spirit. The course was rather generically titled Composition for the English Classroom. I expected the class to be focused around test taking and ways in which to boost students' ability to pass the standards of the state writing test. My hope for that class was to gain knowledge of the type of writing strategies that would help me help my students to boost their writing test scores. What I learned, instead, was something that would permanently alter my teaching and my personal life, the very way that I viewed teaching.

The Feather Circle

The following piece titled "Discovering Truth" is the first Feather Circle writing assignment that I completed, assigned to my entire cohort. "Discovering Truth" is modeled after G. Lynn Nelson's (2004) epigraph from *Writing and Being: Embracing Your Life Through Creative Journaling*.

Discovering Truth: My Feather Story

David said, "If you tell anyone, then the entire family will hate you!"

I was seven and sharing the enclosed space of a bedroom closet with my fourteen-year-old cousin, David. I believed that he was telling the truth. Why wouldn't he? He was my cousin. Why would he lie…to me?

As a child I was always enamored with the idea of truth. I viewed the world with a black and white, right and wrong idolatry. I felt certain that everyone else viewed truth in the same manner I did. I thought that the truth was abundant and apparent behind each pair of eyes I gazed into. I thought that those pair of eyes shared the same truth that I knew.

The stammering untruths of a seven year old…MY untruths as a seven year old…so memorable and cathartic. I will never forget the feeling of the electricity of truth rippling throughout the atmosphere…waiting to be released. Truth contained is a damn of water that waits patiently for its orgasmic release. Truth will wait. Truth will be told.

I believed that he was telling the truth. Why wouldn't he? He was my cousin. He was my molester. Why would he lie…to me?

Now, David's truth had become my truth. We shared a truth through the same pair of eyes…but whose truth? I wondered why my part of truth was being so reluctant to settle. Was there something wrong with me? I panicked. I wanted him to love and accept me. He was my cousin. He was my molester. Why would he lie...to me? My grandfather, now deceased, was like a weather vane. He was good at detecting storms. He sensed the quiet storm brewing within me. Papa pulled me aside one evening and asked, "What is going on between you and David?"

His eyes pierced through mine and straight into my soul. My first instinct was to cry out, "Save me, Papa!" But then I remembered the Truth that I shared with my cousin. Any divulging of our "special" relationship would result in the family hating me for the rest of my life...and I was only seven at the time...rest of my life...that was a virtual eternity!

"Nothing," I confessed as I attempted to hold his gaze. The gritty feel of the untruth rolled off my tongue, leaving a filmy residue on my teeth along with a foul taste in the pits of my palette. It tasted horrible! I held my head to the side, as though the weight were too much for me to bear. My grandfather smelled a rat!

"David!" he yelled out into the deafening silence of the house. My cousin appeared within seconds. "I am calling your father to come and pick you up. Something unsavory has occurred between the two of you," he stated as he pointed between the two of us. "You have taken advantage of my granddaughter and I want you out of my house as soon as possible." I held my breath, waiting for the part where my grandfather banished me from the family. I held my breath as I waited...waited...then I felt it...Truth! Truth encircled me and resided within the strong, sturdy embrace of my grandfather.

"Lil Baby, you don't ever have to lie to me or feel ashamed. You did nothing wrong. Always tell the truth. The truth shall set you free," he spoke while holding me close to him. To this day, I have never felt safer than I did at that moment...sitting in that room with my grandfather and Truth.

Now, I wrote those words as an assignment for a Master of Education class for teachers in secondary English. But this first assignment (a Logo narrative) also required us to choose a symbol that we felt was representative of our current state, and use that symbol as the focus of our piece. I chose Ma'at, the ancient Egyptian goddess of justice, harmony, and truth. In the Duat, the Egyptian underworld, the hearts of the dead were weighed against her single Feather of Ma'at, representing truth. If a heart was deemed unworthy or untruthful, the goddess Ammit devoured the heart, and its owner was condemned to remain in the Duat (Budge, 1969). In selecting this symbol, I wanted to be transparent in my intention of capturing the essence of truth and honesty that my grandfather represented. I also wanted to illustrate, through the use of symbol of Ma'at, that I was ready to acknowledge and accept that truth. Along with this focus, the only other rules of the assignment were the following:

1. Write from the heart.
2. Be "real."
3. Don't be boring.

These requirements may, at first glance, seem trivial and easy enough. But one must consider the prospective risks when sharing a piece "written from the heart" with a cohort full of strangers.

When it was time for us to share our narratives with the class, our professor pulled a feather out of his briefcase. He said: "Whomever holds the feather speaks. Once you have read your piece, pass the feather to the left and the next person will speak. After each person has spoken, there should not be any commentary. Reflect on the words your cohort members have shared and put your comments in a 'Thank You' letter that you may choose to write for him or her."

Listening to everyone's Logo narrative provided insights I would never have been able to achieve if I were left to run the natural course of forming a classroom friendship. Listening to each of my classmate's narrative pieces provided a personal connection to each of them through the ancient art of storytelling.

Then, to further complete that line of connection, I went home and wrote (by hand) a one-paragraph 'Thank You' note to each of my cohort members. And the following inserts are copies of actual 'Thank You' notes that I *received* from two of my cohort members.

Thank You Note #1—Logo Narrative

Dear Eyatta,

Thank you for your logo piece, for sharing your Truth. I love the description of your grandfather as a weathervane, and the 7-year old's perspective you keep throughout. You really do a good job communicating the innocence and uncomplicated perceptions of you at 7 yrs old. "Black & White, good & bad: David was family & he was good. How could he also be bad?"

"Truth" itself becomes a key character in this piece and seems to have as much importance as anyone else. Grandfather Papa knew Truth well. In this piece, we clearly see 7-year-old Eyatta come to know Truth a great deal better than she did before.

Thanks again, and I look forward to more.

Sincerely,

L.A

Thank You Note #2—Logo Narrative

Eyatta—

Thank you for sharing such a moving, personal story. I believe you show courage, intellect, and truth…the pathway to honest expression. There is love in your piece, aching love that reveals itself near the end with your revelation about truth.

Before that, I truly felt your grandfather's eyes piercing me as they had your eyes. Grandfathers can always smell the rats. Thank goodness for that. I love your closing image of you safely coexisting with your grandfather: You and Truth.

Beautiful in the end.

K.M

The process of sharing each other's stories, and then writing notes of thanks to one another, was so powerful. The power of the process allowed us to form a connection that was based on a humanistic perspective that promoted a recognition and acceptance of our differences, allowed us to move past the act of merely *tolerating* another person's race, identity, sexual orientation, religion, or gender. We were a group of strangers who forged a spirit-to-spirit connection, based on the tenets of storytelling and space sharing.

Reading, writing, thinking, and dialogue are core practices of narrative pedagogy. Necessary content appears in the written stories, and students' thinking about the meaning and significance of the stories is elicited. Narrative pedagogy emphasizes how students and teachers learn and experience thinking in actual situations. (Ewing & Hayden-Miles, 2011, p. 212).

The methodology of the Feather Circle was adapted from a Native American means of discussion called a *talking circle*. The circle itself is seen as sacred, according to Wolf and Rickard (2003), representing the interconnectedness of all things: People, earth, moon, and sun (p. 39):

> Traditionally, many Native American communities have used the talking circle as a way of bringing people of all ages together for the purposed of teaching, listening, and learning (Anishinabeg Nation, 1999). Thus, talking circles were a traditional form of early childhood through adult education and provided a way to pass on knowledge, values, and culture. This method of education instilled respect for another's viewpoint and encouraged members to be open to other viewpoints by listening with their heart while another individual speaks. (Sams, 1990, p. 39)

How might such a sacred and powerful methodology be conceptualized in education? I believe that whatever the conceptualization, it operates from a space of respect. It is that cosmology to which I now turn.

Cosmology of Respect: A Theoretical Framework

A cosmology can be thought of as a structure or framework that explains how something operates. To address the research questions I introduced earlier within the chapter, I will use what I call a *cosmology of respect*. In the Feather Circle assignment, the cultivation of a cosmology of respect began with the introduction of the initial writing assignment and "ended" once the last letters of a 'Thank You' note had been read and processed. The writing, sharing, listening, and thanking are integral pieces leading to the enactment of a cosmology of respect.

A cosmology, as referred to in this chapter, is the overarching formation that describes the theory/doctrine of the ways in which respect can be manifested within circles of communication. Empathetic connection embodies respect in multiple forms (Darwall, 1977; Hudson, 1980). Dillon (2003) suggests the various ways of showing respect have the common elements of *attention*, *deference*, *valuing*, and *appropriate conduct*. Attention is shown when a person's mind is focused on an individual's particularities and commonalities (Hajii, 2006, p. 66).

My framework for healing the disconnection so many feel about education has been built around the concept of respect defined here as *the regard that one holds for self and others*. Respect is the capstone of creating a society that operates on the principles of humanistic acceptance and understanding. Respect may indeed be the glue that binds people together and holds one's self-concept. "Respect is essential in a civil society and crucial to positive human relations" (Shwalb & Shwalb, 2006, p. 2). Respect has been called "the single most powerful ingredient in nourishing relationships and creating a just society" (Lawrence-Lightfoot, 2000, p. 13). Respect requires empathy, connection, and symmetry with another person (Hajii, 2006, p. 66). Lawrence-Lightfoot (2000) identified the following six forms of respect, drawing on the work of like-minded scholars:

> **Empowerment** is enabling others to develop the knowledge and self-efficacy to realize their full potential. Students who are active co-creators of their own learning develop the ability, confidence, and motivation to succeed academically (Cummins, 1986).

> **Healing** uses actions and words to counter discrimination, racism, sexism, and oppression. Lawrence-Lightfoot (2000) proposes modeling respect as a powerful curative to the intolerance, inequality, discrimination, and power differentials in schools.

Dialogue taps both heart and mind through active listening, good questioning, valuing inquiry, and thoughtful reflection with another person. Authentic dialogue between student and teacher is never "a crafty instrument for the domination of one person by another" (Freire, 2001, p. 89). Authentic dialogue is not didactic but "real talk" (Belenky, Clinchy, Goldberger, & Tarule, 1986). Didactic talk lacks any sense of a joint effort to share and to reach new meanings. On the other hand, real talk requires careful mutual exchange so that creative and even half-baked or emergent ideas can grow.

Curiosity is the inquisitive interest between two persons seeking a deep understanding of one another. Curiosity requires trust. Teachers provide a safe environment where students are storytellers of their lives. Storytelling is a way of building trust and "growing" respectful relationships.

Attention consists of a profound attentiveness given to a person. When we attend to another's stories, we help the person to feel appreciated, honored, and acknowledged (Cranor, 1975). This provides a foundation for building confidence and courage.

Self-respect is the acceptance of one's own self-identity as intrinsically valuable no matter how others perceive it. This sense of secure self-worth enables young people to develop resilience in coping with life's challenges and problems (Hajii, 2006, p. 67).

My notion of a Cosmology of Respect is a three-fold framework that is enacted through the infusion of the following processes: (1) accessing a vulnerability of the heart, (2) listening from the heart, and (3) communicating through the heart. I use the meaning of heart in the same manner that Palmer (1998) uses it: "in its ancient sense, as the place where intellect and emotion and spirit will converge in the human self" (p. 11). This framework will trouble the ways in which disconnection (emotional, social, and cultural) works as an agent of divorce that retards one's ability to marry the humanistic understanding of all identities. Throughout this discussion (and using the Logo narrative activity discussed earlier in this chapter), I will rely on these aforementioned processes of the Cosmology of Respect to demonstrate the ways respect, community, and narrative writing can create a social and emotional connection to self and others.

Process: Opening the Vulnerability of the Heart

Making connections through the spirit and the heart require *vulnerability*. My Logo piece was written so raw and honestly because my professor first shared his Logo piece with us as an example. While the Logo piece my professor shared was not as candid as the piece I shared, an unprecedented level of transparency existed in his work that I never experienced with any other professor in any other class. His piece not only modeled the level of writing he expected to receive from us, it also served as a model for the level of vulnerability we were "allowed" to display as writers. The pieces we brought in for our Feather Circle all held a similar quality of vulnerability.

Another vital aspect that compelled my cohort and me to write from the spirit and write from the heart was the guiding information we received from the author of our required text. On the first page and first paragraph of *Writing and Being: Embracing Your Life Through Creative Journaling*, the author, G. Lynn Nelson, states his intention for the use of his book:

> This is not a book about writing. This is a book about people writing. It is a book about writing as a tool for intellectual, psychological, and spiritual growth. It is about our language and our being and their powerful interconnectedness, which have often been taken away from us without our even knowing what we have lost. This book is about taking back the miraculous gift of our language and using it as an instrument of creation. (p. 1)

From those first pages, our writing developed as a testimony of our intellectual, psychological, and spiritual growth, as well as our testimony of creating connectedness and community through the vulnerability of sharing our writing.

Process: Listening from the Heart

> But our stories are caught in our throats. We need someone to listen
> to our stuttering, stammering plea to be heard. We need deep listen-
> ing. (Nelson, 2000, p. 44)

The communicative process of our Feather Circle began on the first day
of classes, when our professor walked in to the classroom, after everyone else was seated, and performed a monologue. He made it known to
us, through his level of communication, that he was open to creative and
connective modes of communication. Our professor scaffolded our
process toward communication and connection by guiding us through
writing activities that required us to slowly peel away inhibitions, insecurities, and fear. During the first class, he shared his writings with us.
When we returned for our next class session, we were equipped with our
first drafts of our Logo narratives.

We did not present to the larger group immediately. First, we were
divided into smaller groups, to serve the purpose of making revisions.
These smaller, editing groups also enhanced our levels of student-to-stu-
dent and spirit-to-spirit communication. We were able to share our
pieces with our editing groups, as well as establish a level of trust and
understanding. Bringing trust and understanding into the smaller circles of our editing groups were unspoken requirements; everyone had
written pieces that made them that much more vulnerable and transparent. I was able to recognize the spirit within each of my peers through
the act of reading their literary work.

Once revisions were complete, we were ready for the Feather Circle.
First, we formed the circle, and then we distributed copies by passing
our copies to the left, and taking one copy of each of our peers' work. As
mentioned before, the rules of the Feather Circle bound us to only two
functions: (1) reading our piece and (2) silently receiving the pieces of
others. There was no conversation or applause between piece readings
or during the passing of the feather stick.

There is a magical power that lies in the act of telling a personal story,
a sort of magic of resuscitation. Storytelling is an ancient art form that
unites the human experience through its role as a shaper of voice and
identity, creator of meaning, and transporter of language. The telling of

one's story creates a space for self-affirmation, of proof of existence. In *Warrior with Words* (2000), Nelson asserts that the teaching of writing is also teaching the use of language. Nelson further suggests that "our language greatly determines how we see the world and how we act in the world. Language is both the source of much violence in our society—and its potential cure" (p. 42).

While Nelson defines the sharing of language, and careful use of words, as an important aspect of humanity, sharing, and the promotion of peace, Nelson names listening as an act that is just as powerful. Listening is the journey. The first process of the cosmology of respect, making one's heart open and vulnerable enough to receive, is the primer: the glancing at the map to chart one's course. The last process, communication through the heart, is the destination. The process of listening provides a space for validation of the speaker and also allows the speaker to experience self-validity. I often wonder if something as simple, natural, and free as listening can change the course of the violent acts that are imposed on self and others. Listening is a transformative act. As Nelson (2000) so aptly states: "To listen. Not to grade. Not to psychoanalyze. Not to solve. Just to listen" (p. 45).

Process: Communicating through the Heart

> Personal story leads to authentic communication, speaking from our hearts, from our whole-ness. But authentic communication demands a listener. So story asks of us another change from the orthodox writing class. It asks us to value listening over grading. (Nelson, 2000, p. 44)

The thank-you note process is an act of transformation. The process worked like this: After we listened to everyone read their written pieces, the pieces were distributed so that we each we able to take them home. Once at home, we were to select eight peers and compose a handwritten note of thanks. While writing the thank-you note, our professor asked us to not only comment on the conventional aspects of the piece but to also recognize the piece holistically: We were to comment on the words and the *heart* of the piece.

I call the process an act of transformation because it *felt* like transformation. Writing a Feather Circle piece became meditational, and writing the thank-you note cycled into an intimate connection with another being. I forged alliances with people, if left to the devices of my egotistical snap judgments, I would never have thought interesting enough to speak more than two words to if it had not been for the intimate sharing process of the Feather Circle.

Conclusion

Participating in the Feather Circle was one of the best things that ever happened to me. As a teacher, it prepared me to be more transparent to my students, to allow them to experience me authentically and deeply. According to Palmer (1998), when an educator teaches as a whole person, to nurture the spirit and soul of the students, he or she does not lose professionalism as a teacher. Transformation begins to happen when we allow our students to see our inner self (Wane, Manyimo, & Ritskes, 2011, p. 43).

While I realize that a teacher's reality consists of data, test scores, and standards, it is also my reality that those things do not have to drive the ways in which we teach/relate to our students. To heal, we must learn to connect—with self and with others. Most importantly, we must learn to *respect* experience and personhood. I have discovered, through participation in the Feather Circle, that the journey toward respect begins inwardly. As educators, it is our responsibility to provide a platform for students to actualize themselves as beings who are connected, whole, capable, and worthy of respect. It is also our responsibility to provide them (and ourselves) a safe space for healing. As I have learned, writing has that power to heal, connect, and save lives.

References

Anishinabeg Nation. (1999). *Talking circles.* Retrieved from http://www.geocities.com/CapitolHill/Lobby/1059/talking.html

Belenky, M. F., Clinchy, B. M., Goldberger, N. R., & Tarule, J. M. (1986). *Women's ways of knowing: The development of self, voice, and mind.* New York: Basic Books.

Bruner, J. (1999). Narratives of aging. *Journal of Aging Studies, 13*(1), 7–9.

Budge, E. A. (1969). *The gods of the Egyptians.* (Vol. 1). Mineola, NY: Dover Publications.

Butcher, H. (2004). Written expression and the potential to enhance knowing participation in change. *The Journal of Rogerian Nursing Science, 12*(1), 37–50.

Butcher, H. K., & Buckwalter, K. C. (2002). Exasperations as blessings: Meaning-making and the caregiving experience. *Journal of Aging and Identity, 7*(2), 113–132.

Cranor, C. (1975). Toward a theory of respect for persons. *American Philosophical Quarterly, 12*(4), 309–319.

Cummins, J. (1986). Empowering minority students: A framework for intervention. *Harvard Educational Review, 56*(1), 18–36.

Darwall, S. L. (1977). Two kinds of respect. *Ethics, 88*(1), 36–49.

Dillon, R. S. (2003). Respect. In E. N. Zalta (Ed.), *The Stanford Encyclopedia of Philosophy*. Retrieved from http://plato.stanford.edu/archives/fall2003/entries/respect/>.

Ewing, B., & Hayden-Miles, M. (2011). Narrative pedagogy and art interpretation. *Journal of Nursing Education, 50*(4), 211–215.

Freire, P. (2001). *Pedagogy of the oppressed* (30th anniv. ed.). (M. B. Ramos, Trans.). New York: Continuum. (Original work published 1970)

Hajii. (2006). Four faces of respect. *Reclaiming Children and Youth: The Journal of Strength-Based Interventions, 15*(2), 66–70.

Hanh, T. (1998). *Teachings on love*. Berkeley, CA: Parallax Press.

Hudson, S. D. (1980). The nature of respect. *Social Theory and Practice, 6*(1), 69–90.

Lawrence-Lightfoot, S. (2000). *Respect: An exploration*. Cambridge, MA: Perseus Books.

Nelson, G. (2000). Warrior with words. *English Journal, 89*(5), 42–46.

Nelson, G. (2004). *Writing and being: Embracing your life through creative journaling*. San Francisco, CA: Inner Ocean Publishing.

Palmer, P. (1998). *The courage to teach: Exploring the inner landscape of a teacher's life*. San Francisco, CA: Jossey-Bass.

Pfahl, N. L., & Wiessner, C. A. (2007). Creating new directions with story: Narrating life experience as story in community adult education contexts. *Adult Learning, 18*, 9–13.

Sams, J. (1990). *Sacred path cards: The discovery of self through native teachings*. San Francisco: HarperSanFrancisco.

Shwalb, D., & Shwalb, B. (2006). Research and theory on respect and disrespect: Catching up with the public and practitioners. *New Directions for Child and Adolescent Development, 114*, 1–9.

Wane, N., Manyimo, E., & Ritskes, E. (2011). *Spirituality, education & society: An integrated approach*. Rotterdam, Netherlands: Sense Publishers.

Wolf, P., & Rickard, J. (2003). Talking circles: A Native American approach to experiential learning. *Multicultural Counseling and Development, 31*, 39–43.

On Teaching and Telling

Two Sides of a Teaching (Cassette) Tape

Robin M. Boylorn

As a teenager I never thought about the various ways I sought and celebrated community. In many ways I think I took for granted the straightforward and fully invested ways that I was conditioned to communicate with others. It was, of course, during a time when the technology my family could afford was limited to cordless telephones, an Atari and later Nintendo game system (the original), and a Tandy computer and dot matrix printer my mother bought with all of her savings. It wasn't a lot, even in the early 1990s, but it was enough to allow us to feel full—full of the capacity to have simple luxuries and full of ourselves and the ways those simple luxuries afforded us time together, to talk on the phone anywhere in the house, to take turns playing video games together, and, my favorite, to use the computer, which was so much more "fancy" than the typewriter my mother occasionally let me use. Finally, I had a way of writing stories beyond the handwritten messages I hid in one-subject notebooks I saved from school.

As a 30-something adult who is also a communication scholar I am often conflicted with the ways that computer-mediated communication and technology has both enhanced and inhibited our communication practices and rituals. As Fischer notes in this chapter, we are oftentimes engaged with others through some form of technological advancement that limits the emotional reach of our communication practices. We often forget to be intentional in our communication, to listen deeply, to pay attention to the nuances of what a conversational partner is saying or doing in an exchange, to watch for nonverbal cues, to be an active participant in loving dialogue and ongoing narratives. I miss the times when talking and telling stories happened with eyes touching and hands meeting. I miss the intimacy of old-school communication and pre-technology technology that helped us remember how to connect to each other, as much out of necessity as choice.

I grew up listening to cassette tapes. The plastic square devices held recorded music, melodies, words, and voices embedded on the transparent film of a two-sided tape that could only be retrieved by a cassette player. In some ways the cassette tape is a metaphor for the stories and experiences that can yield community connection and relationships, but are useless without a player, someone to listen and make those stories mean something, someone to allow them to be heard. There are always at least two sides to every story. Following the lead of Eyatta Fischer's chapter, I am reflecting on the inextricable connection between teaching and learning (from) and writing and telling personal stories (to). Borrowing from the time when cassette tapes were the most popular method of recording data, and reaching (out to) others was less convenient, more meaningful, less immediate, more impactful, and deeply connected, I want to explore two sides of using an educational model as a way of accessing and celebrating creativity, connection, and freedom.

In this brief visionary response I am writing as if my words are hidden in a metaphorical cassette tape, holding teaching and writing lessons that can be best understood in the context of my 1980s childhood, 1990s coming of age, and 2000s adulthood, which provides a backdrop of teachers and peers who more often than not did not look like me, in places that did not always acknowledge me, yet I found a sense of belonging and community through shared stories.

The connections I make between teaching and learning are like two sides of a cassette tape; side A is teaching/learning, side B is writing/

telling. While they are both interrelated and part of the same storyline, they distinctly inform my understandings and negotiations of person-hood and pedagogy.

What follows is a brief teaching/learning story, informed by Eyatta Fischer's chapter on "Writing and Telling." I talk about what I thought was a good teacher and how I have adopted "good teacher" practices in my pedagogy. Later I will focus on writing/telling, and like Fischer, I use an excerpt from a class assignment that served as a trigger moment in my learning life and helped me see and situate myself as a storyteller.

Play (Side A): Teaching/Learning

> "To teach is to learn twice."
> —JOSEPH JOUBERT

Rewind (Learning)

Even when I was fairly young I knew there was something delicious about learning. I also knew, instinctively, that stories (at the time "telling stories" was no different from "telling lies") were what brought our family and community together, occasionally, depending on the truth in the telling, disrupting the monotony of weekday routines. People told stories everywhere there was somebody willing to listen: in the grocery store, church aisle, living room, courtroom, WIC line, on the assembly line, stories crossed over lips like invisible tongues. There was something majestic in storytelling. The way that people stopped what they were doing to listen, the way telling stories made your voice change, beckoned with memories and made up parts to fill in the gaps.

I mostly remember women telling stories, though I imagine men talked among themselves. The stories we told were never about the particularities of our lives (our gender, class, raced experiences) but the specifics were never far removed. Being Black, poor, and female was always an embedded element that shaped how the story was told and how it was understood. We could read-discern-comprehend the unspo-ken parts. But the listening was focused on the telling, the detailed scoop of what was going on.

Grown folk would sit at the kitchen table for hours laughing and remembering, telling the same stories over and over again until I had them memorized. They were not intentionally teaching me our legacy, but somewhere between "Chile...you remember when" and "Yes girl," their call-and-response stories inspired spontaneous dancing, belly laughs, and wide open eyes. Stories made everything beautiful, even the tragedies. Listening to them made me want to be a sister storyteller, but the stories I read and learned in school were not the same stories I listened to and witnessed at home. There was a disconnect and I needed a way to bring the sister stories from the front porch to the classroom. As a student it wasn't allowed. As a teacher I would require it.

Pause (Reflecting)

Fischer challenges the assumption that a good teacher is one who "follows the script by producing passing scores, that teaching/learning just enough to pass the test is all that is required, that intra/interpersonal communication has no room in the curriculum, that teaching students to view their curriculum through a critical lens is discouraged, along with teaching to the spirit of a student's identity."

For me a good teacher was one who saw me and knew my name. A good teacher for me was one who made me feel smart and helped me make sense of information by showing me how it was relevant in my day-to-day life. A good teacher, for me, was a teacher who did not make me feel invisible.

Fast-Forward (Teaching)

Being a storyteller has always been my way of setting myself apart. Similarly, I want to be a good teacher—the kind of teacher that students remember years after taking my class. I want to be impactful.

I am still getting used to the notion of being a teacher, an instructor, a professor, teaching, instructing, professing. I want to be an ethical educator (Pelias, 2004). I want to be informed by my conversations and interactions with students (Coles, 1989). I want to teach to transgress (hooks, 1994), meaning I want to teach my students to be critical thinkers and to be engaged in their own learning. I want to continue to learn as I teach.

I can always connect to my students by being transparent, by telling them stories that are memorable and stories that connect what they are learning to what they are living. I was not immediately sure how to use stories to make myself a better teacher, nor did I realize that being a good teacher would help inform my stories, but it did. Being a storyteller helps me make materials accessible to my students, and it helps me make myself accessible to them. Every semester I am committed to creating a community of learning, being, and healing in my classroom. Every semester starts with a story.

Rewind (Learning)

My sister was the oldest and the smartest. Because she did everything first, by the time I did them there was nothing notable about my accomplishments. When I was in the fifth grade my teacher wanted to know why I couldn't be more like "my sister." By the time I made straight As my mama looked at me like that was regular. When I finally made sense of Algebra my sister was taking Geometry. Growing up, learning was connected to being and feeling good enough, and being smart was linked to living up to my sister's brilliance and good behavior. She was quiet; I was a talker. She was good at science and math; I was good at English and handwriting. We could not have been more different. It made sense to me that we were nothing alike, but adults, especially teachers and family members, had expectations that the overlap of genes should have compensated for our dissimilarities. Nevah mind our differences.

Fast-Forward (Teaching)

I wanted to be a writer long before I wanted to be a teacher. In fact, it was never my intention to teach. I had a *lovehatelove* relationship with school and never saw myself as a teacher. Over the years, however, I have learned to love teaching and to embrace my role as a storyteller and story instigator in the lives of my students. We use stories to make sense of things. My goal, as an educator, is not to have my students memorize information that they will later regurgitate for a test and forget immediately thereafter, but I want to tell them stories that help make the concepts make sense, I want to teach them to tell stories that critically engage and challenge essentialist concepts, I want them to write the stories that help them make sense to themselves. Teaching, for me, is not about hierarchies but it is about positionalities. I never try to disconnect myself from my students, my teaching, or my pedagogy. My blackwomanness is as relevant to my interpretation of text as anything else. I don't teach from a neutral lens; I teach from the particularities of my lens/es.

Pause (Reflecting)

My goals as a teacher reflect my needs as a student. I want my students to feel seen, cared for, and protected. Like Fischer, I want my students to experience me "authentically and deeply." However, being open to your students is not without risk. Teaching evaluations and online professor rating sites are full of misinformed, hateful, and sometimes suspicious responses to my nontraditional teaching techniques. Not all students will embrace a classroom where the teacher is transparent (and Black and female and in some cases less than a decade older). I have to negotiate my teaching style, which allows me to embrace and bring my whole self into the room (including and especially the messy parts) to talk through, think through, and write through what it means to be in this world. My classes focus on issues of communication and diversity. We discuss difference and how to talk about taboo topics and how to have conversations about and with people who are "different." Sometimes pain seeps out when we tell our truths. Sometimes empathy and wide arms offer consolation and healing. Sometimes they don't. I have learned to be comfortable with both possibilities. I have learned that while our vulnerability and willingness to be transparent with one another creates a powerful space for connection, you can't force it. And that is OK. Everyone can't be saved. And teachers are not always healers, but they are facilitators.

Play (Side B): Writing/Telling

The following excerpt is taken from an auto/ethnographic writing assignment I was given in graduate school. I attempt here to follow the notion of Fischer's "cosmology of respect," focusing on the processes of being open, listening, and communicating from the heart. My professor's instructions were simple. She asked us to write an auto/ethnography about a difficult experience or memory. I wrote about my deepest childhood secret. The name of it was "Speechless." Later, when sharing our pieces aloud, I skipped over this part.

> I didn't have the words for what had happened to me. I didn't know who to tell or how to tell them. I didn't know the words. Girls in my class had names for theirs, sweet pea, coochie, stinka, cootie cat. Mine did not have a name. Mama always said it was private, my privacy, but she didn't say it had a name. Everything down there was supposed to be a secret. So I didn't have the words to tell her what was happening to me. How I almost relished in the attention of an almost adult who hugged me too tight and rubbed my back under my clothes. I never told her how I was made to sit wide legged and stare at a wall, silently, while my friend, who I trusted, touched my privacy and made me promise not to tell. My reward for the kept secret was soft-spoken words and penny candy. I was only five years old—and I didn't have the words.

While I did not talk about my childhood sexual abuse aloud, I remember marveling at the bravery of my peers who shared similar stories of abuse or pain. I remember thinking, *I'm not brave enough, I'm not strong enough, I'm not ready yet.* Perhaps I was afraid of being judged, or pitied, or not believed. In many ways those same fears may have informed my speechlessness as a child without the words to describe an experience I was too young to understand.

Unlike the Feather Circle exercise Fischer describes, my class did not write letters of thanks to each other. I was, however, grateful for the experience of hearing stories that made me feel less isolated in my pain. I connected with my peers and professor in that class because of the expectation that we tell our truth/s and hear others'. I have similar instincts in classrooms where I am the professor. My vulnerability and transparency makes me human. Our collective vulnerability allows for collective and creative communication around our lived experiences and realities that are both intellectual and embodied. We tell two sides together, we listen deeply for the lessons that language teaches, and we are transformed by the process of doing work that honors the stories and histories represented in the room.

Pause (Reflecting)

Some truths feel dangerous until they are told.

Play

Writers and tellers are teachers.

Stop/Eject.

References

Coles, R. (1989). The call *of stories: Teaching and the moral imagination*. Boston, MA: Houghton Mifflin.

hooks, b. (1994). *Teaching to transgress: Education as the practice of freedom*. New York: Routledge.

Pelias, R. (2004). *A methodology of the heart: Evoking academic and daily life*. Walnut Creek, CA: AltaMira Press.

Chapter 3

Spiritually Centered Caring

An Approach for Teaching and Reaching Black Students in Suburbia

Brooke Harris Garad

Introduction

African American students in suburban schools continue to struggle with the effects of segregation. In racially segregated schools, students and teachers have developed specific practices and pedagogies of caring that exemplify the values of the majority (Patterson, Gordon, & Groves Price, 2008). In predominantly White schools, Eurocentric views and versions of history devalue "other ways of knowing" (Cole, 2011) and Black students are marginalized by systems of domination (hooks, 2003). African American girls, in particular, are placed at the periphery of privilege in Eurocentric suburban schools.

I dealt with my fair share of ignorance and racism as an African American girl in mono-racial Middle America. I grew up in a quiet, safe, diversity-starved suburb of central Ohio and remained the only Black kid in class throughout elementary school. My family lived in a middle-class neighborhood (like everyone else I knew). Almost everybody was Caucasian,[1] Christian, and somehow the same. I always felt different and dreamed of moving to a big city where I could fit in and find people like me. Conflicted, I struggled constantly with my identity throughout middle school and high school. I was neither a Huxtable nor a hoodlum, but few images confirmed that I could be anything in between. For students like me who struggle to succeed (mind, body, and spirit) in schools where the stakes are high on an emotional and academic level, caring teachers can make a world of difference.

In this chapter, I seek to place African American students in suburban schools at the center of an academic discourse on caring in education. I will present different conceptualizations of caring before sharing some of my personal story as auto-ethnographical evidence in favor of an approach I call spiritually centered caring.

Conceptualizing Caring

Care exists in a spiritual paradigm (Dillard, 2006) along with peace and love. Each concept deals with humanizing ourselves and one another with mindful interaction and intention. To care in education is to recognize teaching and learning as processes of the mind, body, and spirit. Yet, to the detriment of a growingly diverse student population in the United States, spirituality is silenced in schools (Wane & Ritskes, 2011) and caring is overshadowed by competition (Noddings, 1992).

One of the most influential scholars of caring in education, Noddings (1992) criticizes an education system that encourages competition and overemphasizes academic achievement. She presents a lack of caring as an impediment to quality and equality in education, arguing that caring for students is essential to their academic success and well-being. Noddings's (1992) caring approach focuses on a *caring relation*, or a connection between two people (the *carer* and the *cared-for*) (p. 15). A caring relation involves mutual recognition and response; caring is completed when two parties participate. Within this framework, caring ceases to exist as an attribute and becomes an interpersonal endeavor. Underpinned by an ethic of care, Noddings's (1992) approach includes modeling, dialogue, practice, and confirmation:

> **Modeling:** When a child knows how it feels to be a recipient of care, he or she is more likely to develop the capacity to care. To model caring is to show a child how to care.

Dialogue: "Dialogue is a common search for understanding, empathy, or appreciation" (Noddings, 1992, p. 23). Dialogue allows us to get to know each other, which sets the foundation for caring relations.

Practice: Putting care into practice ultimately challenges how our schools (which are hierarchically organized and focused on grades, penalties, and rewards) function.

Confirmation: Caring confirmation is genuine and nonjudgmental. It deals with seeing the best qualities in someone and encouraging him or her to be a better version of himself or herself.

Beauboeuf-Lafontant (2002) believes that a caring approach in the Black community is built upon values and objectives different from those outlined above. Many successful Black women educators exemplify a Black feminist or *womanist* epistemology (Beauboeuf-Lafontant, 2002), caring for students in a manner that resembles mothering, sometimes with tough love. This approach is more political than Eurocentric or White feminist caring because caring has more critical implications in marginalized communities. In these contexts, caring means enacting a *political clarity*: teaching students about and preparing them for the harsh realities of racism, sexism, and other "isms" that exist beyond the schoolhouse. Beauboeuf-Lafontant (2002) argues that Black teachers working in their own community have a collective commitment to caring because progress as a people is linked to the success of every member. Her model of womanist caring includes embracing maternal roles, enacting political clarity, and recognizing the risk involved in teaching the political. I consider this approach culturally relevant caring (see Ladson-Billings, 1995). Patterson et al. (2008) also compare the frameworks of Noddings and Beauboeuf-Lafontant. The authors argue that Noddings's notion of caring is colorblind. Centered on "individual nurturing that emerges from the mother-child relationship" (p. 99) and couched within White ideals of morality and ethics, Noddings's conceptualization of caring fails to account for institutionalized racism and structural inequalities that cannot be challenged on an individual level. While the authors provide an example of this model's efficacy in predominantly White settings, they show how it can marginalize Black students and teachers who operate from a different epistemological understanding and approach to caring. A visual representation of the differences described by Patterson et al. (2008) is depicted in Table 1.

Table 1. Comparing Traditional To Culturally Relevant Caring

	Traditional Caring	Culturally Relevant Caring
Scholar	Noddings	Beauboeuf-Lafontant
Approach	White feminist	Womanist
Stance	Colorblind	Color conscious
Key Components	Modeling, dialogue, practice, confirmation	Embrace of the maternal, political clarity as goal, an ethic of risk
Application	Caring based on "individual nurturing"	Caring centered in the community

Presented in this way, there is a clear color line dividing what I have termed a traditional caring framework and a culturally relevant caring framework. In a world where theoretical differences are not so neatly defined, how would teachers and students in predominantly monocultural/mono-racial schools fit into or employ these frameworks? A caring framework for African American students needs to include political clarity and color consciousness, or the recognition of race as a key factor affecting the educational success and well-being of students. How can teachers of diverse cultures enact political clarity and color consciousness with African American students?

The importance of seeing each student as a member of a cultural or racial community as well as an individual is emphasized in Nieto's (2008) explanation of *critical caring*. In the chapter "Nice Is Not Enough: Defining Caring for Students of Color," Nieto suggests critical care where kindness falls short. Similar to the way a colorblind pedagogy is a disservice to African American students, a charitable approach is disempowering. Even well-intentioned concessions about academic performance are detrimental because setting the bar low will ensure low achievement. Nieto (2008) writes:

> I have seen numerous cases in which "nice" teachers expected less of their students of color, believing that by refusing to place the same rigorous demands on their students of color as they do on white students, they were making accommodations for the students' difficult home life, poverty, or lack of English-language proficiency. Such "accommodations" may unintentionally give students the message that teachers believe these students are incapable of learning. (p. 29)

Part of practicing critical caring means rejecting a hidden curriculum about race and ability despite socially constructed expectations of subpar performance among students of color. It involves recognizing socioeconomic inequalities but avoiding assumptions about students' situations. Believing in and confirming the talent and potential of every student, while expecting academic excellence, is key to critical caring with political clarity and color consciousness.

Considering the case of teachers and students in my suburban alma mater, how does a European American teacher prepare African American students for experiences that are unique to the African American community? Practicing political clarity and color conscious caring within one's own community is arguably easier than doing so with students from different cultural or racial backgrounds. I contend that spirituality is the starting point for teachers to build the capacity to care critically for students of backgrounds different from their own.

Some argue that spirituality has no place in schools, but I believe it is innate in every individual and therefore omnipresent. Motha (2011) describes spirituality as "our intuitive sense of nurturing, what we know is right in understanding, combining the head (intellect) with the heart, right in intention and effort and virtuous in action" (p. 54). She adds that spirituality is "an organic total integration of the individual, regardless of race, gender, culture or religion" (p. 63). If we consider spirituality as innately intuitive and unique to each individual, we begin to understand how a spirituality centered approach to caring could benefit from aspects of both traditional and culturally relevant caring frameworks.

Building upon the ideas of Beauboeuf-Lafontant (2002), Nieto (2008), and Noddings (1992), I propose a caring approach centered in spirituality. This spiritually centered caring approach takes a color conscious and justice oriented stance, it considers caring to be individually spiritual and community oriented, and it proposes inquiry, dialogue, *integrity of being,* and *critical affirmation* (see hooks & West, 1991) as its key components. Table 2 highlights the commonalities and differences among the caring frameworks and lists the key components of my approach, which I will explain in the sections that follow.

Table 2. Extending Caring Through Culture And Spirituality

	Traditional Caring	Culturally Relevant Caring	Culturally Relevant Caring	Culturally Relevant Caring
Scholar	Noddings	Beauboeuf-Lafontant	Nieto	Harris Garad
Approach	White feminist	Womanist	Anti-racist	Spiritually centered
Stance	Colorblind, change oriented	Color conscious, justice oriented	Color conscious, justice oriented	Color conscious, justice oriented
Key Components	Modeling, dialogue, practice, confirmation	Embrace of the maternal, political clarity, an ethic of risk	Critical care	Inquiry, dialogue, *integrity of being,* and *critical affirmation*
Application	Caring as a relation that is individually oriented	Caring as a relation that is community oriented	Caring for individuals of racial and cultural communities	Caring as individually spiritual *and* community oriented
Expressly spiritual?	No	No	No	Yes

An expressly spiritual element is missing from established concep-tualizations of caring. Although Noddings (1992, 2008) writes extensive-ly about spirituality in education and the need to care for the whole child, her explanation for an ethic of care is not *centered* in spirituality. Beauboeuf-Lafontant (2002) highlights the role of love in a womanist approach to caring but does not describe love the way I conceptualize spirituality, as the grounding and generating force for how and why we care. Nieto's (2008) critical caring sings with a fighting spirit but does not honor the power of spirituality in shaping our caring approach.

For many, spirituality is a highly individual set of principles or prac-tices intended for the common good. Faith groups that pray, meditate, or maintain silence for common causes believe in the power of spiritu-al intention to heal or help ourselves and others. One might argue that there is a vast difference between right faith and right action; perhaps the steps of the status quo are paved with good intentions. Still, I argue that spiritual-centeredness is essentially humanizing. A spiritually centered approach to caring encourages individual nurturing—or tending to the spirits of students and oneself. It also operates on an assumption of the selflessness of spirituality. As such, spirituality has the potential to be rec-iprocally individual and centered in community. Spiritual-centeredness is a solid foundation for enacting political clarity and working toward spirit justice and social justice.

As an African American girl who attended school in the suburbs, my spirit was injured (see Siam, 2011) by the cultural mores of the majori-ty. But I found teachers who reached me on a deeply personal and spir-itual level. From these teachers, I learned that caring involves a connection between two human beings, a relation that recognizes the universality of some experiences and resists the barriers of race and culture. By sharing my stories in the following section, I hope to eluci-date salient aspects of how to conceptualize and practice spiritually centered caring.

Caring for the Spirit: My Personal Stories

How do my educational experiences inform my perspective on caring for African American students in the suburbs? To answer that question,

I will share a few stories from my past using Ladson-Billings's (1994) story/scholarship method. I have written with my voice as a student and then responded with my voice as a teacher. This strategy provides a platform for inquiry into my own memories, an analysis of my reflections within a larger societal and scholarly context, and a demonstration of how to practice spiritually centered caring with inquiry, dialogue, integrity of being, and critical affirmation.

Story I. Whose English?

Dear Ms. Brooke,

My Multicultural English class was interesting today. Ms. Mead made us sit in a circle (with no desks) and talk. We were supposed to talk about an important moment in our lives, but no one was taking the assignment seriously. I did. I talked about November 19th, 1995, the day Dad died. People in the class got quiet and started to listen. Then they shared their own personal stories. In some ways, the class makes us closer, but most of the time I don't like it. I like that we write poems and talk, but I don't like that no one takes it seriously. I admit it doesn't feel like a real class, and most of the Black kids take it, so everyone thinks it's easy. Multicultural English really is different from any other class I've taken.

From this reflection, I recognize the systems of domination (hooks, 2003) that characterized my educational experiences. A hierarchy of knowledge is present and palpable in the actual and hidden curriculum of our schools in the United States. I remember taking only one multicultural class, and the stigma surrounding it significantly shaped the experience. I ask rhetorically (due to the confines of this chapter): How can we change the perception that non-dominant discourses (or multicultural voices) are not serious or rigorous? How can we incorporate alternative ways of knowing and pedagogies into mainstream schooling? Knowing what I know now about multicultural education and culturally relevant pedagogy, this is how I might respond to my younger self:

Dear Young Brooke,

I think it's exciting that you're taking a Multicultural English class. Your teacher is on to something. Did you know that lots of very smart scholars value talking (dialogue) as part of the learning process? It is revolutionary to recognize that your peers have answers to a lot of profoundly difficult questions. Not everything you learn needs to come from a book or an "expert"—the world is made up of truths. If you stay in the class, continue to work hard, and take it seriously, perhaps you can help change the perception of the class. For now, try to focus on the benefits of learning in a different way. Sometimes we don't know the value of what we're learning until years later.

In my response, I try to demonstrate critical affirmation by praising Young Brooke and pushing her to consider her capacity to change perceptions about her Multicultural English class. Without becoming inaccessible, I couch my comments in a social context and provide a counterexample to a dominant discourse about Truth. In this subtle way, I hope to convey an appreciation for cultural differences and ways of knowing. This could set the foundation for becoming an ally for an African American student.

Story II. Se Habla Español

Dear Ms. Brooke,

I cried in Spanish class today. Yo lloré. I can't explain exactly why I was upset, but we reached a point in our conversation and it became clear that I'm different. I'm the only Black kid in class and sometimes I feel like no one understands my point of view. It's painful to feel misunderstood, and I'm embarrassed to have cried in front of everyone. My mom always tells me not to let 'em see me cry—or sweat. But, one good thing came of the crying. My Spanish teacher and I had a heart to heart. She came to my next period class to see if I was OK. She knocked on the door and pulled me into the hallway to ask what happened. We talked for a few minutes and I tried to explain how it felt to always be the odd-one-out. I was truly touched that she cared enough to try to understand. Do you understand?

This reflection confirms (for me) that caring relations can be the difference between a memorable teacher and one who is easily forgotten. While the catalyst for the crying remains nebulous after so many years, I remember with clarity the conversation with my teacher. I believe we shared a spiritual understanding of one universal human experience: emotional pain. When students are struggling with hard-to-understand emotions or simple sensations of unease, how can a caring educator respond?

Dear Young Brooke,

No llorés, mi hija. Don't cry. I want you to know that I do understand. I've felt out of place and misunderstood on many occasions. Do you know that I didn't have an African American woman teacher until graduate school? Some of my favorite teachers were very different from me, but they took a special interest in me. Your Spanish teacher sounds like a great person. You're lucky to have someone who cares about more than just your grades.

I think you should spend some time thinking about what happened in class and write a story or a journal entry about it. If you can find a way to express your emotions to the rest of your class, they could surely benefit from your point of view. In general, it's a great thing to be honest with yourself about your feelings. Try not to lose that ability. It's a skill, just like speaking Spanish.

In my response, I try to highlight integrity of being. After listening to Young Brooke, reflecting on my own experiences, and telling my own story about feeling similarly, I am able to be myself and encourage her to remain true to herself (even when her voice is silenced). As someone who considers writing a spiritual practice, I encourage Young Brooke to write to make sense of her sentiments and find solace.

Story III. Hit Me on the Hip

Dear Ms. Brooke,

Today was the first day of school and I already got into trouble. My pager went off in yearbook class! The pager beeped so loudly and I didn't react right away because I didn't know it was mine. My teacher took the pager away and put it in her desk. I had to stay after class for a lecture and I can tell that I made a bad first impression. I know I shouldn't have had the pager, but everyone has one. What's the big deal?

Dear Young Brooke,

I understand that most of your friends have pagers, but the truth is, you're not supposed to have it at school. I appreciate your remorse, but I must agree with your teacher. You broke a rule and deserved a consequence. Can you understand that perspective?

Nowadays, many people associate pagers with drug dealers. Did you know that? Even if the stereotype is wildly ill-fitting, your teacher doesn't know you yet, so he or she is working out of the stereotypes he or she may believe about you. But I believe whether or not he or she gets to know you,

you're a great girl. So until then, you better be on your best and brightest behavior, not for the teacher but for yourself. If not, you'll have to explain yourself not only to me, but to your whole family.

Young Brooke, I need to say something serious now. I know that you often feel misunderstood at a school where few of your classmates are Black, but try to remember not just why you are there, but who you are. Your parents made many sacrifices so that you could attend a good school. Your grandparents didn't even have the right to go to school with White children! Can you imagine? My dear girl, you owe it to yourself and your family to shine. Now that I've said that, I need you to know something else: I also got a lecture on the first day of my junior year of high school. My teacher told me later that she thought I was "trouble." It took awhile for me to earn her respect, but I did it. You know, the saying is true: "we all make mistakes." But the way you conduct yourself after a mistake is what speaks volumes about your character.

With this dialogue, I wanted to highlight critical affirmation. Again, I praised and pushed back. For me, the word *critical* involves a political consciousness. African American teachers practice political clarity by sharing counternarratives (Roberts, 2010) and personal stories about racial inequality. Critical affirmation should account for injustices, but it should also openly criticize the behaviors that perpetuate stereotypes and keep people on the losing side of the struggle for justice.

As a high school student, I learned a lot about the world and its injustices, through experience. As a teacher I seek to unlearn the pedagogies that cause spirit injury and work toward justice for myself and those for whom I care. By sharing the stories and counter-stories of my young and older self, I sought to explicate and demonstrate the key components of an approach to caring that is centered in spiritually.

A Spiritually Centered Approach to Caring: A Letter to My Colleagues

Dear Colleagues:

It's time we talked to ourselves about how we might really support and care for the spirits or our students, not simply their minds. To practice spiritually centered caring, you will need to begin with a *soundness of spirit*, to engage in inquiry, dialogue, and critical affirmation with an integrity of your own being. This means that you must work toward a continual process of self-reflection where you tell your own stories and *listen* to your students' stories with *empathy*, not sympathy. We can captivate our students if we are willing to critically affirm them, if we are willing to reciprocally praise *and* push back.

Spiritually centered caring involves a process of *self-inquiry*. Upon meeting a student, we should ask, "Who is he or she?" and be aware of our assumptions. We could conduct inquiry into our own feelings, wondering: "Will a recent news report about a member of this community affect how I feel about or interact with him or her?" Inquiry also involves recognizing how our past (recent and distant) shapes our opinions and epistemologies. We should ask, "Who am I in relation to this person?" The answers should involve *color consciousness*, the recognition of Whiteness as well as the racial identities of people of color. To couch the practice in political clarity, resist making determinations about anyone based on race or religion, sexual orientation, immigration status, or simple hearsay. Allow an acknowledgment of the humanity and spirituality of each student to be the starting point for your interaction with them.

Asking ourselves difficult questions is part of inquiry, just as articulating and accepting the answers is part of *dialogue*. Dialogue in spiritually centered caring is a collective process of exploration and discovery. We learn about ourselves and others when we engage in dialogue. We set the foundation for caring relationships by making ourselves vulnerable to the possibility of judgment, but open to clarity and understanding. The words we choose position us along a continuum of political clarity and color consciousness. Using nonjudgmental speech reflects understanding and sets the groundwork for *becoming an ally*.

We need to be honest, humble, and vulnerable to make ourselves and our teachings accessible (hooks & West, 1991). hooks and West (1991) encourage scholars to share stories even when we are unsure of the reactions of our audience. This integrity of being means maintaining a trueness to self. Within a caring approach that accounts for spirituality, integrity of being involves allowing ourselves and our students to be imperfect but whole.

If we accept that we are imperfect but whole, we can practice critical affirmation. Describing her friendship with Cornel West, bell hooks says, "you and I have...the willingness to engage intellectually with the kind of critical affirmation where we can talk, argue, disagree, even become disappointed in each other, yet still leave one another with a sense of spiritual joy and renewal" (hooks & West, 1991, p. 2). When we practice critical affirmation with a soundness of spirit, even a reprimand can feel like care because it *is*.

In the spirit of caring,

Brooke Harris Garad

Conclusion

When I was growing up, my mother told me that life is not fair. She taught me that my brothers had certain privileges because they were boys, but all of us had to work harder than our White peers to prove ourselves at school. She and my father, like many African Americans, learned the same values. She believed that telling the hard truth is part and parcel of a caring pedagogy for African American children (Beauboeuf-Lafontant, 2002).

African American students in suburbia and beyond need caring teachers to help them navigate the injustices of our society and world. Beauboeuf-Lafontant (2002), Nieto (2008), and Noddings (1992), among others, have challenged us to take the whole child into account, to be more than simply nice to students, and to make our practice political. I believe that we need to make our practice spiritual.

Spirituality is the starting point and ultimately the catalyst for building the capacity and willingness to care across cultural differences. Spiritually centered caring is an individual and community-oriented process of inquiry, dialogue, integrity of being, and critical affirmation. It requires us to center ourselves in a soundness of spirit that will help us to know how to teach when we are unsure.

Note

1. I have since learned that the term *Caucasian* is a remnant from problematic racial classifications (Mukhopadhyay, 2008). But during my childhood, Caucasian was the preferred or politically correct term. See Mukhopadhyay, C. C. (2008). Getting rid of the word "Caucasian." In M. Pollack (Ed.), *Everyday antiracism* (pp. 28–31). New York: New Press.

References

Beauboeuf-Lafontant, T. (2002). A womanist experience of caring: Understanding the pedagogy of exemplary black women teachers. *Urban Review, 34*(1), 71–116.

Cole, S. (2011). Situating children in the discourse of spirituality. In N. N. Wane, E. L. Manyimo, & E. J. Ritskes (Eds.), *Spirituality, education & society: An integrated approach* (pp. 1–14). Rotterdam, Netherlands: Sense Publishers.

Dillard, C. B. (2006). *On spiritual strivings: Transforming an African American woman's academic life.* Albany: SUNY Press.

hooks, b. (2003). *Teaching community: A pedagogy of hope.* New York: Routledge.

hooks, b., & West, C. (1991). *Breaking bread: Insurgent Black intellectual life.* Boston: South End Press.

Ladson-Billings, G. (1994). *The dreamkeepers: Successful teachers of African American children.* San Francisco, CA: Jossey-Bass.

Ladson-Billings, G. (1995). Toward a theory of culturally relevant pedagogy. *American Educational Research Journal, 32*(3), 465–491.

Motha, J. (2011). Spirituality and its relevance for the contemplative educator. In N. N. Wane, E. L. Manyimo, & E. J. Ritskes (Eds.), *Spirituality, education & society: An integrated approach* (pp. 49–66). Rotterdam, Netherlands: Sense Publishers.

Mukhopadhyay, C. C. (2008). Getting rid of the word "Caucasian." In M. Pollack (Ed.), *Everyday antiracism* (pp. 28–31). New York: New Press.

Nieto, S. (2008). Nice is not enough: Defining caring for students of color. In M. Pollack (Ed.), *Everyday Antiracism* (pp. 28–31). New York: New Press.

Nieto, S. (2006). Proceedings from the Longfellow Lecture. *Teaching as political work: Learning from courageous and caring teachers.* Yonkers, NY: Sarah Lawrence College.

Noddings, N. (1992). *The challenge to care in schools: An alternative approach to education.* New York: Teachers College Press.

Noddings, N. (2008). Spirituality and religion in public schooling. *Yearbook of the National Society for the Study of Education, 107,* 185–195.

Patterson, J. A., Gordon, J., & Groves Price, P. (2008). The color of caring: Race and the implementation of educational reform. *Educational Foundations, 22* (3/4), 97–116.

Roberts, M. A. (2010). Toward a theory of culturally relevant critical teacher care: African American teachers' definitions and perceptions of care for African American students. *Journal of Moral Education, 39*(4), 449–467.

Sium, A. (2011). My Name is "Mohamed," but please call me "John": Canadian racism, spirit injury and the renaming of the indigenous body as a right of passage. In N. N. Wane, E. L. Manyimo, & E. J. Ritskes (Eds.), *Spirituality, education & society: An integrated approach* (pp. 139–156). Rotterdam, Netherlands: Sense Publishers.

Wane N. N., & Ritskes, E.J. (Eds.). (2011). Introduction. In N. N. Wane, E. L. Manyimo, & E. J. Ritskes (Eds.), *Spirituality, education & society: An integrated approach* (pp. xv–xxiii). Rotterdam, Netherlands: Sense Publishers.

Care as a Racialized, Critical, and Spiritual Emotion

Samara D. Madrid

To care in education is to recognize teaching and learning as processes of the mind, body, and spirit. (Harris Garad, p. 67)

Brooke Harris Garad's preceding chapter on spiritually centered caring
for teaching and reaching Black students in suburbia highlights the
significance of emotion and spirituality in teaching and learning. As
noted in the quote above taken from her chapter, teaching and learning
is not simply a cognitive process but is also an embodied spiritual-
emotional process, where the teacher recognizes the connectedness and
oneness, at a deeper human level, with the students they encounter in
their daily lives within the classroom. As a scholar of emotions in early
childhood, I am interested in thinking through the relationship between
conceptualizations of care and emotions in this response to Harris
Garad's chapter.

Harris Garad begins her chapter by dismantling and revealing ways
of caring that have been dominant in the field of education and then follows with an auto-ethnographical account of her lived experience as a
young African American student in a predominantly White suburb.
She carefully crafts, taking from White feminist (Noddings) and Black

feminist (Beauboeuf-Lafotant) perspectives, a spiritually centered model of caring. By doing so she adds to a small but growing field of work that challenges prevalent ways of caring in classroom spaces, demonstrating the importance of both emotional and spiritual work in the education of African American children by White teachers. Teaching and learning is an emotional endeavor. Teaching and learning is a spiritual endeavor. It is also a highly racialized endeavor. As such, when we consider care and spirituality we also must uncover how race, power, oppression, and dominance construct teachers' understandings about how "to do" these epistemological and ontological ways of *knowing, feeling, and being* with their students (Ahmed, 2004; Boler, 1999; Zembylas, 2008; Zembylas & Chubbuck, 2009).

As Harris Garad makes visible in her chapter, it is not enough to simply love and care for our students: We must first understand, through a critical lens, how these emotions are embedded in our social and cultural histories, especially when working with students whose racial identities differ from our own. The work presented in this thoughtfully written chapter allows us to reconsider and reconceptualize the following three points when contemplating how to teach the mind, body, and spirit of children from various racial, ethnic, socioeconomic, and religious backgrounds:

- Care as a Racialized Emotion
- Care as a Critical Emotion
- Care as a Spiritual Emotion

In the sections below, I will locate Harris Garad's work in the recent literature around each of these ideas (racialized care, critical care, and spiritual care) while considering what this work offers and what is left for us to stretch our understandings as scholars, teachers, and students who are committed to caring spiritually for ourselves, our students, and our community.

I begin each section with a piece taken from Harris Garad's chapter that pushed me to think more deeply about these topics and/or challenged my conceptions about care and spirit in educational spaces. I hope to invite a textual conversation of sorts among Harris Garad's work, my own work, and the work of scholars in the field to propose that we can view care as a site of racialized and political existence, a site of tension and transformation in critical consciousness, and a site that recognizes our collective divinity and spirituality.

Care as a Racialized Emotion

Practicing political clarity and color conscious caring within one's own community is arguably easier than doing so with students from different cultural or racial backgrounds. (Harris Garad, p. 70)

Harris Garad raises an important point when one practices color-conscious caring with students who come from communities different from our own: *It is easier to care when the person appears to be like us.* This makes the act of caring not a neutral emotional practice but a politically charged emotional practice that is related to our social and cultural ways of "doing" emotion (Gergen, 1999; Lutz, 1988). Her chapter illustrates the cultural nature of emotion as she considers how White feminist ways of caring are based on "mutual recognition and response" while Black feminist ways of caring are based on "embracing material roles and enacting political clarity." Thus, "care" is not a universal emotion with a universal rule about how we should display it. Definitions about what it means to care and whom we should care for vary based on our cultural assumptions. This becomes problematic when we carry these deeply rooted ways of "doing" care into our classroom interactions.

Harris Garad's work extends the work of other feminist scholars who study race and emotion such as Ahmed (2004) and Boler (1999), who postulate that our emotional investments and attachments are racialized, politicized, and embedded within power relations. This stance contradicts the commonly accepted notion that emotions are individualized states of feeling that we "have" rather than "do." These more recent perspectives, however, do view emotion as socially mediated practices and discursive constructs bound by language, culture, and ideology. The question then becomes not "What *is* care?" but "What does care *do*?" "Who does it silence?" "Who does it oppress?" "How is it a site of social control?" Sara Ahmed, in her book *The Cultural Politics of Emotion* (2004), examines how the emotion of love has been used by dominant racial groups to justify racial divisions and the emotion of hate toward those who might disrupt their historical dominance and power. That is, we fight for our racial community because we love/care for them. From this standpoint, hatred toward other racial groups who threaten to displace or challenge White power is viewed not as hate, but rather as a *love* for their own. This love then becomes a justified emotion (i.e., in the name of love) and held up as a positive moral attribute of the person and community.

And this is where the problem of "care" resides. Through the disguise of caring for "our people" and "our community," people simultaneously use emotion to justify feelings of discomfort and hate toward those who are different from them and who threaten their historical and political ways of caring for their deeply *cared for* ideological beliefs. Ahmed (2004) further suggests that "Emotions show us how histories stay alive, even when they are not consciously remembered; how histories of colonialism, slavery, and violence shape lives and worlds in the present" (p. 202). Harris Garad shows us how White teachers (and all teachers) of African American students in suburbia must use political clarity and consciously consider how their racialized emotions and dominant notions of care can ultimately oppress and silence the histories of students from different racial backgrounds. More importantly, White teachers must not only be willing to consider their racialized ways of caring but also be willing to speak about how their own emotional investments and attachments to their *caring ideologies* reinforce and reinscribe White ways of doing emotion in the classroom context.

Care as a Critical Emotion

> Part of practicing critical caring means rejecting a hidden curriculum about race and ability despite socially constructed expectations of subpar performance among students of color. It involves recognizing socioeconomic inequalities but avoiding assumptions about students' situations. (Harris Garad, p. 70)

As I reflected on the statement above by Harris Garad, I was reminded of Boler's (1999) pedagogy of discomfort and Chubbuck and Zembylas's (2008) critical emotional praxis as tools for teacher emotion that can be marshaled for social justice work in educational spaces. Emotion, when used reflexively versus reactively, can allow teachers to interrogate their assumptions about inequalities and race in the classroom. More importantly, these two theories rest on the notion that emotional discomfort rather than emotional comfort can push or motivate teachers to engage in social justice work.

Chubbuck and Zembylas (2008) posit, "The interplay between justice and emotions is complicated, however. It is not about individuals having the right kind of feelings as this would essentially make an individual's judgment of right and wrong dependent on the existence of specific emotions" (p. 275). The existence of positive or negative emotions should not be used as a gauge for teachers when considering what are just and unjust classroom practices. More importantly, having a positive or negative emotion does not mean that injustices are removed or resolved. In fact, as illustrated by Harris Garad, feeling "care" can often lead to actions and reactions from teachers that support unjust outcomes, such as charitable care and/or holding expectations of subpar performance for specific groups of students.

White teachers of African American students in suburbia must be willing to sit with their uncomfortable feelings when contemplating just and unjust classroom practices and ways of caring in schools. When learning about and discussing critical pedagogies and issues of social justice, teachers often have emotional ambivalence as they attempt to reconcile old core values with new knowledge about race, power, and privilege (Zembylas, 2008). The difficulty for most teachers is in recognizing that ambivalence as well as the fear of the unknown is a common reaction when one's deeply held ideologies are disrupted. For example, in my own ethnographic research on teacher emotion and socially just practices (Madrid, 2011; Madrid, Baldwin, & Frye, 2013) the classroom teacher experienced worry, struggle, and discomfort as new knowledge disrupted her understandings about what were "right" and "just" practices for her preschool students. This discomfort was intensified when she realized she could not rely on her emotional responses to determine what was just and unjust (i.e., this feels *right* so it must be *just*). "Socially just" teaching and learning can be a fearful and/or defensive process for teachers especially when exposing the hidden curriculum and revealing how classroom practices may be promoting injustices.

Critical emotional praxis is the ability of the teacher to "question emotionally charged, cherished beliefs, exposing how privileged positions and comfort zones inform ways in which one recognizes how he/she has been taught to see/act (or not to see/act), and empowering different ways of being with/for the other" (Zembylas & Chubbuck, 2009, p. 354). Through using emotional discomfort rather than emotional comfort in the classroom, as typically experienced by those in privileged and powerful positions, the teacher is able to open up a space where authentic conversations about social inequalities can occur and students from historically marginalized groups are allowed to express their thoughts and emotions around the injustices they've experienced both in and out of school. Teacher care from this perspective includes the teacher's ability to *lean into the discomfort* and *bear witness* to these injustices even when it disrupts the teacher's customary and comfortable ways of knowing/feeling.

Care as a Spiritual Emotion

> Spiritual-centeredness is essentially humanizing. A spiritually centered approach to caring individual encourages individual nurturing—or tending to the spirits of students and oneself. It also operates on an assumption of the selflessness of spirituality. (Harris Garad, p. 72)

Spiritual-centeredness is the salient aspect that distinguishes Harris Garad's model of teacher care from other scholars. She offers a spiritual solution to the problems of care and emotion that I've examined in this visionary response. Integrity of being, critical affirmation, and political clarity are practices embedded in her model of teaching and learning. I would also offer the notions of *vulnerability* (Brown, 2012) and *witnessing* (Boler, 1999) to the list of components that inform spiritual care. This was illustrated in Harris Garad's stories and counter-stories as she recounted her Spanish teacher's courage to "bear witness" to her emotional pain as a Black student in a predominantly White school. It was also illustrated by her own willingness to be courageously vulnerable with her teacher, her self, and her peers.

According to Ahmed (2004), "Healing does not cover over, but exposes the wounds to others: *The recovery is a form of exposure.* The visibility produced by recognition is actually the visibility of the ordinary and normative or the visibility of what has been concealed under the signs of truth" (p. 200). Spiritual healing and human connection are grounded in vulnerability and exposure, to be seen with all of our *perfections and imperfections* and know that we are still worthy of love and belonging just as we are at that very moment of exposure (Brown, 2012). The link among vulnerability, spirituality, and caring is that both the student and the teacher can be authentic in their emotional and intellectual responses (or even fearful of exposing their vulnerability) with the knowledge that emotional pain and struggle are the connective threads that make us human and part of humanity. Being able to reveal our stories and concealed emotional pain is the path to reclaiming our spirit in and out of the classroom.

Witnessing is the other side of vulnerability as it makes demands on the teacher to *hear and hold* the stories of students who have experienced injustices and emotional pain. This is key when thinking about how teachers can support students in spiritually affirming and healing spaces. Testimonies of racism, classism, and sexism are to be held with political clarity and selflessness, not with sympathy and self-centeredness. It requires the teacher to move past individual self-reflection or spectating (which often leads to surface level sympathy) to a humanizing level where the teacher is actively present with the student as an advocate who also considers the political and historical implications of the testimony. Boler (1999) suggests that "witnessing, in contrast to spectating, is the process in which we do not have the luxury of seeing a static truth or fixed certainty" (p. 186). Spiritual witnessing is the ability of the teacher to *nonjudgmentally* be with and see the student recognizing and affirming injustices, while simultaneously caring for the collective spirit of all those who have experienced such injury.

Concluding Remarks

Harris Garad's spiritually centered caring approach uncovers dominant assumptions about who and what we are as spiritual beings, breaking the illusion that we are separate and making visible what has been concealed. She forces us to consider our collective histories and memories, acknowledging that we are greater than this individual social construction that we call "self." Spirituality is "recognizing and celebrating that we are all inextricably connected to each other by a power greater than all of us" (Brown, 2012, p. 64). It is my hope that Harris Garad's model is used by White teachers of African American students in suburbia to reexamine their racialized emotions, critical emotions, and spiritual emotions with the goal of reclaiming connection and spirituality in education. It is also my hope that, more broadly, all teachers will consider the implications of emotion in the teaching and learning of students who are different from them with the following understanding: "Justice is not simply a feeling. And feelings are not always just. But justice involves feelings, which moves us across the surfaces of the world, creating ripples in the intimate contours of our lives. But 'where' we go with these feelings remains open to question" (Ahmed, 2004, p. 202). I believe the answer lies in our emotional work as teachers and caring spiritual beings.

References

Ahmed, S. (2004). *The cultural politics of emotion*. New York: Routledge.

Boler, M. (1999). *Feeling power: Emotions and education*. New York: Routledge.

Brown, B. (2012). *The gifts of imperfection: Let go of who you think you're supposed to be and embrace who you are*. Center City, MN: Hazelden.

Chubbuck, S. M., & Zembylas, M. (2008). The emotional ambivalence of socially just teaching: A case study of a novice urban schoolteacher. *American Educational Research Journal, 45*(2), 274–318.

Gergen, K. J. (1999). *An invitation to social construction*. Thousand Oaks, CA: Sage.

Lutz, C. (1988). *Unnatural emotions: Everyday sentiments on a Micronesian atoll and their challenge to Western theory*. Chicago: University of Chicago Press.

Madrid, S. (2011). Emotional intersections: Learning how to feel as a social advocate. *The Voice: The Journal for Campus Children's Centers, 6*(3), pp. 5–6.

Madrid, S., Baldwin, N., & Frye, E. (2013). Professional feelings: One early childhood educator's discomfort as a teacher and learner. *Journal of Early Childhood Research*. DOI: 10.1177/1476718X13484240.

Zembylas, M. (2008). Engaging with issues of cultural diversity and discrimination through critical emotional reflexivity in online learning. *Adult Education Quarterly, 59*(1), 61–82.

Zembylas, M., & Chubbuck, S. M. (2009). Emotions and social inequalities: Mobilizing emotions for social justice education. In P. Schultz & M. Zembylas (Eds.), *Advances in teacher emotion research* (pp. 343–363). New York: Springer.

Chapter 4

Less Religion, More Spirituality

Spiritually Relevant Pedagogy in the Global Era

Gilbert Kaburu & Chris Landauer

Introduction

In this chapter, we shall first propose a philosophical and pedagogical stance namely Spiritually Relevant Pedagogy, its definitions and assumptions. Second, we draw on our unique life experiences as a framework for how we look at the differences between spiritualities and religiosity. Finally, we explore the ways in which spiritualities can be integrated into teaching and learning.

We feel that it is important to emphasize that while spiritualities can be found through religion, they can also be discovered independent of religion. We refer to spiritualities (as opposed to spirituality) as a philosophical stance. We believe that human beings are a lot more complex than we make them out to be, and as such, there is often more than one spirituality at play, enmeshed, working in tandem or in dissonance with each other based on the different contexts that we navigate.

Writing from a spiritual perspective, we affirm that there are multiple subjective realities, and we dispute claims to universal application. With this in mind, we offer a take on spiritualities and religion in education, based on our personal experiences growing up in Uganda (Gilbert) and the United States (Chris). In our stories, we aim to look at syncretism and cultural universals that exist across various cultures and religions that may be useful to bridge some of the gaps that have been created between religious and cultural groups locally and globally.

By creating space for spiritualities within education, we allow students to bring their whole selves to the learning environment, rather than having to leave a part of themselves outside of the realm of education (Dillard, 2006). Like holistic education, SRP "attempts to nurture the development of the whole person [including] the intellectual, emotional, physical, social, aesthetic and spiritual" (Miller, Karsten, Denton, Orr, & Colalillo Kates, 2005, p. 2). We believe that by creating space in school for spiritualities we can better serve the needs of students and help integrate and connect them with the energy of other people and places across the planet and beyond. Moreover, "addressing spirituality in the curriculum can mean reawakening students to a sense of awe and wonder. This can involve deepening a sense of connection to the cosmos" (p. 2). In a day and age where many are absorbed by technology and social media, we believe that it is important to maintain and preserve a connection with the living world around us.

Spiritually Relevant Pedagogy

We are imagining a new spiritual philosophy and pedagogy as a different way of teaching that embodies the mind, body, and spirit. It is a paradigm in which the specific name that defines one's spirituality is less important than the principles that guide it. Spiritually Relevant Pedagogy (SRP) is a shift from the detached exclusivity of many forms of organized religious practice and is inclusive of the many ways that spiritualities can manifest.

In articulating this pedagogy, we appropriate Gloria Ladson-Billings's (1995) Culturally Relevant Pedagogy (CRP). An influential scholar in education, she draws on Patricia Hill Collins's (1991) postmodern Black Feminist epistemology and critical race theory. Like culturally relevant teaching, a Spiritually Relevant Pedagogy seeks to develop students academically, support cultural competence, and support critical or sociopolitical consciousness. It shares the three propositions that Ladson-Billings (1995) articulates: (1) *self and others,* the philosophical belief in the educability of all students, and teachers' self-perceptions as community members giving back; (2) *social relations,* which aims at building an equitable and reciprocal teacher-student relationship that seeks to build a community of learners where sharing, rather than competitive individual achievement, is encouraged; and (3) *knowledge,* where knowledge is reconstructed, recycled, shared, and viewed critically with multifaceted assessments. Wisdom, as separate from knowledge, also has value as a way of knowing. The U.S. society has privileged Western individualist intellectual epistemes (what may be referred to colloquially as *book smarts*) over other cultural ways of knowing, owning, expressing, and storing knowledge. On the contrary, Spiritually Relevant Pedagogy, as a philosophy and pedagogy, values wisdom beyond simply what can be measured on standardized examinations. It posits that there are other ways of knowing that are relevant, but not always valued, in educational settings. There is a big push for quantifiable and logical knowledge accumulation, but little space to tell stories or be creative, or express wisdom in other ways. This biases the learning space toward one way of learning that puts students in competition with one another.

Whereas Culturally Relevant Pedagogy alludes to the recognition and integration of spiritualities and implicitly argues for the importance of non-mainstream epistemologies, SRP extends the discourse by placing spiritualities at the center of educational discourse.

As we examine Spiritually Relevant Pedagogy (SRP), it is important to demystify it and articulate its characteristics.

- It differentiates spiritualities from religiosity.
- It recognizes the spiritualities' potential to unite, rather than divide, people of different religious backgrounds, that is, "spirituality could be the positive force to counter the ills of religion" (Ritskes, in Wane, Manyimo & Ritskes, 2011, pp. 19–20).
- It recognizes and values the centering of spiritualities of the teacher and the students and creates a learning community

in which everyone can feel comfortable to share their joys, fears, and vulnerabilities without feeling threatened or judged.

- It recognizes multiple ways of knowing and valuing different people's knowledges.
- It allows a space in which the most valuable things in our lives can be shared, recognizing our whole selves as being an integral part of the learning process.
- It values content knowledge as an essential aspect of schooling.
- It values using knowledge to heal the world, not to manipulate it (Palmer, 1993).
- It recognizes that while spiritualities might be inherent and present for many, they are not always drawn upon in education, teaching, and learning. Thus, there is a need for philosophical and pedagogical reform that provides spaces for spiritualities.

A critical message of SRP is that we do not have to leave a part of ourselves outside of the school setting as we engage our multiple roles as teachers, administrators, or scholars; neither do we demand of that from our students. In this regard, we must connect the curriculum to our students' lives outside of school to tap into the things that matter to them.

SRP acknowledges that all knowledge is value laden. Who legitimizes knowledge and in whose favor are important questions that must be critically dissected in both local and global contexts. Therefore, there is a need to recognize the partial nature of knowledge to aim for culturally relevant and anti-oppressive pedagogy (Ladson-Billings, 1995; Kumashiro, 2009).

SRP requires us to en-center spiritualities in our curriculum, pedagogy, and praxis. It entails, where culturally appropriate, building time into the school day for meditation, allowing enough waiting time where students can ask questions or reflect on prior knowledge instead of quickly moving on to the next unit and integrating these valuable knowledges into the curriculum. It requires us to recognize that students bring with them personal experiences from their homes and communities that are relevant for teachers to draw on. It requires us to ask why "students are taught long before they enter the academe to resist any questions concerning spiritual issues" (Palmer, 1993, p. 379). Why are students "told from an early age that school is not a place to bring their question of meaning: take them home, to your religious community, or to your therapist, but do not bring them to school"? (p. 379). We posit that if students are provided space and opportunities to practice spiritualities in the educational setting, they will begin to develop their whole self.

Using SRP entails approaching teaching and learning discourses as multiple and dynamic, and as improvisational and fluid spaces where learning occurs in different ways and contexts. The importance of spiritualities is in helping structure learning in a present-orientation, where students can "be" or "exist" in the moment, instead of racing through the checkpoints of schooling with their eyes on their future orientation (Bloome, Puro, & Theodorou, 1989).

We know our work may be perceived as controversial and uncomfortable for some. Having said that, by drawing from our own life experiences as a means to recognize that all people bring unique and important experiences to the school setting we find reason for advocating SRP and for sharing the philosophies that undergird it.

Embracing One's Spirituality = Living One's Philosophy

Palmer (1993) writes about the distortion of the Christian traditions by those who "contain the 'knowledge' of Jesus in a compartment labeled 'religious' and engage in other forms of knowing as if there were no connection" (p. 49). Despite our apprehension for organized religion, we are spiritual people. Spirituality "lies beyond rational conceptualizations and thoughts about God" (Cole, in Wane et al., 2011, p. 5). Spirituality allows for truth to be found in many forms. Palmer (1993) acknowledges that "if truth is personal, then creeds and institutions are only the objectified shells of the truth-seeking life that pulses in every human heart" (p. 50). This puts into perspective how insignificant the objectified names are that people in different parts of the world put on their beliefs, when the focus might instead be on how similar the *intentions* are. There is no need to assign only one name to our spirituality (Wane et al., 2011). People of different faiths and spiritual backgrounds have a lot more in common than we often will admit. Palmer (1983) reassures us that "where analysis aims at breaking the world into its elements, prayer aims at seeing beyond the elements into their underlying relatedness" (p. 19). The universal concepts that many religions share provide the basis for common understanding and mutual coexistence.

Rodriguez and Fortier (2007) contend that "social-cultural structures are viewed in dichotomous terms. That is, one is *either* a Christian or not, one *either* an Indian or not, and so on" (p. xi). We view spiritualities as being holistic and allowing space for multiple identities. We recognize that spiritualities can exist in many forms. Simple moments of reflection and observation are one way to help us begin to develop our spiritual selves. In addition, building relationships with those around us is an essential element of the learning environment.

As a research philosophy, spiritualities, ontologically, seek to make connections with the entire community and to connect with something higher than the human ego. They seek for humility in questioning claims to universal application, and posit for multiple and subjective realities. As an epistemological concept, we refer to a spiritual paradigm as subjective and purpose-driven. Methodologically, it is about empowering different perspectives and multiple voices by building relationships, expressing feelings, using our intuition, practicing active listening, and engaging in continuous self-reflection. Its inquiry aim is about making connections with others, discovering self in others, and discovering others in self (Hanh, 1997). It draws on life experiences to see that knowledge is personal, communal, and dialogic. Knowledge is accumulated in cyclical, reciprocal, infinite ways that recognize the fact that we are always becoming. SRP seeks to be reflective, deep, and empathetic, and it suspends judgment with the recognition that there is always a lot to learn from others (Rogoff, 2003). A spiritual philosophy values inclusion and relational participation between an individual and his or her work. Ethically, the spiritual paradigm from which we write tilts toward revelation of special problems and solutions that can be personal or communal (hooks, 2000).

The spiritual philosophy also calls on us to resist the dominant practices that privilege the mind over body and written over oral communication (Muhungi, in Wane et al., 2011). It encourages us to avoid disembodying ourselves, living in our heads and using our bodies as transport for our brains (Robinson, 2006). SRP involves us reflecting on our own biographies, our spiritualities, and how they inform our work. This includes areas of privilege and oppression that are dynamic and complex, for the oppressor in one instance may be the oppressed in another, and vice versa. Our goal is to reimagine a holistic education that centers spiritualities and disrupts the taken-for-granted objective assertions that continue to plague not just the academy but also education generally, looking at it from our own perspectives growing and studying in the United States and Uganda.

We contend that a researcher's background and experiences do have a relevant, indeed significant, place in academic work. Drawing on our life experiences and cultural memories, we hope that our different and yet similar life experiences will enhance understanding and ground our knowledge of how spiritualities have shaped our understandings.

We Speak from Our Own Tongues

Chris Landauer

> "I'm not sure I can tell the truth...I can only tell what I know." (James
> Clifford, 1986, p. 8)

I grew up in a predominately White, middle-class suburb of Columbus, Ohio, where Christianity was the dominant religion, although it existed as an undercurrent rather than something that overtly overshadowed all aspects of the community. I did not regularly attend a place of worship of organized religion when I was growing up. I would go to church occasionally on Christmas or Easter. My path toward spirituality, therefore, was not inherited but rather is evolving over time through my experiences and observations, though certainly I had to have been influenced by the culture around me.

My initial observations of religion growing up were the many actions of members of organized religious groups had not met the ideals they promoted. As an adolescent I started to look at religion as something that had historically divided people, led to wars, and often created separation. I would see wars on television that, to a large extent, were being fought over religion. Religion, from my experience and observations growing up, had become an institution more closely affiliated with politics than a place to practice spirituality. As a result, I began to view religion with skepticism. I grew frustrated with what I perceived as people using religion as a justification for wrongdoings, or as a pardon for their transgressions. As I have gotten older, I can now acknowledge that at the root of many of the organized forms of religion, there is a spiritual intent. But I remain concerned that, in practice, religion has not always fulfilled its promise for me.

Having attended public school, religion didn't always show up explicitly in my educational experience. Still, in reflection, there were spaces that provided opportunities for being spiritual. For example, my schooling offered an extensive arts program that I felt offered me spaces to express myself without judgment and provided an outlet for alternative funds of knowledge. I also had many wonderful teachers who made space for personal expression, who took time to cultivate meaningful relationships that helped open spaces for learning. One particular class with which I felt a connection was called Political Radicalism, and speakers from every side of the religious and political spectrum were brought in to speak to us. What made this experience so unique was that the teacher created a space where students were not told what to believe, but rather we were encouraged to explore and ask questions. I felt affirmed instead of indoctrinated. The teacher respected the students in a way that allowed us to explore, without judgment, those things with which we felt a connection. Being exposed to such a wide variety of people and opinions, and learning in a space that encouraged discussion and debate, helped to foster empathy in me and opened my eyes to be more accepting of others. This experience deepened my connection to the amazing variety of people that make up the human race, yet it also provided a reminder about how much we all have in common, teaching me that I should care about others and their passions, as well as their struggles.

Many of my teachers, like the one described above, embodied a sense of spirituality in how they fostered a connectedness with their students. Classes like this gave me a voice. Today, as a teacher myself, I continue to see the importance of spiritualities in the learning process, and I draw on my own experiences in classrooms growing up to encourage my students to think critically and to care for others. Building meaningful relationships, I believe, is the key to education. This includes not only relationships between teachers and their students but also teachers building meaningful relationships with their colleagues, as I believe education cannot and should not be an isolated endeavor. People must be made to feel cared for, valued, and a part of something purposeful. Educators, in creating a school and classroom culture that allows for the expression of spiritualities, can help students feel connected to one another and to the planet. Education can provide young people opportunities for self-reflection and contemplation, collaboration and a shared purpose with their peers, or quiet time with nature that can perhaps, in some ways, act as antidotes for the ills of society. My own experiences in classrooms where I felt connected to something bigger have shaped the way I view the role of spiritualities and have affected our shared vision of a Spiritually Relevant Pedagogy.

Gilbert Kaburu

> Hundreds of millions of Africans are lurching between an unworkable Western present and a collapsing African past. Their loyalties are stretched between predatory governments and disintegrating tribes, between arbitrary demands of dictators and incessant pleadings of relatives, between commandments of the Bible and obligations to the ancestors. At its heart, the great experiment in modernity that continues to rattle Africa goes on inside individuals, as they sort out new connections with their families, their tribes, and their countries.
> —BLAINE HARDEN, *AFRICA: DISPATCHES FROM A FRAGILE CONTINENT*

I was born in Tororo, Eastern Uganda, in a polygamous family of many mothers and 26 children. *Mzee* (Swahili for "Elder"), as my father was called, was the quintessential African patriarch: a commercial farmer and retired senior police officer who had served his country for the majority of his adult life. Mama left her job as a police receptionist to raise us. Mzee had multiple and often conflicting spiritual roles: He was the clan leader and a church elder at the same time. As a clan head, he prayed to the ancestors and gave libations to them. He invited traditional medicine men to help diagnose any problems we faced and to help us overcome them. When the crop yields were poor, or cows were stolen, or even sometimes when we or the farm animals fell sick, he consulted a medicine man or two to help mediate on his behalf. In the Protestant Church to which we went for prayers as a family every Sunday, one of Mzee's best friends was the bishop. Mzee ushered us into the sitting room every evening where he said prayers that often lasted an hour or even two. This consisted of him leading a sermon and then asking God to bless the meal. It was quite common for religious leaders from the Protestant Church and even the Jehovah's Witness to come home for evening fellowship. As a young child growing up in this spiritual domestic space, I still had the space to chart my own route. Well, I rebelliously tried to.

Whereas some may take a hypocritical perspective of this, I choose to take a pragmatic view. Looking back, I realize Mzee practiced a syncretized version of spirituality that enabled him to shuffle in and out of Christian and African spiritual rituals. Perhaps it was his way of resisting the socially marked and policed views of religion. Perhaps it was his way of breaking down the boundaries of what was considered private and what was considered public.

I look to Uganda today and see how the colonial legacy of Christian religion pushed any other forms of spirituality to the margins. On the surface, Christianity has become the public (and official) spiritual philosophy. However, when one peels the onion, one can see how powerful African spiritualities are to the lives and meaning-making processes of the people. But Africans continue to infuse and adapt their traditional spiritual values into their Christian and Islamic beliefs. My professor of African Studies, Dr. Kelechi Kalu, often talks about the need to en-center African spiritualities as a strategy against the rampant corruption in the continent. His advice is simple yet interesting: Let's have the leaders swear into office to an African traditional spiritual medium using African spiritual instruments and not to God or Allah with the Bible or Koran. Let's replace the Bishops and Muftis with medicine men and diviners. The point he makes (in a rather subtle way) is that the African politician is yet to take "foreign religion" seriously and until we as African peoples are true to ourselves, we cannot be true to others. Neither can we expect this of our students.

Growing up in a school culture where official knowledge came from the teacher or textbook, I resisted the thought that knowledge was fact. In my view, knowledge was not relational, contested. I still remember so well when, during a fully charged debate, I asked my (very religious) teacher a question: "What if there is more than one God? What if there is no God at all? What if we died and found out that the God we are worshipping is the wrong God?" Given these seemingly unanswerable questions, literature in English became my refuge. It was the only place where I could make intertextual connections. And it was not about finding the right answer, but asking the right questions. My literature teacher allowed us the space and freedom to ask these questions. In more ways than one, she is the reason I am a teacher today.

As mirrors of society, this view of public/private is still manifested in Ugandan schools, offices, and even churches. I often ask myself: Why is everything African presented as inferior—voodoo and witchcraft? Why do Africans praise Jesus or Allah to the extent of sounding fatalistic but fear witchcraft and consult African medicine men "in the dark"? As an educator, I ask: How does this play out in the classrooms? I seek to have my students challenge the taken-for-granted assumptions about what it means to know and how we know. In my teaching, I encourage my students to make intertextual connections with reading materials and use them as avenues to ask the hard (and often uncomfortable) questions about spiritualities and about social injustices. My goal as an educator is to help students become critical consumers as well as creators of knowledge aware of and capable of using their inherent agency to transform their communities. Ultimately, the transformation of Africa has to start with the quality of students that come out of our schools. My life experiences with spiritualities and my vision for African education have informed this concept of spiritually relevant pedagogy and our re-imagination of a pedagogy that is all-inclusive and empowering.

Integrating Spiritualities in the Classroom

What is the use or purpose of an academic life if it doesn't provide a
healing space within which love is generated and promoted? (Dillard,
2006, p. 75)

The institutional structures that define educational systems globally
deserve interrogation. Both in the United States and in Uganda, educational institutions have continued to ignore or blatantly act against
opportunities for centering or nurturing a spiritual life. Using rewards
and punishments, schools continue to shape our views of self and the
world by implicitly and explicitly teaching us to work against or in
competition with others. There still is a discrepancy between what is offi-
cially taught and the "hidden curriculum" that gets left out (Apple,
2004). Using a Spiritually Relevant Pedagogy means interrogating the
curriculum, pedagogy, and the entire academic structures for how
knowledge is transmitted. Mitigating against this hidden curriculum
means teaching students the skills to be critical thinkers, to be able to recognize and critique oppressive aspects of knowledge, to question injustice, to create opportunities for purposeful interaction, and to work
collaboratively toward social justice (Palmer, 1993).

Whereas some scholars call it love (hooks, 2000), others refer to it as
care (Ladson-Billings, 1995), and still others refer to the concept as devo-
tion, in our view, it matters little what one calls it: Spiritualities can
express themselves in many forms. And as we elaborate below specific
considerations for teachers who might value the inclusivity of the term
spiritualities and seek to engage a more Spiritually Relevant Pedagogy,
we also suggest that the philosophy that undergirds it must be one that
is inclusive of such diversity.

*First, it is important for educators to remember that our children are
humans first and students second.* As such, we need to care about them,
their lives both in and out of school (Kinloch, 2010). When we do that,
we partake in the spiritual journey of teaching and learning that is liberating as well as healing (Dillard, 2006; Palmer, 1993). It should also be
emphasized that spirituality begins with loving the self before it is pro-
jected to others. By teachers caring for themselves, they "become the doctor who heals himself and heals the other" (Hanh, 1997, p. 28).

Spiritualities are enhanced and complemented by dialogue. From our autobiographical stories in this chapter, the reader might glean what both existed and was wished for in our educational experiences. One of those things was the desire for dialogue. Dialogue involves students as well as teachers *actively listening* to what others have to say, and empathizing (though not necessarily agreeing) with one another all the time (Dillard, 2006). Dialogue is about understanding that our world-view is affected by our lived experiences, and that culture shapes and is shaped by us. It is acknowledging that when we dialogue *with* spirit and *about* spirit, and when we remember the things that bring us together, we begin to see ourselves and others more clearly (Hanh, 1997). And when we do, we begin to regain our humanity.

Third, spiritualities can be defined in diverse ways. We contend that being spiritual is not necessarily synonymous with being religious, and so too is it that one can be religious without necessarily being spiritual (Krippner, 2003). Spiritualities are not found only in religious settings but can also be found in the simple moments of everyday life, in spending time with others, or with nature, or in creatively expressing oneself through the arts. In other words, while religion and spirituality are often linked "many streams nourish and support the river of your life" (Hanh, 1997, p. 85). So is it true of spiritualities and the ways they might manifest in our teaching and learning.

Spiritually Relevant Pedagogy means *using knowledge to heal the world, as opposed to dismantling and commodifying it.* It means recognizing that human beings are one species sharing the same planet, and that we have a responsibility to nurture and heal one another and to view the world as sacred. Spiritually Relevant Pedagogy means using a critical lens to interrogate the assumptions and normalized values that propagate or preserve hegemonic discourse (Kumashiro, 2009; Ladson-Billings, 1995; Palmer, 1993).

How can we move beyond grades and checklists that are not always the best way to assess learning? A way to develop spiritualities within education is by *promoting collaboration among students.* The current educational structures, both in the United States and in Uganda, are set up to promote individual accomplishments. As a result of the corporate structure of the educational system, students are incentivized to compete with one another instead of being invited to work together. Standardized testing has created a competition for funds that encourages rote memorization and regurgitation, rather than reflective or critical thought that draws from students' real-life experiences. Sloan (in Miller et al., 2005) writes, "it is common knowledge that we all, children and adults alike, learn more easily and remember better those things we are really interested in. But this basic pedagogical principle has all but disappeared in the present craze for standardized testing in every subject at every level" (p. 37). Moore (in Miller et al., 2005) notes: "Our current focus on facts and science skills highlights a certain dimension of human reality but overlooks others. An emphasis on mind has generated a neglect of soul" (p. 9). There must be a balance. While grades and test scores can often be helpful measures of student achievement, they do not always show the entire picture and, therefore, we must be careful to remember that students are not simply data or numbers, but rather are thinking and feeling human beings.

In a context with a proliferation of technology at school and at home, the use of technology for emotional stimulation can have adverse effects on a child's spiritual and social development. As Sloan (in Miller et al., 2005) shows, it is "crucial that the child have opportunities for acquaintance with living nature and an abundance of simple natural objects for play materials, both of which call forth a wealth of open-ended, mobile, and living images and pictures in the child's consciousness" (p. 33). This puts a lot of responsibility on parents and teachers to be conscientious about what kinds of toys and play materials are kept in the home and at school and to purposely create engagements with nature.

A Spiritually Relevant Pedagogy means that instead of de-emphasizing or cutting the arts and extracurricular activities (which is happening in both Uganda and the United States), we allow time for multiple modes of acquiring knowledge and valuing the different talents that students bring to school, beyond what have been normalized to be higher-level academic courses. To create avenues for well-balanced individuals all realms of knowledge must be included.

SRP also involves continuously reflecting on our own positionalities, areas of privilege and disadvantage, and ways in which these concepts are dynamic, fluid, and always changing. As individuals we are never complete, but always becoming. SRP encourages questioning the history and formation of one's nation and the ideals on which it was supposedly founded. It entails being cognizant of the fact that culture as a concept is always evolving in ways that impact individuals, as well as being affected by the individuals. Furthermore, SRP demands reflection on how even within our work as devoted educators, we may unintentionally propagate oppression (Kumashiro, 2009; Ladson-Billings, 1995). SRP calls educators to constantly interrogate their own biases about their spiritual beliefs, as well as their assumptions about what their students may or may not believe.

Implementing a Spiritually Relevant Pedagogy necessitates shifting from a material value system to a system that values intrinsic qualities (Kasser, 2011). bell hooks (2000) contends that "although we live in close contact with neighbors, masses of people in our society feel alienated, cut off, alone....Materialism creates a world of narcissism in which the focus of life is solely on acquisition and consumption" (p. 105). Implementing a Spiritually Relevant Pedagogy means moving beyond individualism in the classroom to a more collective discourse in which we understand the balance between the needs of the individual and those of the wider community. In the Ugandan setting this might mean teaching students the need to navigate the delicate balance between the values of African humanism (Ubuntuism) in which understanding oneself is predicated on understanding the wider community and individual needs and aspirations (Appiah, 1992; Mandela, 1994; Tutu, 1999). This could involve caring for others, attending ceremonies, and looking after elders and relatives. In the American setting, this might consist of encouraging collaborative service learning projects that allow students to spend time working together and volunteering in the community.

Conclusion

We attempted to articulate in this chapter the importance of a Spiritually Relevant Pedagogy as a philosophical shift toward en-centering spirituality in education. The guiding theme of this discussion is that spiritualities come in many forms, and structures in education that tend toward exclusivity need to be reconsidered for how they might better include the multiple and various ways people make sense of their existence on this planet. The societal structures that oversee the educational systems, both in the United States and Uganda, too often continue to create a climate that centers on competition and individualism, pushing spiritualities to the periphery. By changing the philosophy and pedagogy within education, we may be able to change the outcomes for both the inner and outer lives of our students. In teaching that allows spaces in classrooms for multiple expressions of spiritualities (whether through collaboration, dialogue, multiple modes of learning, or quiet contemplation), we can help move human existence in a direction of healing education.

References

Appiah, A. (1992). *In my father's house: Africa in the philosophy of culture*. New York: Oxford University Press.

Apple, M. (2004). *Ideology and curriculum* (3rd ed.). New York: Routledge.

Bloome, D., Puro, P., & Theodorou, E. (1989). Procedural display and classroom lessons. *Curriculum Inquiry, 19*(3), 265–291.

Clifford, J. (1986). Introduction: Partial truths. In J. Clifford & G. E. Marcus (Ed.), *Writing culture: The poetics and politics of ethnography* (p. 8). Berkeley: University of California Press.

Collins, P. H. (1991). *Black feminist thought: Knowledge, consciousness, and the politics of empowerment*. New York: Routledge.

Dillard, C. (2006). *On spiritual strivings: Transforming an African American woman's academic life*. Albany, NY: SUNY Press.

Hanh, T. N. (1997). *Teachings on love*. Berkeley, CA: Parallax Press.

Harden, B. (1990). *Africa: Dispatches from a fragile continent*. New York: Norton.

hooks, b. (2000). *All about love: New visions*. New York: William Morrow.

Kasser, T. (2011). Produced by the center for a new American dream [Video file]. Retrieved from http://www.youtube.com/watch?feature=player_embedded&v=oGab38pKscw

Kinloch, V. (2010). *Harlem on our minds: Place, race, and the literacies of urban youth*. New York: Teachers College Press.

Krippner, S. (2003). Spirituality and healing. In D. Moss, A. McGrady, T. C. Davies, & I. Wickramasekera (Eds.), *Handbook of mind-body medicine for primary care* (pp. 191–201). Thousand Oaks, CA: Sage.

Kumashiro, K. (2009). *Against common sense: Teaching and learning toward social justice* (2nd ed.). New York: Routledge.

Ladson-Billings, G. (1995). Toward a theory of culturally relevant pedagogy. *American Educational Research Journal, 32*(3), 465–491.

Mandela, N. (1994). *Long walk to freedom: The autobiography of Nelson Mandela*. Boston: Little, Brown.

Miller, J. P., Karsten, S., Denton, D., Orr, D., & Colalillo Kates, I. (Eds). (2005). *Holistic learning and spirituality in education: Breaking new ground*. Albany, NY: SUNY.

Palmer, P. J. (1993). *To know as we are known: Education as a spiritual journey* (3rd ed.). San Francisco, CA: Harper.

Robinson, K. (2006). Ken Robinson says schools kill creativity [Video file]. Retrieved from http://www.ted.com/talks/ken_robinson_says_schools_kill_creativity.html

Rodriguez, J. (2007). *Cultural memory: Resistance, faith & identity*. Austin: University of Texas Press.

Rogoff, B. (2003). *The cultural nature of human development*. Oxford: Oxford University Press.

Tutu, D. (1999). *No future without forgiveness*. New York: Doubleday.

Wane, N. N., Manyimo, E. L., & Ritskes, E. J. (Eds). (2011). *Spirituality, education & society: An integrated approach*. Rotterdam, The Netherlands: Sense Publishers.

Infusing Identity Enactment as a Component of Spiritually Relevant Pedagogy

Khosi Kubeka

> Walking, I am listening to a deeper way.
> Suddenly all my ancestors are behind me.
> Be still, they say. Watch and listen.
> You are the result of the love of thousands.
> —LINDA HOGAN (B. 1947)

Placing spirituality at the center of teaching and learning is what Kaburu and Landauer are honoring and calling for in this chapter. It is a call that is long overdue. Spiritually Relevant Pedagogy (SRP) speaks to the need to create spaces for students from diverse cultural backgrounds in an effort to convey the essence of humanity from one person to another. It is thus " a shift from the detached exclusivity of many forms of organized religious practice and is inclusive of the many ways that spiritualities can manifest" (Kaburu & Landauer, p. 90). It is a way of tuning in to the part of us that is connected to our inner and higher selves that we call source, God, Spirit, Buddha, among others and integrating this in our learning, teaching, and research practices. It therefore pushes boundaries and the foundation of education in powerful ways. Furthermore, SRP "attempts to nurture the development of the whole person [including] the intellectual, emotional, physical, social, aesthetic and spiritual" (Miller, Karsten, Denton, Orr, & Colalillo Kates, 2005, p. 2). This is in line with the *Soka* education philosophy, forwarded by Daisaku Ikeda (1996), which seeks to promote "the capacity to find meaning, to enhance one's own existence and contribute to the well-being of others, under any circumstance" (p. 2). This capacity then is what is meant "happiness."

Not only do I echo their call, I extend the dialogue by making a case for an infusion of the notion of *identity*, especially within the context of education in post-Apartheid South Africa. Here, I am not referring to the traditional Western theorization of identity that places people in boxes of quantifiable stages and definitions. I am referring to subjective experiences of identity as understood, interpreted, and enacted by the teachers and students in their pedagogical interactions. I am referring to spaces of interaction wherein students and teachers seek to celebrate and discover (a) Who am I? (b) From where do I originate? (c) How do I honor that which is my source? (d) Given who I am, what then is my mission in this world? For reasons I will outline below, engaging with these questions becomes particularly pertinent in post-Apartheid South Africa.

As a researcher, my work focuses on how youth transition to adulthood within unstable and changing social contexts (familial, communal, and national levels) and the impact of these on developmental outcomes such as sense of identity, mental health (self-esteem), educational experiences, and the propensity to engage in risk-related behavior (delinquency and early sexual behavior). As an educator who adheres to a developmental approach to teaching, I use a holistic approach in my engagement with students. My approach is informed by my belief in *Soka* (value creation), a humanistic education philosophy that views students as "cluster[s] of unsurpassed jewels" (Ikeda, 2012, pp. 1–4). In other words, I seek to treasure each student as a human being who brings with him or her richness of knowledge and experience that needs to be tapped and nurtured within the formal learning environment.

In my interactions with students, especially those of African ancestry (both in and outside the classroom), I get to learn even more deeply about the heavy burden of experience stemming from the challenges of navigating a university space that, for most, is foreign. I use the term *foreign* deliberately to point out that navigation of spaces and systems of education and work for people of African ancestry is like moving from one's own country to a foreign land. The transition from home to institutions of higher education means that we/they alter aspects of self and ways of being in order to adapt. In South Africa, most youth grow up in townships and rural communities and are from families not rich in material terms, but rich in terms of their cultural heritage (rooted in African norms) and a sense of collective identity and community. Most of my students are first in their families to enter higher education. While this is a cause for celebration and family pride, it also makes it difficult for their loved ones to fully appreciate the struggles they go through at university; It is therefore difficult for families to provide support when needed.

These are brilliant, articulate, and talented young people who have a lot to offer the learning environment they have chosen to enter. However, they struggle to deal with the strain of an advanced-learning environment where they are expected to keep up with the predominantly Western, often complex ways of understanding the world, leaving little or no room for self-expression and situating their own experiences within the material they are expected to engage with. This kind of teaching and learning does not take into account or allow them to honor their rich indigenous knowledge and heritage. This imposition of Eurocentric epistemologies at the expense of the students' sense of self has been a form of assimilation. Furthermore, as Kaburu and Landauer posit, there is a "big push for quantifiable and logical knowledge accumulation, but little space to tell stories or be creative, or express wisdom in other ways. This biases the learning space toward one way of learning that puts students in competition with one another" (p. 91). Their self-esteem is therefore diminished by their inability to measure up to the competitive environment. In addition, the flaunting of material and economic privilege they often witness and the subtle racial attacks are psychic violence they are subjected to on a daily basis. They fall apart because they realize that the system is so powerfully well-guarded that they cannot change it. The result is an experience of identity confusion.

As a Black woman scholar who has been through the process of re-socialization as it were in a similar kind of schooling environment in the

1990s, I can relate to what these students are going through. This makes my work and mission as a scholar both personal and sacred (Dillard & Okpalaoka, 2011). The feelings of self-doubt and a sense of inadequacy that I have identified among my students shaped my experience as well. They were demons I had to constantly battle throughout my college career. I define it as a constant battle because despite these feelings, my desire to learn more and my ambitions to further my education and become a scholar were also fueled. In addition to often feeling inferior, I found myself having to navigate two worlds: The White world (dominant culture) and the Black world of home and community. It was a strain because I felt like I was forced to change who I was to adapt to ways of thinking and living as I became more formally educated. In the process, these adaptations undermined my culture, my heritage, my essence of Blackness. It is here where my battle with my own form of Du Bois' (1903) double consciousness began. Du Bois argues that one of the ways in which double consciousness manifests itself is in the internal conflict between being African and Western simultaneously. Double consciousness is an awareness of one's self as well as an awareness of how others perceive you and the conflict between them. The danger of double consciousness resides in conforming and/or changing one's identity to fit how others perceive you.

Even though I battled with feelings of inadequacy, I was more resilient than many of the students I witnessed dropping out of formal schooling. This resilience was because, in early adolescence, I was fortunate enough to be introduced to the teachings of Steven Bantu Biko, Malcolm X, Martin Luther King Jr., and others. In particular, Biko's Black Consciousness ideology ignited a strong resolve in me to explore and affirm my identity as a Black woman. Black Consciousness is predicated on the belief that because Black people are often confined to poor living conditions, they develop a state of alienation and rejection of self that tends to associate anything good to Whiteness. This self-negation usually begins in childhood and persists throughout one's life. The only way to rid one of this sense of unworthiness is by refuting the notion that Black is a deviation from the "normal," which is White (Biko, 1978). What it teaches are virtues such as self-love and self-value as a Black person. Embracing this ideology provided a strong foundation for an affirmation of a strong sense of Blackness that I would later draw upon as I grappled with the challenges of university life. In my role today as an emerging scholar at my university, my personal experience and journey become an inspiration for the African heritage students I engage with on a daily basis. Part of my mission is to raise their consciousness, as a way of instilling and cultivating a strong sense of pride and confidence so that they know and internalize the truth, which is that they are worthy and have the right to quality education and socioeconomic opportunities that will improve their life chances.

During the Apartheid era, the Black Consciousness ideology formed a central and critical part of the credo of most anti-Apartheid political and social movements, whose mission was to fight against the subjugation of Black people in the country. The objective was to raise racial awareness and critical consciousness among Black people, wherein the latter was encouraged to refute the perception perpetuated by the Apartheid government depicting Black people as unworthy as a racial group. These tactics served as the impetus for the mobilization of the masses for political action in Black communities across the country.

However, in the post-Apartheid era, beginning with the first democratic elections in 1994, Black Consciousness and radical political action gave way to sentiments of national unity, reconciliation, interracial group tolerance, and contact under the umbrella of "the New South Africa" or the "Rainbow Nation." Farred (2006) describes the rainbow in this context as symbolizing "the disjoining of the 'old' South Africa from the new; the rainbow of the present represents a 'racially' complementary harmony as opposed to the Apartheid past where the disunion of the various peoples was the predominant racist logic" (p. 231). The push for the creation of a non-racial nation, in essence, served as the substitution of race as a principal representation of identity with "racelessness." While advocating a racial identity premised on Black Consciousness would have defeated the purpose of cultivating a non-racial environment, schooling in the post-Apartheid era had to be reframed so that it is keeping with the spirit of unity and reconciliation, while at the same time redressing the inequalities of the past. The way in which this was articulated in the society (both rhetorically and in terms of policy) was the promise of providing (or attempting to do so) access to quality education among the previously marginalized racial groups. This resulted in the designing and implementation of educational policies geared toward the *integration* of a previously racially segregated educational system. However, as Soudien (2004) asserts, what has taken place in the schooling system in South Africa is not integration, but *assimilation* wherein the "values, traditions and customs of the dominant group frame the social and cultural context of the school . . . and presume[s] that subordinate groups represent a threat to the standards of the dominant group and that the dominant group is culturally superior" (p. 92). This has calamitous consequences for the members of the subordinate groups because they are compelled to (yet again) abandon their own identities and cultures and accept, usually under duress, the superiority of the culture and, by implication, the identities of the groups into whose social context they are moving (p. 93). In this case, it is often Black people who find themselves in environments in which their cultural identity is viewed as inferior or not legitimate. We heard evidence of this in the stories presented in the preceding chapter. As Kaburu so convincingly shared, Soudien (2004) presents evidence of how such practices have been detrimental to Black learners. Given that they grow up in a society where opportunities for social mobility are not hindered as they deliberately were for their parents and previous generations, they are the ones who have to move into the previously forbidden, mostly only White spaces wherein they are expected to leave behind their own identities and adopt those of the superior culture. How was this orchestrated? Soudien (2004) argued that the fact there has been a flight of children out of the former Black schools to the English-speaking (former White) school system is telling. This is because there has been no movement of White students into former Black schools. English-speaking former White schools are more popular among Black learners and parents. Former Black-only schools are notorious for poor-quality education. While most Black learners enter the formerly White schools, which changes the racial composition and structure of the schools, the racial profile of teachers and authorities does not change (Soudien, 2004).

I argue that the dynamics of schooling as it impacts on the identities of Black learners extends to higher education spaces as well. It explains why many students of color experience a depletion and fragmentation of their sense of identity within institutions of higher learning. Black students are forced to leave parts of who they are, their sense of identity, when they enter spaces of higher education. This results in fragmented selves that are not culturally or spiritually grounded—and that have negative implications for personal and intellectual well-being. This is why advancing a Spiritually Relevant Pedagogy is needed and might extend its core mission to include a "putting together" of fragmented identities that have been sacrificed in the name of integration, particularly for students of color. The advancement of spiritualities within education is crucial in that it enables students to bring their *whole* selves to the learning environment, rather than having to leave a part of themselves outside of the realm of education (Dillard, 2006). As such they are able to reconnect with their inner being so that they can be grounded and centered and not easily swayed by the contrasting experiences presented by the contradictory environment they are navigating. In other words, such spiritualities will facilitate a space for them to just simply **be**!

Kaburu and Landauer put forward philosophical principles that educators can use to integrate a Spiritually Relevant Pedagogy in their teaching and engagement with students. Here, I illustrate the ways that identity construction and enactment can be infused within the considerations at the end of their chapter for teachers and educational professionals regarding Spiritually Relevant Pedagogy:

1. *"It is important for educators to remember that our children are humans first and students second."*

    Engaging with students as well-rounded human beings as opposed to numbers is crucial. It requires compassion and willingness to get to know their ethnic and cultural background and personal circumstances and how these inform their academic performance. Part of seeking to understand who they are and where they come from involves having a sense of their subjective understanding of their identity. It means showing interest in those cultural practices they have been socialized into and how they particularly navigate time and space. It means actually affirming these ways of being and knowing and encouraging students to articulate them in their work. It also means seeking to understand the uses and value of such cultural heritage in dealing with personal challenges and stress and encouraging students to continue to draw upon these healing practices away from home.

2. *"Spirtualties are enhanced and complemented by dialogue."*

Kaburu and Landauer view dialogue as central in SRP, wherein both students and teachers actively listen to and share personal experiences based on compassion and empathy. In my undergraduate courses on context, identity, and youth developmental well-being, I implement what I call Roundtable Dialogue Sessions. Here students are encouraged to form groups with other students from diverse racial, cultural, and religious backgrounds. The objective of these sessions is to get students engaged in collaborative and intellectual discussions based on topical issues relating to youth identity, health, and education as covered in the course. It is an opportunity not only to expand their understanding of ideas and concepts but also to share their diverse experiences of navigating change and its impact on their sense of self.

3. *"Spiritualities can be defined in diverse ways."*

I concur with Kaburu and Landauer: Spiritualities do not have to be couched or expressed within religious settings or dogma. Celebrating one's heritage and cultural, personal, and social identity is also a form of spiritual practice.

4. *"SRP means using knowledge to heal the world . . . by promoting collaboration among students."*

I have combined Kaburu and Landauer's final two points as they are intimately connected as we think about identity development and dialogues of healing. Using the same Roundtable Dialogue assignment mentioned previously, my students are first encouraged to engage with the prescribed reading material individually. They are asked to highlight the major questions or point that stands out to them as they read and bring that into the dialogue reflection space to share with their group. This makes for a stimulating and critical group discussion that students enjoy and look forward to. It is within the roundtable dialogue session spaces that students get an opportunity to *then critically reflect with their peers* on their "positionalities, areas of privilege and disadvantage," as Kaburu and Landauer suggested: Such collaboration helps them to both see and experience how their perspectives have been shaped by their ancestral and historical experiences and are also always constantly evolving. And those are the sorts of spiritualities we can all live with.

References

Biko, S. (1978). *I write what I like*. New York: Harper and Row.

Dillard, C. B. (2006). *On spiritual strivings: Transforming an African American woman's academic life*. Albany: SUNY.

Dillard, C. B., & Okpalaoka, C. L. (2011). The sacred and spiritual nature of endarkened transnational feminist praxis in qualitative research. In N. Denzin & Y. Lincoln (Eds.), *The Handbook of Qualitative Research* (4th ed., pp. 147–162). Thousand Oaks, CA: Sage.

Du Bois, W. E. B. (1903). *The souls of black folk*. Chicago: A.C. McClurg and Co.

Farred, G. (2006). "Shooting the White girl first": Race in post-Apartheid South Africa. In K. M. Clarke & D. A. Thomas (Eds.), *Globalization and race: Transformations in the cultural production of Blackness* (pp. 226–248). Durham, NC: Duke University Press.

Ikeda, D. (2012). "Encouragement for Soka Educators." *SGI Newsletter*, 8660: 1–4. Japan: Soka Gakkai.

Ikeda, D. (1996). *Columbia daigaku deno SGI kaicho no koen* [SGI President Ikeda's Lecture at Columbia University]. *Seikyo Shimbun*, June 16.

Miller, J. P., Karsten, S., Denton, D., Orr, D., & Colalillo Kates, I. (Eds). (2005). *Holistic learning and spirituality in education: Breaking new ground*. Albany, NY: SUNY.

Soudien, C. (2004). Constituting the class: An analysis of the process of "integration" in South African schools. In L. Chisholm (Ed.), *Changing class: Education and social change in post-Apartheid South Africa*. Cape Town: HSRC Press.

Chapter 5

Occupy Classrooms

Teaching from a Spiritual Paradigm

Angela Cartwright Lynskey

Introduction .

We are unstoppable; another world is possible.
—OCCUPIERS AT ZUCCOTTI PARK, NYC

Using Dillard's (2006) spiritual paradigm, and drawing from Palmer (1993) and hooks (1989), my students and I engaged in an inquiry project about the World Trade Organization (WTO) and the Occupy Movement. In addition to learning content related to multinational corporations and citizens' rights, students were encouraged to form and interrogate their own opinions, find their unique voices, and experience the healing of a positive identity based in academic success. The success of my students' inquiry into the Occupy Movement had little to do with the instruction I provided them. Truth be told, I gave them little direct "instruction" during our time together. Their success was based in their commitment to know, and make known to others, the complexities of international trade and the Occupy Movement. Their engagement, inquiry, and articulation were inspired by a spiritual paradigm. Dillard (2006) describes a spiritual paradigm as embodied, political, risky, cultural, sacred, grounded in truth, dialogic, liberating, and redemptive. An inquiry unit designed around these components provided my students with an engaging learning experience, as well as an opportunity to reinforce positive aspects of their identities. My hope is that our personal transformations will act as catalysts for transformations, rooted in a politics of related truth, which will create change throughout our school, community, and larger society.

Transformative Learning

The goal of the academy is transformation (Dillard, 2006). We are transformed when we experience "a shift of consciousness that dramatically and permanently alters our ways of being in the world" (Dei, in Cole, 2011, p. 2). Dillard's spiritual paradigm is wonderfully situated to encourage transformative teaching and learning. When students begin to see themselves and the world clearly, even differently, a transformation has occurred within them. Their transformation can act as a catalyst for the transformation of others. When my students began to interrogate themselves and the systems that form the infrastructure of their world, they began the process of transformational learning; when they experienced success with academic and activist identities, the transformation continued; when they used their insights and voices to encourage others to challenge their assumptions, their own transformational learning came full circle.

Dillard's (2006) conception of transformation can be seen as an extension of Palmer's (1993) description of education as transcendence. He explains that "an education in transcendence prepares us to see beyond appearances into the hidden realities of life—beyond facts into truth, beyond self-interest into compassion, beyond our flagging energies and nagging despairs into the love required to renew the community of creation" (Palmer, 1993, p. 13). He rejects the interpretation of transcendence as escape and instead argues that it "is a breaking-in, a breathing of the Spirit of love into the heart of our existence, a literal in-spiration that allows us to regard ourselves and our world with more trust and hope than ever before" (p. 13). Palmer's beautiful words wisely point us to a different state of consciousness, but Dillard's push us toward a different state of being. Education from a spiritual paradigm challenges us to become something more than what we were before we encountered it. It calls us to move from working toward a more just and peaceful world to choosing to radically walk in it now. My students and I attempted to walk in new spaces of transformative education during our inquiry projects on the World Trade Organization and the Occupy Movement. Our work within a spiritual paradigm encouraged us to engage with our world on a deeper level, one that inspired us to privilege the sacredness of humanity and the communal nature of truth, respect embodied and cultural knowledges, embrace of the risks of learning for a politics of liberation, and engage in redemptive dialogues.

Inquiry for Transformation: Current Affairs in the Spiritual Paradigm

Current Affairs is a half-credit elective offered to juniors and seniors as an option for completing the three-credit Social Studies graduation requirement. Current Affairs replaced an Ohio Graduation Test remediation course, and many of the students who enrolled in these courses had struggled to experience academic success in the past. Of the students whose experiences are chronicled in this chapter, 11 of them were English Language Learners, two students were identified as learning differently, and nine of them had yet to pass the Social Studies portion of the Ohio Graduation Test. Sixty-five percent were male, with 35% being female. Sixty-three percent were White, 16% were Latina/o, 12% were African American, 6% were Somali, and 2% were multiracial.

Before the school year began, I had tentatively planned to do a unit on the World Trade Organization to coincide with its General Meeting; the unit would culminate in a debate during which students would interrogate the efficacy of the WTO. While the broad idea had been developed early, the preparatory activities were planned in response to developments in our classroom and in our larger society. We first investigated common problems associated with global trade using resources from *Rethinking Schools*. Students read and discussed scenarios about a variety of trade disputes, then formulated what they believed to be appropriate responses. The purpose of these exercises was to demonstrate that some issues are so complex as to make simple solutions nearly impossible. Additionally, the activities encouraged students to begin formulating their own value systems in relationship to economic profit and human rights, upon which they would rely for the duration of the unit.

Sacredness and Truth: Privileging Relationships and Connecting with the Content

Challenging students to acknowledge and critique the systems that often position human rights against economic profit was a way to invite students into a space of sacredness and truth, which are pillars of Dillard's (2006) spiritual paradigm. Sacredness and truth are in some ways strangers to the public education classroom of today, with its market-based models and standardized-test ranking of students. These two concepts, so important to the development of both individuals and societies, are among those most often missing from the classroom. From their intangibility to their interrogation of dominant systems and worldviews, the very essence of sacredness and truth are challenging to the academy. Making space for these ideas is at the root of a spiritual paradigm.

When engaged in our inquiry project, I provided materials for my students that encouraged them to interrogate the assumptions that human rights can be preempted by economic growth, and that the two are even comparable. While encouraging them to form their own conclusions, I intentionally selected sources that would lead them to (re)evaluate the assumptions that form the foundation of systemic inequalities. Some students chose to continue to support the status quo, while others opted to challenge it. Regardless of their conclusions, I tried to make the space of the inquiry sacred. While I believe there is an incontrovertible link between truth and justice, even economic justice, I also tried to appreciate the communal nature of truth. Palmer (1993) describes teaching as creating "a space in which obedience to truth is practiced" (p. xii). Despite the dominating sound of words such as *obedience* and *truth*, Palmer's vision is one situated squarely in a partnership model. When asked to identify the truth that must be obeyed, he responds that we must be faithful to the truth "that emerges between us" (p. xii). My students found as much truth as they could together, stretched as many of their boundaries as they could at this time; for their efforts and their honesty, I honored their truth by respecting the communal process they participated in when seeking it. While I did not necessarily agree with all of their opinions, I recognized that they were born out of earnest consideration and reflected as much challenge to their worldview as my students were equipped to handle at that time.

Critical scholar-educators are increasingly suspicious of the dominant model of education that reinforces the assumption that human rights are comparable to profit (Eisler, 2005; O'Sullivan, 2005). These critiques are rooted in privileging humanity in a system designed to dehumanize in pursuit of profit. Sloan's (2005) interrogation ultimately led to a rejection of the dominant model of education in favor of one that encourages educators and students to become more fully human. Similarly, O'Sullivan's (2005) alternative model of emancipatory hope challenges educators (indeed, all citizens) to see past the dominant market model into what he calls the "Big Picture" (pp. 69–71). When we focus only on the bits of knowledge that will be tested, we miss the interconnectivity of whole disciplines to our lives. We must help our students learn how to see their place in the larger world, including the past and the future. O'Sullivan's (2005) voice is both poetic and prophetic as he reminds us that "standard of living does not add up to quality of life" and equally so when he concedes that "critique without vision leads to despair" (pp. 70–71). His lament stems from a society with unsustainable and inhumane priorities, as well as the cynical voice that claims nothing else is possible. O'Sullivan's antidote to despair is in his interpretation and application of the concept of "strange attractors," which are the creative elements in society that lead to transformation (pp. 73–76). He calls educators to see themselves as strange attractors and "situate ourselves in a 'great work'" in which we ask "great questions" (pp. 73–76). For many students, questions of *what* and *how* are not great; they are not inspiring, not transformational. Educators who desire to engage in transformational learning with their students must ask the difficult questions of *why*, and even more significant, *how could it be otherwise* in their pursuit of great work. Teaching and learning are much more meaningful activities when one approaches the processes and outcomes with an eye for the role they can play in transforming society.

In encouraging my students to interrogate the dominant production-based interpretation of the World Trade Organization, I was challenging them to ask *why* and *could it be otherwise* in regard to our ranking of profit over people. Challenging the hierarchies upon which oppression is built is at the heart of Eisler's (2005) alternative transformational model of holistic education. It is based on relationships, which she privileges equally with reading, writing, and arithmetic goals in education. Her model is called Partnership Education, as opposed to the current model she identifies as Dominator Education. Eisler's premise is that both what we teach and how we teach it train our students to interact with others in certain ways. Her model challenges educators to reassess how, where, and what we teach for the elements of hidden curriculum that undermine the importance and development of healthy relationships. Healthy interpersonal relationships, priorities, and definitions of success are integral to transformative education. Partnership Education seeks to create a template for information based on "linking rather than ranking," challenging the hierarchal structure of the Dominator model (Eisler, 2005, p. 51). Challenges to Dominator Education thus include challenges to both epistemology and methodology, focusing instead on the more relational truths and inquiries of the partnership model.

After becoming familiar with trade disputes and developing our value systems upon which to evaluate them, the second step in our inquiry was to introduce the World Trade Organization as a possible solution to or authority in global trade disputes. We analyzed both positive and negative arguments about the WTO and students selected a position for the upcoming debate. The position statement for the debate was *the benefits of the WTO outweigh the negative effects*, and students had to determine whether they agreed or disagreed. Despite the fact that students were participating in the daily preparatory assignments, I became concerned about the quality of the debate. The WTO, free trade, fair trade, and economic progress balanced by human rights were very abstract concepts for my students. They had no emotional buy-in, and thus lacked the passion to fully engage the difficult material.

Sloan's (2005) evaluation of the destructive aspects of modern life is insightful when considering student apathy. In his argument, Sloan asserts that our overstimulation has prevented us from developing the capacity to fully appreciate any of the stimuli. Because my students were distracted by simpler and flashier stimuli, they could not make a connection with the content. Sloan's use of Rousseau's lament regarding modernity aptly describes the situation of my students: "Of all the things that strike me, there is none that holds my heart, yet all of them together distract my feelings, so that I forget where I am and who I belong to" (p. 40).

Throughout the academy, there is an increased acknowledgment of the need to integrate the spirit into our learning environments to enhance engagement and learning. In his foreword to *Spirituality, Education & Society: An Integrated Approach,* Abdi (2011) laments,

> As the authors in this important endeavor clearly expound, the noticeable absence of spirituality from the educational research and from contemporary spaces of school, is to say the least lamentable, and the coming of this work and other treatises that should follow it, are essentially needed, and should awaken, one must hope, in all those whose perception of public education as a primary public good is authentic and present, an urgent sense of advancing the place of spirituality in all learning situations, relationships and outcomes. (p. xiii)

His concern is shared by many scholars and educators (Dillard, 2006; hooks, 2000; Palmer, 1993; Rendon, 2000; Shahjahan, 2004; Tisdell, 2007; Wane & Ritskes, 2011).

Sloan (2005) continues the critique of a spiritless education, asserting that educators can no longer accept the system that "would homogenize, standardize, and regulate the human being and the environment also for the purposes of control and exploitation" (p. 43). When we approach our students, and teach them to approach others, as valuable only in their capacity to produce, we do a great disservice. The standards-based, assessment-driven atmosphere of education today comes dangerously close to devaluing our students' whole selves. Moore (2005) concurs, acknowledging that our educational system's "emphasis on mind has generated a neglect of soul" (p. 9). Current educational practices encourage students to learn the correct answers to politically and economically expedient questions; while these practices may create good consumers, even students, they are not creating good citizens and lifelong learners.

Moore (2005) rejects the product-driven quest for knowledge at the expense of wisdom, reminding readers that education "cultivat[es]...a certain kind of ignorance," privileging not knowing in the same way it privileges knowing (p. 15). He suggests that a holistic spiritual education provides "healing" through "the discovery of what the soul wants" (p. 13). Scholar-poet Alice Walker (2006) takes up his argument, asserting that "the soul wants to know the truth; what is really going on" (p. 215). Our students will be inspired to learn when we ask them questions that matter about the issues that are important to them; encouraging them to question the value systems so often portrayed as the natural state of affairs is a worthwhile place to start. The dominant model of education, representing the dominant ideology of society, portrays the value of economic growth as equal to the value of human life. Students must be taught that they can interrogate those assumptions in pursuit of a more just world.

To increase my students' interest, I decided to use a medium effective with them and show *The Battle in Seattle*, a film about the protests that collapsed the 1999 World Trade Organization Ministerial Conference. The film chronicles the experiences of a variety of fictional, but composite, characters as they navigated the unrest in Seattle. My students enjoyed the film to the point that I had to make them leave for their next classes. One unintentional consequence was that many students wanted to change their position after they saw the film. I did not allow them to switch sides in the debate for a variety of reasons. Practically, it is difficult to have a debate when all participants are arguing the same thing. However, there was a deeper reason that also influenced my decision. Their initial analyses had been based in their responses to data. After seeing the film, the data remained unchanged; however, my students' perception of it was significantly altered. I desired for them to grasp the importance of how our filters, born of our life experiences, affect the way we see the world.

Embodied and Cultural: Acknowledging Our Boundaries

Because many students desired to change their debate position after viewing it, we had a class discussion about our experience with the film. Students described which scenes and characters had affected them most, and we analyzed the extent to which the film could be described as propaganda. A significant issue in our analysis of the film and its impact on us was the extent to which we saw ourselves reflected in the characters. Though my students were not familiar with the concept of positionality, we had a brief discussion of how our experiences shape the way we see the world. Students understood this simplified version and were able to identify how our life experiences may have influenced our perspective on the issues associated with free trade. Multiple students referenced their class positioning and the impact it had on their access to economic opportunities. Other students referenced nationality and race, as they relate to access and privilege, when explaining their positionality. The film portrayed youth, along with the middle and working classes, as resisters to oppression; my students saw themselves in those characters and imagined themselves in those scenarios. Their allegiance was shifted from abstract ideas about economic growth to personal experiences of resistance.

My students' awareness and descriptions of the way their embodied experiences affected their perception and interpretation represented an integral aspect of a spiritual paradigm. Dillard (2006) describes embodiment as being present and letting your embodied experience, or positioning, be evident. For adolescent learners, this can look different than it does for scholars and educators. My students began the process of embodiment as it pertains to a spiritual paradigm. They engaged in an interrogation of why they perceived the world as they did and of recognizing their role in systems of oppression. They did not engage in theoretical critiques of how these systems have been (re)produced, nor did they hypothesize ways in which these systems could be disrupted. However, they began to be aware that these systems exist, and that they have concrete impact on the lives of real people.

In addition to embodiment, Dillard (2006) describes a spiritual paradigm as being cultural. Her conception of the cultural component of a spiritual paradigm is that practitioners do not deny their own boundaries, but neither are they restrained by them; instead, practitioners seek to stretch both their own and others' boundaries. Anzaldúa (2003) also asserts the importance of breaking boundaries when she describes their limitations. She describes the dangers of being one who cannot not move past her own boundaries, saying she "can't hold concepts or ideas in rigid boundaries...rigidity means death" (p. 180).

While we did not explicitly interrogate our own cultural boundaries during the inquiry project, we did attempt to identify the genesis of our own perspectives. As they were largely culturally based, our reflection was the beginning of our journey into stretching our own boundaries. By acknowledging how our embodied and cultural experiences informed our understanding of the world and our own value systems, my students and I were beginning to inhabit the embodied and cultural aspects of a spiritual paradigm; we acknowledged how our comfort zones were created and began to step outside of them. I found that when I framed our content within investigations of current social issues, my students were able to make a connection with the issues beyond the cognitive realm. Applebaum (2004) describes emotional connections as "the first tools that educators employ to arouse critical awareness of social injustice" (p. 71). Refusing to be limited by boundaries is a crucial component of transformational learning in a spiritual paradigm.

After the film engaged their emotions and challenged their boundaries, my students were ready for a passionate debate. When they prepared their individual argument sheets, they re-assessed previously examined sources with unexpected vigor. They were no longer simply completing an assignment to receive a grade; they were invested in the larger issues their assignment represented. They made astute observations and organized themselves into cohesive units to effectively articulate their positions. When the official debate ended, as we had reached the conclusion of the formal structure, they began an informal discussion of the issues of fair versus free trade, as well as human, environmental, and sovereignty rights. They did not arrive at any solutions to trade disputes, or the larger issues of human rights, nor did any students concede the argument to the alternate perspective; however, the debate provided them with information that enabled them to participate in an authentic dialogue in which they heard and learned from each other.

Dialogue: Respecting the Truth We Found Together

Dialogue is a necessary component of a spiritual paradigm (Dillard, 2006). Dillard's conception of the communal and sacred nature of truth requires that those who seek it participate in dialogue with others. She identifies dialogue as the beginning of the beloved community, which interrogates and creates truth together. Dillard (2006) draws on hooks's (1989) conception of dialogue to describe the process through which communal truth is made: "Dialogue implies talk between two subjects, not the speech of a subject and an object. It is humanizing speech, one that challenges and resists domination" (p. 22). Many would assume all dialogue would meet these qualifications, particularly in an educational setting. However, hooks's explanation is significant, as it rejects the domination and knowledge-imperialism that characterizes inauthentic dialogues (Jones, 2004).

Palmer's (1993) musings on truth in community are significant in a discussion of dialogue as a necessary component to a spiritual paradigm. His philosophy of dialogue lies in its intent, which he identifies as the desire to bring people together, not further divide them. Redemptive dialogue is achieved when we engage in "a rich and complex network of relationships in which we must both speak and listen, make claims on others and make ourselves accountable" (Palmer, 1993, p. xii). For dialogue to be authentic, participants must be committed to a mutual understanding. Palmer's focus on relationships and responsibility resonates with aspects of a spiritual paradigm (Dillard, 2006). Cole (2011) echoes Dillard's privileging of relational spirituality, asserting that responsibility is a necessary component of spirituality. Walker (2006) speaks to the responsibility of knowledge, arguing that "knowledge kept secret ceases to be knowledge; it becomes dogma and superstition. Knowledge actually requires sharing in order to exist" (p. 162). Sharing knowledge and seeking truth through dialogue can be seen as an antidote to oppressive systems. bell hooks (2000) asserts that the hoarding of knowledge is usually linked to a desire to hold power over another, which is in direct opposition to the true aims of dialogue and transformational education.

When my students were engaged in our inquiry project, there were many moments of intense disagreement. However, students maintained their composure and our sense of classroom community by privileging their relationships as classmates over their desire to be "right." They heard each other and addressed each other's perspectives respectfully, though none were swayed from their positions. During the unit, my students asked difficult questions, made astute observations, and began to settle into their positions. Regardless of their position in the surprisingly passionate debate, I was impressed by their ability to approach the problems of international trade from a variety of angles. My pride was based in their ability to demonstrate passion about something, but not at the expense of their relationships.

I was pleased with the results of the planned unit; I felt that my students had made much progress with both the spoken and unspoken curriculum identified for the unit. They had analyzed documents, formed opinions about trade issues and international organizations, and had supported them both in writing and orally. They had achieved all of these curricular objectives while at the same time privileging relationships and interrogating oppressive assumptions. I was also quite interested in one of the unintended and unplanned learning opportunities. While we were studying the World Trade Organization to prepare for our debate, the Occupy Wall Street Movement began to gain momentum. We decided to compare the 1999 Battle in Seattle with the current Occupy Movement protests. Students identified many similarities, from chants to tactics, which both sets of demonstrators used. As with the World Trade Organization, students analyzed their own embodied and cultural positionality in their evaluation of the Occupy Movement. When our analysis of the World Trade Organization ended, our class moved on to other topics; however, as student interest remained high, we continued to have periodic "check-ins" with the Occupy Movement, during which we discussed major events and developments.

My family travelled to New York City for the Thanksgiving holiday, and on Friday, November 25, we visited Zuccotti Park. We spent a couple of hours with the Occupiers, interviewing them and recording their experiences. Despite our attempts, the New York City Police and private security guards encircling the park declined to give comments, even off-camera. The experience was surreal, exhilarating, and heartbreaking. We witnessed three marches arriving at the park, one arrest, and countless acts of Occupiers sharing material support. Because of the continued interest of my students in the movement, I decided to use the footage as the catalyst for an Occupy unit.

Political: When Students Become Teachers

The decision to pursue a unit on the Occupy Movement, and especially to use footage of myself interviewing Occupiers, was not easy. The Movement had become quite politicized, with much rhetoric along partisan lines. The political battles that had embroiled our state just weeks before had pitted teachers, and other public employees, against the governor and state senate. Voters had sided with public employees, but the experience had been damaging. Some community relationships remained adversarial and teachers were wary of topics with political implications.

Many classroom teachers can be hesitant to politicize their classrooms, particularly in states embattled by politicians using public employees as pawns. However, the politicization of public education is unavoidable. Levine (1995) argues that schools, due to their purpose, structure, and content, are "highly political institutions" (pp. 56–57). Teachers, classmates, and school administrators are an integral part of the experiences that shape students' perspectives and identities. Though the implications may be daunting and require sensitivity and diligence, educators should remember the larger societal function of public education. Freire (1970a, 1970b) and Giroux (2001) famously argue that emancipatory education is the site of societal transformation. Introducing Freire's theoretical work, da Veiga Coutinho (1970) places the practical impetus on teachers, arguing, "there is no neutral education. Education is either for domestication or for freedom. Although it is customarily conceived as a conditioning process, education can equally be an instrument for de-conditioning. *An initial choice is required of the educator*" (p. vi; emphasis added).

Preparing students for their roles as citizens is an example of the often-politicized unspoken curriculum in our schools today. Darling-

Hammond (2002) highlights the importance of teachers embracing the intrinsically political nature of our work by asserting "teaching is a moral and political act, and teachers can play a key role in facilitating positive social change" (p. 2). Politicizing your classroom within a spiritual paradigm means acknowledging the unintentional politics already at work and then embracing a politics of transformation for peace and justice (Dillard, 2006). Santora (1995) concurs and also offers guidance for creating a transformative politics for the classroom, saying, "As teachers it is risky for us to remain passive. We have a responsibility for building classroom communities that confront controversy and take responsibility for creating a better community, one that values diversity and human integrity and fights inhumanity" (pp. 21–22). Her words remind us that embracing the political nature of our work does not mean indoctrinating our students for the benefit of a particular party or side in the culture wars, but instead encouraging our students to embrace a politics of mindfulness and the interconnectivity of all humanity.

Despite the political circumstances that surrounded our inquiry, I decided that I needed to embody a politics of transformation in my classroom. By selecting the topic, and by using primary source material created during my presence at Zuccotti Park, I was indicating my own position on the Occupy Movement. Navigating evident positioning is a complex matter for public educators desiring to work from a spiritual paradigm. While my commitments to social justice and emancipatory education are evident in my own scholarship, I do not always explicitly state them in my role as a public educator. In the increasingly politicized and ideological environment of public education, teachers who desire to provide their students with a transformational education must inhabit the borderlands of working for the (re)construction of the system while still within the system. My students, my co-teacher, and I knew our subject matter was potentially controversial due to its politically charged nature. Despite the potential pitfalls, we all decided the work was important.

We chose to continue in our work, knowing that it might be controversial, but feeling that the risk was worth it. Intentionality is a significant part of the politics of a spiritual paradigm. When describing the intrinsically political nature of a spiritual paradigm, Dillard (2006) points to Martin Luther King Jr., Mahatma Gandhi, and Alice Walker as practitioners of a spiritual paradigm who all embraced clear political goals for their work. Indeed, they are at least as notable for their activism as they are for their spiritual commitments and practices. Dillard (2006) also identifies a significant caveat in her assertion that each of these transformational scholars/activists was unapologetic about the political goals in their work. A spiritual paradigm is intentional, not accidental.

I intended to show the video clips to my students on Monday when we returned to school, but technical difficulties delayed it until Tuesday. Thankfully, a student in the class was quite adept at computer and video technology, and he was able to reformat the footage so that I could play it at school. While he worked on it Monday, my students interviewed me about my experiences at the Occupation site, and then we watched online videos of notable Occupation moments from the last couple of weeks. The refresher was just what we needed; the next day, students entered the room asking if we got the footage reformatted. When I told them their classmate had been successful, they cheered! We watched the footage and tried to identify potential costs and benefits of the Occupy Movement. Based on students' observations, they selected their positions and opted to participate in either an in-class debate assessed by a building administrator or a guest-teaching presentation to a Senior English class. When we realized that their groups were quite uneven, student volunteers moved themselves; their willingness to argue different perspectives and branch out of the safety of our classroom made me very proud. They were beginning to see themselves as competent, not just as learners but also as teachers.

The coup de grace to my doubts and the moment that reminded me why I became an educator occurred when a student, who had experienced little success in his academic career, returned from a two-day absence. He approached me with a textbook (from a different class, as my course does not have one) full of bookmarks. He had read through the Constitution, marking every passage he felt pertained to the right to peaceful protest and petition. In addition, he had copied down the Web address of a site that had legal advice and guidelines for peaceful protesting. He told me he did it at home, saving the Web address on his flash drive, as well as writing it for me. My inclusion specialist commented that this was the most interest she had ever seen him take in school.

During our research days, students were unusually focused. We had class meetings at the beginning of each period, reviewing our specific goals for the day and how they fit into the larger project goals. I asked for and gave updates regarding significant events (large-scale arrests, evictions, etc.) of the Occupy Movement each day, as well as sharing art and other media about the larger issues represented by the Occupy Movement. For each event or media, we analyzed it from both sides of the debate, constructing interpretations that could be used by each side. However, the majority of the class time was spent in student groups with peripheral teacher presence in case of questions. Student leaders emerged as individuals volunteered to be team captains. Interestingly, more than one team captain was a student who had previously been academically unengaged and unsuccessful. Attendance increased, as did the submission of daily work in the form of project updates.

Risky: In Pursuit of Joy

Despite my concern of starting a controversy in our school and community, and my students' concerns about inviting others into our classroom community to evaluate their debate and presentations, we continued in our inquiry. Choosing to continue in spite of the potential for controversy is another facet of Dillard's (2006) spiritual paradigm. Working from a spiritual paradigm is risky; it requires courage as the practitioner is required to walk in spaces that do not yet exist, especially in the areas of fairness and social justice. I felt the risk when my administration informed me that the debate judging would also serve as my yearly evaluation. My students felt the risk when they articulated their own analyses of complex issues in front of people not a familiar part of the safety of our classroom community. Our risks were intertwined; in some ways, our worth, our identities as teacher and students, would be judged by classroom outsiders simultaneously. While these risks may be on a smaller scale than those associated with university scholarship from a spiritual paradigm, including issues of publishing and tenure, they were quite real to us. However, the risks associated with working from a spiritual paradigm are worth it when one considers the possible rewards. Dillard (2006) describes the results as joyful, and as Walker

(2006) reminds us, "to be revolutionary means, by definition, to be willing to sacrifice" (p. 149), in pursuit of joy. The work my students did, and
the success they experienced, was the joy that I pursued and found in
the inquiry experience.

Redemptive: (Re)Making Ourselves

Student products from the inquiry project were amazing, with grades
ranging from B+ to A+. Students approached their debates with seriousness and conviction, but they argued calmly and within the boundaries
of a traditional debate. Presentations included a variety of activities
designed to acquire and maintain their students' attention. Both types of
product included areas in which students with different strengths could
be successful. Students who excelled in media skills developed handouts;
students who excelled in the fine arts created visual aids; students who
excelled in research provided materials; a student who excelled in the per-
forming arts developed a rap; students who excelled in oration delivered
material. Each student was a valued, and unique, member of the self-gov-
erning group. Their competence and initiative were their own; they were
successful, and I was privileged to witness it. We were all freed from pre-
conceptions of our roles as both teachers and learners; we experienced
success and satisfaction together, on our own terms.

The personal and social successes of my students are representative
of Dillard's (2006) assertion that the spiritual paradigm be redemptive.
As the classroom can be a place of wounding for many students, it is
imperative that we offer them opportunities to heal there, too. Academic
healing, as is the case with all healing, is a community concern; hooks
(2000) describes the relational nature of healing, saying "rarely, if ever,
are any of us healed in isolation. Healing is an act of communion" (p.
215). For society to be redeemed, the wounded must first be healed. The
community of students in my class engaged in a healing process as
they grew and were redeemed together to reclaim their "school" identities. Some became classroom leaders, some had their voices heard by
their peers and/or authority figures, and some were positioned as good
students, knowledgeable individuals, and competent articulators—all
for the first time. The healing that comes from being seen, and seeing

yourself, in this way can redeem the educational experience and encourage continued academic success, and in this case, continued activism.

When the wounds are healed, students can begin the difficult work of becoming. The same experiences that provide healing can also provide inspiration. During our inquiry project into the Occupy Movement, students exercised much decision-making power and self-regulation. I gave them broad guidelines for research and general templates for how to share their findings, but they formed their groups and designated their own roles. These experiences as knowledgeable and competent leaders were critical to the development of positive identities for my students. As its own discipline, identity formation is of interest to educators because of the role education has in socialization (Marshall, 2006). We begin to value certain traits based on our membership in social groups (Reynolds & Prior, 2006). The social influence on individual values creates a dynamic where an intensely personal quest is made public. Students arrive in the classroom with a personalized store of potential selves, but will nurture and develop only those that receive praise or acknowledgment (Thoits & Virshup, 1997). Given a choice, most students will not choose an identity that leads to social exclusion. The critical factor is how individuals determine which characteristics to value. When educators provide experiences in which students' most positive potential selves are valued and encouraged, we are supporting the adoption of those selves as important parts of students' identities.

Edmiston's (2007) words are significant when he argues that students who repeatedly experience academic failure will begin to see themselves as incompetent, but those who experience success will internalize a competent identity. Positive identity formation is important for all students, but evidence suggests that it may be even more crucial for students who might need more support in making positive choices (De Haan & MacDermid, 1999). As students take their place in the adult world, those who will be the most successful are the students who enjoyed the most practice with responsibility. If we want students to be effective citizens, we must provide them with practice in the safety of the classroom.

In addition to providing practice for adulthood, positive identity development in the classroom is critical for students of difference. As students of difference are culturally situated in ways that they can neither select nor reject, and have little power to participate in the naming and framing of, they frequently experience what Du Bois (1990) describes as "double consciousness" (p. 45; see also hooks, 1995). Double consciousness is the process through which one sees oneself through the eyes of another, while continuing to be aware of one's own self-perception. Banks (1996) uses *marginal man* to describe similar processes. In the marginal man theory, individuals of difference are constantly moving between two worlds as they are forced to exist in both the dominant and marginalized cultures. Due to experiences of oppression, students of difference may in some circumstances reject their identity of difference (Banks, 1996; see also Mura, 1999). During our inquiry unit, however, students of difference were encouraged to embrace their identities of difference and utilize their knowledge of multiple perspectives to add to the complexity of the debate. Students who were able to speak of the effect of race, class, or nationality on their perspectives added richness to the narrative that would have been missed without their unique contributions. In the relational and cooperative environment of our inquiry project, difference was valued because it added to the strength of the group.

Education as Liberation: Concluding Thoughts on the Importance of a Spiritual Paradigm

Dillard (2006) includes liberation as necessary for a spiritual paradigm. She, like Aime Cesaire (1994) and Thich Naht Hahn (2008), recognizes the need to liberate both the oppressed and the oppressor. We each have in us the seeds of both, and they are both damaging to the individual and society. Critical theorists, such as Freire (1970a, 1970b) and Giroux (2001), helped make visible systemic inequalities of hegemony, and the role of public education in (re)producing and (de)constructing them. Freire (1970a, 1970b) argued that educators must choose to teach in ways that disrupt the reproduction of the status quo, but he cautioned that literacy skills are only emancipatory when they give people the tools to awaken and liberate themselves. While there was little concrete liberation in our classroom inquiry into the Occupy Movement, I believe the seeds of critical media literacy, self-reflection, and the articulation of analyses will bear liberatory fruit in my students. Our inquiry project gave them space to interrogate their own perspectives and the role of systemic inequality in their society; it also provided them with a sense of competence as a knowledgeable authority. As these seeds grow, they will have a transformational effect on my students and the communities of which they are a part. The identities they can create around these experiences are exemplary of the social function of public education in a democracy.

As scholars and educators, we are to be committed to Banks's (1996) conception of transformative academic knowledge, which "consists of concepts, paradigms, themes, and explanations that challenge mainstream academic knowledge...[and] key assumptions that mainstream scholars make about the nature of knowledge" (p. 16). The lessons to be learned from hooks (1989), Palmer (1993), and Dillard (2006) are important for educators and scholars who seek to use the spirit in the quest for transformation. Simply bringing together the elements of information, opportunity, and participants is not, in and of itself, enough to encourage transformational learning. Learners, and teachers, must be invested; relationships must be committed and protected; and inquiries must be intentionally critical. It is the spiritual component that inspires students and educators to do the difficult work of transformational learning.

Transformational learning is difficult because it requires change. Williams (1997) captures some of this complexity when she describes "a community [engaged in] this most difficult work of negotiating real divisions, of considering boundaries before we go crashing through, and of pondering our differences before we can ever agree on the terms of our sameness" (p. 4). Dei's (2000) conception of synthesis as a process during which systemic assumptions are (re)evaluated, as opposed to simply inviting new participants into discussions operating under those assumptions, is also crucial to understanding how transformational learning can occur. Dillard's (2006) spiritual paradigm, and the related concepts of transcendent education, communal truth, and authentic dialogue, provides guidelines that educators can use to transform their pedagogy in pursuit of societal change. As Palmer (1993) asserts, "If teaching is to be reformed in our time, it will not be the result of snappier teaching techniques. It will happen because we are in the midst of a far-reaching intellectual and spiritual revisioning of reality and how we know it" (p. xvii).

References

Abdi, A. A. (2011). Foreword. In N. N. Wane, E. L. Manyimo, & E. J. Ritskes (Eds.), *Spirituality, education & society: An integrated approach*. Rotterdam, Netherlands: Sense Publishers.

Aloe, M. (Producer), & Townsend, S. (Director). (2007). *Battle in Seattle* [Motion Picture]. United States: Screen Media.

Anzaldúa, G. (2003). La conciencia de la mestiza: Towards a new consciousness. *Feminist theory reader: Local and global perspectives*. New York: Routledge.

Applebaum, B. (2004). Social justice education, moral agency, and the subject of resistance. *Educational Theory, 54*(1), 59–72.

Banks, J. A. (1996). *Multicultural education, transformative knowledge, and action*. New York: Teachers College Press.

Cesaire, A. (1994). Discourse on colonialism. In P. Williams & L. Chrisman (Eds.), *Colonial discourse and post-colonial theory: A reader* (pp. 172–180). New York: Columbia University Press.

Cole, S. (2011). Situating children in the discourse of spirituality. In N. N. Wane, E. L. Manyimo, & E. J. Ritskes (Eds.), *Spirituality, education & society: An integrated approach* (pp. 1–14). Rotterdam, Netherlands: Sense Publishers.

Darling-Hammond, L. (2002). Chapter one: Learning to teach social justice. In L. Darling-Hammond, J. French, & S. P. Garcia-Lopez, *Learning to teach for social justice*. New York: Teachers College Press.

da Veiga Coutinho, J. (1970). Introduction. In P. Freire, *Cultural action for freedom*. Cambridge, MA: Harvard Educational Review.

De Haan, L. G., & MacDermid, S. M. (1999). Identity development as a mediating factor between urban poverty and behavioral outcomes for junior high school students. *Journal of Family and Economic Issues, 20*(2), 123–148.

Dei, G. (2000). Rethinking the role of Indigenous knowledges in the academy. *International Journal of Inclusive Education, 4*(2), 111–132.

Dillard, C. B. (2006). *On spiritual strivings: Transforming an African American woman's academic life*. Albany, NY: SUNY.

Du Bois, W. E. B. (1990). *The souls of Black folk*. New York: Vintage.

Edmiston, B. (2007). Mission to Mars. *Language Arts, 84*, 4.

Eisler, R. (2005). Tomorrow's children: Education for a partnership world. In J. P. Miller, S. Karsten, D. Denton, D. Orr, & I. C. Kates (Eds.), *Holistic learning and spirituality in education* (pp. 47–68). Albany, NY: SUNY.

Freire, P. (1970a). *Cultural action for freedom*. Cambridge, MA: Harvard Educational Review.

Freire, P. (1970b). *Pedagogy of the oppressed*. New York: Continuum.

Giroux, H. A. (2001). *Theory and resistance in education: Towards a pedagogy for the opposition*. Westport, CT: Greenwood Publishing.

Hahn, T. N. (1998). *Teachings on love*. Berkeley, CA: Parallax Press.

hooks, b. (1989). *Talking back: Thinking feminist, thinking Black*. Boston: South End Press.

hooks, b. (1995). *Art on my mind: Visual politics*. New York: New Press.

hooks, b. (2000). *All about love: New visions*. New York: William Morrow.

Jones, A. (2004). Talking cure: The desire for dialogue. In Megan Boler (Ed.),*Troubling Speech, Disturbing Silence* (pp.59-71). New York: Peter Lang.

Levine, D. (1995). Overview: Building a vision of curriculum reform. In D. Levine, R. Lowe, B. Peterson, & R. Tenorio (Eds.), *Rethinking schools: An agenda for change* (pp. 52–60). New York: New Press.

Marshall, J. M. (2006). Nothing new under the sun: A historical overview of religion in U.S. schools. *Equity and Excellence in Education, 39*, 181–194.

Moore, T. (2005). Educating for the soul. In J. P. Miller, S. Karsten, D. Denton, D. Orr, & I. C. Kates (Eds.), *Holistic learning and spirituality in education* (pp. 9–16). Albany, NY: SUNY.

Mura, D. (1999). Explaining racism to my daughter. In T. B. Jelloun, *Racism explained to my daughter*. New York: New Press.

O'Sullivan, E. (2005). Emancipatory hope: Transformative learning and the "strange attractors." In J. P. Miller, S. Karsten, D. Denton, D. Orr, & I. C. Kates (Eds.), *Holistic learning and spirituality in education* (pp. 69–78). Albany, NY: SUNY.

Palmer, P. (1993). *To know as we are known: Education as a spiritual journey*. New York: HarperCollins.

Rendon, L. I. (2000). Academics of the heart: Reconnecting the scientific mind with the spirit's artistry. *Review of Higher Education, 24*(1), 1–13.

Reynolds, F., & Prior, S. (2006). The role of art-making in identity maintenance: Case studies of people living with cancer. *European Journal of Cancer Care, 15*, 333–341.

Santora, E. D. (1995). The drama of dominance and diversity: A multicultural curriculum framework for secondary social studies/language arts core. (ERIC Identifier ED387379).

Shahjahan, R. (2004). Reclaiming and reconnecting to our spirituality in the academy. *International Journal of Children's Spirituality, 9*(1), 81–95.

Sloan, D. (2005). Education and the modern assault on being human: Nurturing body, soul, and spirit. In J. P. Miller, S. Karsten, D. Denton, D. Orr, & I. C. Kates (Eds.), *Holistic learning and spirituality in education* (pp. 27–46). Albany, NY: SUNY.

Thoits, P. A., & Virshup, L. K. (1997). Chapter five: Me's and we's: Forms and functions of social identities. In R. D. Ashmore & L. Jussim (Eds.), *Self and identity: Fundamental issues*. New York: Oxford University Press.

Tisdell, E. J. (2007). In the new millennium: The role of spirituality and the cultural imagination in dealing with diversity and equity in the higher education classroom. *Teachers College Record, 109*(3), 531–560.

Walker, A. (2006). *We are the ones we have been waiting for: Inner light in a time of darkness*. New York: World Press.

Wane, N. N., & Ritskes, E. J. (2011). Introduction. *Spirituality, education, and society: An integrated approach*. Rotterdam, Netherlands: Sense Publishers.

Williams, P. J. (1997). *Seeing a colour-blind future: The paradox of race*. London: Virago Press.

Spiritual Occupations

Reflections on Pedagogies and Everyday Stories of Globalization

Carmen Liliana Medina

Constructing a pedagogical context to reflect and construct critical practices around the Occupy Movement opens up the possibility of reframing classrooms to engage in examining the complex relation between local and global power, local and global resistance, and local and global knowledge production. Nevertheless, these pedagogical experiences cannot be understood in relation to an abstract global movement but instead in relation to pedagogies where we foreground an understanding of the unique consequences and the individual stories of those affected by the power of global multinational power. This is a pedagogy, as Dillard (2012) suggests, that centers "the sacred nature of experience" (p. 70) to map how our individual stories are embedded in other people's stories and our understanding of the world. Reading and reflecting on Angela Cartwright Lynskey's chapter "Occupy Classrooms: Teaching from a Spiritual Paradigm," I kept coming back to a personal story that helped me interpret both the author and her students' work from a deep personal connection. I feel this connection emerged because of the ways the students in her classroom continuously moved between an understanding of a worldwide political movement and the particular lives and stories of individuals (including the students) whose lives are affected by contemporary oppressive politics of privatization, consumerism, and marginalization. I bring Lynskey and her students' work *a mi casa* (to my home) to make sense of the important work that happened in this classroom and to highlight the potential of rethinking local knowledge production in relation to our lives and the lives of others around the world.

Spirituality has always been a complicated aspect in my life. I grew up in Puerto Rico in a family with a father who has a strong male-oriented set of Marxist's beliefs, including his claim that God does not exist. My mother is Catholic and was raised as a traditional Puerto Rican woman. But in many ways, she has refused to live her life and raise her daughters under the same values and social conditions that were imposed upon her. She lives creating a balancing act between her respect for her parents' traditional ways of raising her and new ways of defining what it means to be a Puerto Rican woman, mother, and teacher. One interesting thing to me about my parents is that while my Marxist father always has a radical thought to explain how systems of oppression and colonization work toward Puerto Rico (and I agree with him most of the time), it is my Catholic mom who always has a pair of tennis shoes ready to go to march in any demonstration in favor of workers rights, anti-colonial manifestations, anti-privatization of public institutions, or any other call that speaks in favor of justice on the island. It always feels that my mother has a different sense of what it means to take action that is grounded in her soul and faith and that as hooks (2003) reminds us comes from a different sense of community and compassion grounded in a spiritual practice that "enhances the struggle for liberation" (p. 164).

One of these moments for my mother was the recent 2010 students' strike at the University of Puerto Rico. The students were fighting against a disproportionate tuition raise and the privatization of services within the university. All campuses had joined the strike and the students had "occupied" all campuses with an organized network of support to survive days living inside each campus. The government did not expect the level of organization and strategic planning from the students. The immediate reaction from the government was to send a mandate that prohibited the entrance of any food or goods for the students occupying all campuses. This created a high level of *indignación* from many human rights groups within and outside of the university community who challenged the government mandate and encouraged people from outside the university community to bring food and to peacefully offer it to students. This meant crossing the lines of police that surrounded the gates of each campus and peacefully challenging their authority. On one of those days, I called my mom as I usually do on Sundays. She answered the phone and told me it was a very rainy day, and I asked her what she was up to. She told me she was making an *asopao* (a Puerto Rican thick soup) for the students at the UPR. She then went on to tell me that she had gone to the closest University of Puerto Rico campus to our house, stood at the gates, and asked the students what they wanted to eat. The students told her that on that rainy day and living in tents that an *asopao* would be perfect. So, she went home and made them a big pot of *asopao* that she brought to them later on. "And the police?" I asked her, and she said, "They are humans too and looked the other way." As she told me the story I was so incredibly proud and moved by her deep sense of compassion but more so by what Dillard (2012) describes as her faith in change, a faith that does not comes from any radical philosophy but from an spiritual understanding of what it means to (re)member what's sacred in our journey as a Puerto Rican family and in this case our local public university. A sacred place where she, her husband, grandchildren, and most of her family have been and will be able to go and afford an education, a sacred place that is an amazing center for cultural, academic, and intellectual production and a sacred place where most of the island's social justice and community advocates have been formed. It is her understanding of the sacred space of public education, the riskiness to protect and act on its behalf, and the cultural memories of this place that ground her sense of social action. This understanding is connected to a larger community resistance struggle including those who have respect for our only public higher education institution, one that neoliberals are attempting to privatize and make inaccessible to those who benefit from it the most. It makes sense, as Freire (1970 taught us, to think that privatizing, controlling, and developing a corporate model within the most powerful center for local knowledge production will have devastating consequences for our identity as an island: It'll be a top priority in conservative political agendas to dismantle the university as a way to exercise control on the island. This "occupy movement" (or *el Movimiento de Los Indignados* as it is called in Spanish), and the webs of local and global social action that were at the core of this movement, exemplifies one of the realities of what Occupy Movements are speaking against around the world and that are at the core of what Lynskey presents in her chapter. Her pedagogical solidarity to engaging with the world at a deeper level and that she describes as "one that inspired us to privilege the sacredness of humanity and the communal nature of truth, respect embodied and cultural knowledges, embrace of the risks of learning for a politics of liberation, and engage in redemptive dialogues" (p. 117) speaks to me of the importance of rethinking pedagogies of global interconnectedness and solidarity—a pedagogy that honors the power of collective social actions and the ways in which individuals, like my mother, act in everyday oppressions. Reading Lynskey's chapter I was reminded of my mom's story and how our lives are touched by people who are currently engaged in multiple forms of resistance, "occupations," and solidarity that are emerging around the world and how it is our sense of compassionate, emotional, political, and spiritual consciousness that drives us to act and continue. Lynskey, reflecting on Dillard's (2006) work in relation to her pedagogical project, explains that "Education from a spiritual paradigm challenges us to become something more than what we were before we encountered it. It calls us to move from working toward a more just and peaceful world to choosing to radically walk in it now. My students and I attempted to walk in new spaces of transformative education during our inquiry projects on the World Trade Organization and the Occupy Movement" (p. 117). Their walk toward transformation is not an isolated activity; I believe that with Lynskey and her students there are people around the world who are walking in similar directions. Examining how these multiple paths and trajectories toward social consciousness intersect and interact to create a more just world in contemporary times seems to me like a powerful humanizing pedagogy.

Recently, I have begun to redefine my work in critical literacy in elementary public schools in Puerto Rico using globalization as a new form of colonization as my framework for inquiry. Reframing the traditional idea of *literacy strategies* into *critical literacy as strategizing practice* (Medina & Wohlwend, in press), I am interested in exploring what's new and what's just another form of historical oppression toward traditionally marginalized communities in this "globalization" and multinational power. Critical globalization studies sociologist Santos (2006), in his piece "Globalizations," articulates a complex sociopolitical analysis to make visible the ways in which the idea of globalization masks more than it reveals. What it doesn't reveal is how people in traditionally marginalized communities continue to be at the bottom of hierarchies of power and oppression that are not any different than other historical moments. He goes into conceptualizing the idea of "insurgent cosmopolitanism" that inspires my idea of *critical literacy as strategizing practices*, to describe social actions that engage in resistance against the inequalities that are produced by top-bottom models of globalization, more specifically corporate markets. Nevertheless, what I see missing within some of these contemporary ideas coming from sociology is the spiritual importance in such acts of insurgency. Lynskey's chapter, grounded in the complex ecology of work in pedagogy, justice, and spirituality, is a view of action that integrates who we are and engages our histories at a deeper level in ways that could help us reformulate our relation to new forms of colonization and multinational markets domination. As Bauman (1998, 2007) suggest the consequences of globalization are unequal and fragmented but also material particularly to historically marginalized communities. The pedagogical possibilities that Lynskey provides us through her students' voices allow us to clearly see the multifaceted and networked ways in which people in their local communities can respond, react, and transform as they "talk back" and act upon their own and other people's actions to oppressive systems in a way that humanizes and reframes the idea of global citizenship. If we believe dominant corporate global power exists, is a pedagogical global resistance possible as we become aware of people's localized social actions across communities? My mother's actions say yes—and Lynskey and her students do, too.

References

Bauman, Z. (1998). *Globalization: The human consequences.* London: Polity Press.

Bauman, Z. (2007). *Consuming life.* Malden, MA: Polity Press.

Dillard, C. (2012). *Learning to (re)member the things we've learned to forget: Endarkened feminisms, spirituality and the sacred nature of research and teaching.* New York: Peter Lang.

Dillard, C. B. (2006). *On spiritual strivings: Transforming an African American woman's academic life.* Albany, NY: SUNY.

Freire, P. (1970). *Pedagogy of the oppressed.* New York: Continuum.

hooks, b. (2003). *Teaching community: A pedagogy of hope.* New York: Routledge.

Medina, C., & Wohlwend, K. (in press). *Literacy, play and globalization: Converging imaginaries in children's critical and cultural performances.* New York: Routledge.

Santos, B de S. (2006). Globalizations. *Theory, Culture and Society, 23*(2–3), 393–399.

Chapter 6

Can One Ever Be Wholly Whole?

Fostering Biracial Identity Founded in Spirit

Ashley N. Patterson

Introduction

My great-grandmother was born in the Midwest near the turn of the last century, a product of a forbidden relationship between a White doctor and a Black house girl. She was adopted by a Black family from the same city and grew up, fair-skinned and light-eyed, knowing who her biological parents were and being aware of her biracial heritage but claiming only her Blackness. I was born to two parents who racially identify themselves as Black, but I myself was not aware of my Blackness as a thing to claim until I was five years old and a member of a predominantly White kindergarten class. It is from this perspective, that of a self-identifying Black woman with a racially diverse familial past and present, that I write this chapter.

My understanding of race relations in America is informed (and in some ways knowingly limited) by my lens as a Black woman, but the perspective I offer here is also founded in a belief in the necessity of spirituality. I am not alone in this belief and share this perspective with scholars whose ideas I will highlight throughout this chapter. A spiritual self is one who is cognizant and embracing of all aspects that make up that self. If we seek to understand one another—as teachers, students, relatives, strangers—or ourselves with any degree of completeness, a context of spirituality as described here must be at the core of that understanding. A level of spirituality must be achieved if the self-identification of an individual is to be healthy and complete and encompassing of the entire person. Considering the biracial person in particular, this stance is important because there are a number of factors at play—such as mass media, demographic boxes to be checked, available common language—that attempt to force the individual to honor only fractions of oneself at a time, denying the opportunity to celebrate one's whole person. Some may question why I believe it a necessity to take such a stance. My response is that an identity is a critical thing for a person to have because it is the place from which an individual sees himself or herself, the world, and his or her place in the world. I am joined in this response by many fellow thinkers including Alice Walker, bell hooks, and Cynthia Dillard, to name only a few. It is necessary for race to be incorporated into that identity because we live in a world that is fundamentally concerned with race, and the ignoring or minimizing of this fact does nothing to lessen its stronghold or to facilitate navigation around it.

In this chapter, I begin by presenting a review of the literature considering what has been said about racial identity development in youths in general and about biracial identity development in particular. I attempt to incorporate a standpoint of spirituality into the work that has already been done. Using commentary drawn from popular culture, I then share models of a range of potential challenges and victories that the biracial person faces when attempting to racially identify himself or herself. These examples serve as frames within which I offer suggestions for how influential parties can be a service and not a setback to biracial youth who are in the process of forming, exploring, or solidifying their racial identities. By positioning spirituality in the forefront of my remarks, I hope to limit the potential fracturing of inherently whole persons as I consider the challenge of identifying as biracial in today's American society.

Racial Identity through a Spiritual Lens

It must be said that race is a socially constructed method of categorization and that there are no biological justifications for racial separations (Omi & Winant, 1994). While the biological support for categories of race have been refuted and found to be nonexistent, this does not diminish the fact that people choose races (both for themselves and for others) and in doing so choose ways they believe they should act, ways they should belong, and ways they should accept or reject the belonging of others. Culturally, race continues to play a major role in the way people interact with one another, in the way people look at each other, and in the way people see themselves. Americans in particular are engaged in a constant struggle to release themselves from the constraint of racial attributes imposed on them by others while also fighting just as hard to retain the divisions that race serves to uphold. This leaves the biracial person in a position that makes him or her vulnerable to crossfire spent in the name of pledging allegiance to one racial group.

The healthy development of an identity allows for movement through life, in and out of a variety of spheres, while simultaneously maintaining a sense of self. That grounding sense of self is threatened when one is not quite sure how to think of himself or herself in self-identified terms, let alone when called to do so against the many backdrops one stands in front of throughout each day. As Erikson (1950) explains, to complete the process of identity development, youth must answer questions such as, "Where did I come from?" "Who am I?" and "What do I want to become?" He further insists that the steps taken to form an identity are not a marker of the natural process of maturation; rather, identity must be sought after and worked toward if it is to be achieved. As Muss, Velder, and Porton (1996) describe of Erikson's work, the end goal of the identity formation process is "the establishment of a meaningful self-concept in which past, present, and future are brought together to form a unified whole" (p. 51). It is this whole that must be kept intact for the individual's self-concept to be most meaningful. Viewing the individual and his or her identity through the lens of spirituality aids in the preservation of that whole. And, at least in the United States, for one's identity to be complete, it must include, to some degree, the issue of race.

Though America's ideas about race may not lend themselves to a single colloquial definition, they are undeniably pervasive. As have other scholars, Omi and Winant (1994) cite the 1982–83 legal proceedings of Susie Guillory Phipps to prove this point. Phipps attempted to have her birth records amended to change her legal race from Black to White on the grounds that she was only 3/32 Black and was denied this opportunity by a court of law. The authors provide this example as an illustration that "demonstrates how deeply Americans both as individuals and as a civilization are shaped, and indeed haunted, by race" (p. 54). Though they contend that race is neither something we should rise above nor an idea that is developmentally stagnant, they are clear in their assertion that it plays a role in the everyday lives of all participants in American society. To play the game of life, the rules of which have been predetermined, race simply must be acknowledged. Racial identity, however, is more than just checking off a particular box on a census form. As Helms (1993) defines racial identity, it is "a sense of group or collective identity based on one's perception that he or she shares a common racial heritage with a particular racial group" (p. 3). There are several competing theories as to the nature of the development of racial identity. Drawing from some of these theorists, Helms (1993) offers three racial identity components: personal identity, reference group orientation, and ascribed identity. She explains that personal identity deals with how one feels about himself or herself; reference group orientation "refers to the way in which one uses particular racial groups...to guide one's feelings, thoughts, and behaviors"; and ascribed identity describes the way in which one consciously racially categorizes himself or herself (p. 5). It is not difficult to see how these three components could be in conflict when one has biracial heritage, but a calming of that conflict is exactly what must be achieved for the individual to adopt a racial identity founded in spirit and wholeness.

Poston (1990) argues just this in his proposal for a new model describing the identity development process of biracial persons. He notes several problems with the models proposed by Helms and Cross that specifically address persons who identify monoracially including the following: the models imply a choosing of one race over another; the models set up dominant and minority cultures in an "either/or" binary that does not account for biracial persons possibly coming from both; they do not allow for multiple, intertwined identifications; and they require some level of acceptance of the minority culture. Each of these limitations act as spiritual barriers to a biracial person achieving a sense of wholeness. Moving beyond the model proposed by Poston, Renn (2004) offers a range of ways in which multiracial persons may racially identify, each of which accounts for the fact that each individual ultimately chooses the racial identification that best suits him or her as a unique person. Efforts to theoretically describe the identity formation process, a process taking place on social, spiritual, emotional, and cognitive planes, are far from quieted.

As Renn (2004) describes, there is disagreement among theorists as to the ultimate goal of biracial identity. She explains that one camp of theorists holds that a fully developed biracial identity will be similar to those identities of monoracial peers. Another group insists that biracial identity is notably different from monoracial identity in that "a distinct biracial/bicultural, mixed race, interracial or multiracial identity is the goal," with some members of this group also theorizing that biracial individuals will also come to embrace their "otherness" as something special (Renn, 2004, p. 13). The third group outlines the goal of biracial identity to be "an individual's ability to engage in a variety of 'border crossings' between and among social contexts defined by race and ethnicity" (p. 13). Each of these groups of theories place emphasis on a different outcome of a developed racial identity, but none of them stresses the fact that the ultimate goal of self-understanding is to be able to analyze and either edit or accept—and eventually embrace—all parts of oneself so that this understanding can serve as the compass by which the individual navigates his or her journey through the world. By knowing oneself, one can work to preserve the wholeness that makes up that self, allowing that preserved whole to be a healthy, effective individual, member of a family, participant in a community, and contributor to society. When considering how spirituality is connected to this wholeness, I must first illustrate the definition of spirituality I am enacting.

There are many working definitions of spirituality used by many thinkers for many different purposes. In the context of this discussion, the meaning of spirituality is found in wholeness. Wholeness is the ability to feel comfortable in your skin regardless of your surroundings because your true, complete self is active. Even when those around you do not agree with or personally complement you, wholeness can be maintained if a strong sense of inner security and peace has been established. As Lemkov (2005) adds, "Wholeness suggests that one's life, experience, and learning are coextensive, and that learning is thus life-long" (p. 17). She goes on to define learning as "a prolonged journey in consciousness, in self-unfoldment" (p. 17). hooks (2000) describes wholeness as the ability to simultaneously embody characteristics of being in the center and in the margin. When one can look "both from the outside in and from the inside out," a balanced whole can be achieved (p. xvi). The benefit of embodying this wholeness is that it allows one to be maximally functioning in daily life; spirituality in this sense provides one with the otherworldly skills needed to navigate the material world in which we live. A firm belief in and understanding of oneself as an entire person allows for faith in intuition and in the "sixth sense" that allows us to interpret things that we may not be able to see, feel, taste, touch, or hear, but that we still *know* are there. The question posed in this discussion is this: Is it possible to attain a station of wholeness if one's identity is fractured? Through the highlighting of examples of biracial persons who are visible in various realms of popular culture including music, sports, fashion, and movies, this question will be explored and possible answers proposed. By sharing comments made by biracial persons themselves, I will explore challenges and victories that are likely experienced by others. Comments by musical artist Lenny Kravitz and actress Halle Berry will provide insight into the process of deciding on a name for one's racial identity. Quotations drawn from Spike Lee's film *Get on the Bus* will illustrate conflicts that arise when one's chosen racial identity is not universally accepted. Finally, remarks by reality TV personality Jade Cole and professional athlete Blake Griffin will serve as examples of ways in which one can become empowered by the racial self-naming process.

Are My Choices My Own?

Lenny Kravitz: What We Have to Learn

> My mother told me that you need to embrace both sides of your cul-
> ture, but understand that society's going to view you only as Black.
> And she told me that when I was six.
>   —LENNY KRAVITZ, GRAMMY AWARD WINNING ARTIST

Lenny Kravitz was born in the racially charged 1960s to a Black mother and a Jewish father. His mother, actress Roxie Roker, played one-half
of the first interracial couple to be featured on prime-time television. She
endured the reality of the judgment and oppression felt by interracial
couples of the time both in life and on the screen. It was upon this background that she attempted to advise her young son who was first alert-
ed to the fact that something was not "normal" about their family
makeup after attending school for the first time. The unspoken message
of Roker's comment, almost a warning, is that biracial persons do not
have control over how they will be categorized by people who only see
their skin color. Behind the scenes, the mother expected her son to love
both his Jewish and Black heritages, but she also wanted him to develop the thick skin necessary to exist in the world as a Black man. Rebecca
Walker shares a heritage similar to Kravitz born of a Black mother,
author Alice Walker, and a Jewish father. She reflects on her childhood
that was void of a message like the one Roker gave to her son. Walker
(2005) explains, "Growing up, I was in fact a black child and I had to
navigate being a black child in a racially stratified world. For any of my
caregivers to ignore this basic truth was, in my opinion, to ignore the
reality of my daily existence and thus be unable to help me figure out
how to move skillfully through it." As Walker would likely agree, while
Roker would have been doing her son a disservice to not encourage him
to know where he came from—the cultural history that makes him
who he is—she would have been doing an equal disservice to lead
him to believe that others would be as celebrating of his racial diversity as she encouraged him to be.

Mental health professional and mother of two biracial children,
Brown (2001) explains, "racial self-perception is not something that is

inborn....Rather, it is formed through the ongoing interaction with a person's immediate and extended social environment" (p. 43). The people that made up the social environment when Kravitz grew up in the 1970s, like those that constitute the social environment of today, are preoccupied with race and, as previously stated, driven by categorization. It was not until the 2000 Census, 210 years after the government began tracking the population by racial categories, that Americans were afforded the opportunity to select more than one racial category by which to identify themselves. Prior to this time, each person had to make a singular selection. Under his mother's guidance, Kravitz would have marked the box for Black, posing a challenge as Brown (2001) sees it because in doing so he would have to take on some components of the Black American experience including having to internalize "the prevalent values of our society, which include the devaluation of black people" and "the mores and culture of the Black community [that] frequently clash with the values of White society" (p. 44). If the biracial person chooses a monoracial category in name only, society may assume that he or she has also taken on the features described above although that may not be the case. In doing what society seems to expect by choosing to self-identify monoracially, the biracial person may actually be entering into a contract including fine print by which he or she is not prepared to abide.

Halle Berry: I Had to Decide for Myself

> "Oh, my God. Oh, my God. I'm sorry. This moment is so much bigger than me. This moment is for Dorothy Dandridge, Lena Horne, Diahann Carroll. It's for the women who stand behind me, Jada Pinkett, Angela Bassett, Vivica Fox. And it's for every nameless faceless woman of color that now has a chance because this door tonight has been opened. Thank you. I'm so honored."
> —HALLE BERRY, FROM HER 2001 ACADEMY AWARDS BEST ACTRESS
> ACCEPTANCE SPEECH

In her speech, Halle Berry (who was raised almost exclusively by her White mother) shared her winning honor with "every nameless faceless woman of color" whom she saw as mutually benefitting from the honor bestowed on her. Irrespective of the culture of the home within which she was raised, Berry professed pride in and allegiance to her darkened skin color and racialized category. Further, she counted her two-year-old daughter, whose father is French-Canadian, among those women of color as well. Why is this so? In a recent interview with *Ebony* magazine, Berry shared, "I'm Black and I'm her mother and I believe in the 'one-drop theory'" (in Dubois, 2011, p. 82). She went on to say, "I had to decide for myself and that's what she's going to have to decide—how she identifies herself in the world. And I think, largely, that will be based on how the world identifies her. That's how I identified myself" (in Dubois, 2011, p. 82). The judgments of others based on her outward appearance most strongly influence how Berry sees, names, and identifies herself.

Introduced as a way to legally segregate and enslave offspring of Black slaves and White slave owners, the legacy of the "one drop" rule remains in that it is rare for a biracial person with phenotypic Black markers to be able to be identified as White by those not privy to his or her "true" racial makeup. Persons with one White parent who look Black—or simply just darker than White—are not readily given access to their Whiteness by stranger passersby. In public, what can be visually observed is more influential than the home culture shaped by the adults by which one was raised. Persons who are not seen by others as being phenotypically White are not automatically afforded the unspoken privileges that accompany an assumption of one's Whiteness. Consider the fact that President Barack Obama, son of a Kenyan father but raised in a home with a White mother and White grandparents, will not be known historically as a White president or even as a biracial president. Because his skin is brown, Mr. Obama will forever be titled our first *Black* president. As Lenny Kravitz shared in a PBS interview with Tavis Smiley, "We say he's the first African American President, that's cool, you know, he is. But it's always first *Black* president or *Black* president Obama. The man has another fifty percent that we're discounting here, and that's what we have to learn." This discounting of parentage—and all of the traits that are influenced thereby—serves to muddy the waters in which biracial persons are to behold a clear image of themselves. However, let us not be settled with that murkiness and consider that clarity, in the form of a spiritual foundation to the under-standing of that biracial image, is possible.

Gatekeepers of Spiritual Wholeness

Excerpt from Get on the Bus: It's Just Different

GREG: I remember one time I stole some candy from a grocery store, OK? The manager saw me, caught me red-handed. So he calls my mom.

JAMAL & FLIP: [With anticipation] Oooooooooo.

GREG: My mom comes to the grocery store—oh, God! [Pauses, shaking head and opening eyes wide in reflecting on memory.] You know, my mom must've lectured me for two or three hours, man.

JAMAL: [Bewildered] Lectured you?

GREG: Yeah.

JAMAL: You didn't get a beatin' or nothing?

GREG: No. Unh-uh.

JAMAL: Not, like, a smack or nothin'?

FLIP: His mother's White.

JAMAL: [Understandingly] Oh!

GREG: Yeah, my mom's White. So what?

FLIP: Nothin,' I'm just tellin' him how it went down.

GREG: It's not relevant. Is it relevant? You have a problem with it?

FLIP: No! I was just telling him our mothers' different, OK? Our moth-ers whip ass. Your mother lectures. That's all I'm sayin' [with laughter].

—FROM SPIKE LEE'S 1996 GET ON THE BUS

In this excerpt from Lee's film chronicling the fictional cross-country bus ride of a group of men on their way to the 1995 Million Man March, Greg provides this input to the conversation just after Flip and Jamal, both Black men with two Black parents, shared stories of having been beaten by their mothers for various childhood infractions. In his comment of clarification to Jamal, Flip is effectively dichotomizing the worlds of children with White mothers and children with Black mothers. His indication is that there are some aspects of the lives of children from these two groups for which a common ground cannot be found because they are necessarily different. In this way, the difference, the thing that one is *not* according to the viewpoint of the ostracizer, is more defining of someone than any characteristics the person does possess.

The biracial person seeking to identify himself or herself monoracially is in a quandary in that he or she faces potential rejection from his or her peers who have two parents that are both of the race that only one of the biracial child's parents can claim. As Brown (2001) explains based on a study conducted with almost 200 biracial people within the context of a predominantly Black community, "having a White parent and therefore being seen as 'not black enough,' participants were frequently suspect in regard to racial group allegiance" (p. 85). At the same time, however, Brown observed that biracial students growing up in White communities often received "negative attention—racial slurs, taunting, rejection, and at times bodily harm" (p. 84). In monoracial settings, the "otherness" of the biracial person is brought to the forefront more readily than any commonalities he or she undoubtedly shares. Biracial persons are asked and expected to make choices concerning racial self-identification, but they are also prohibited from making certain decisions. The wholeness of the biracial person is in jeopardy when loyalties to racial identification are torn between two options while simultaneously being called into question on the grounds of legitimacy.

Excerpt from *Get on the Bus: Enthusiastic Immersion Enthusiastic Acceptance*

GREG: I already told you, I consider myself Black.

FLIP: Hang on, no disrespect.

GREG: No no no. Just because a person is White does not mean that I dislike him.

FLIP: I'm not talkin'—

GREG: Or just because a person is Black…does not mean that I like him. I consider myself Black just like Bob Marley was Black.

FLIP: I'm not talkin' about Bob Marley.

GREG: He was so-called "mulatto." I consider myself Black.

JEREMIAH: Hey, hold it. Wait a minute. The man is Black. Why don't you just let him be?

FLIP: He is also White.

JEREMIAH: If this was slavery, think ol' massah would care that he was half-White? He'd be a slave. Just like the rest of us.

FLIP: Yeah, but he'd be a house slave. Pimpin' around the big house. While the rest of us be talkin' about grits, this fool would be eatin' potatoes. He'd have breast of chicken, we'd have neck bones. Our women would be blistered up and stickin' from pickin' cotton. His would be all bathed, smellin' good and nine times out of ten, the honey he'd be hittin' skins with, she'd be a White girl.

JEREMIAH: Hold it. Just hold it a minute. How about the grits? Grits was for the White folks up in the big house. Slaves would be lucky to get corn mush. And as for hittin' skins with a White girl…a Black man could get lynched for even thinkin' a thought like that.

FLIP: Come on Pops. You know what I mean.
—From Spike Lee's 1996 Get on the Bus

This scene shows Flip, a self-identifying Black man with two Black parents, engaged in an attack on the racial identity of Greg, a self-identifying Black man with a White mother and a Black father. Greg makes an argument for the justification of his right to choose his race in mentioning international music icon Bob Marley, who was born of a White father and a Black mother but whose Blackness goes generally unquestioned. This does not impress Flip and he immediately deflects the reference. Instead, so concerned with limiting the legitimacy of Greg's self-identity, Flip brings to the conversation the historical context of slavery in the attempt to solidify Greg's existence as an "other," or, more specifically, not a Black man. Yet, he does not have accurate historical facts about his culture, the culture to which he is vehemently attempting to deny Greg membership. Flip exists blissfully in his Blackness, ignorant of the truths of his cultural past that shape the present condition of race relations to which he is actively subscribing. These misconceptions are manifested in his aggression toward Greg. Jeremiah, an older gentleman who has more accurate knowledge of the struggles experienced by Black men in the times of slavery, refutes Flip's hypothetical accusations with truth. At the end of the exchange, Flip appeals to the unspoken cultural comradeship that he assumes he has with Jeremiah, a fellow Black man, in saying *"You* know what I mean." He is drawing the conclusion that the two share some sort of universal understanding in being Black that excludes Greg. However, it seems that for Jeremiah skin color is not enough to signify like-mindedness.

The exchange witnessed in this selection gives the impression that the biracial person who identifies monoracially will always have his cultural legitimacy called into question. It is difficult to exist as a whole spiritual being if the person you have constructed for yourself is not accepted by those among whom you have to exist. Greg considers himself to be Black, but Flip is not granting him access into that community. It is hard enough to try and navigate the American social scene as a Black person. How much harder must it be to do so when people assume you are Black but that is not how you identify yourself or, similarly, when you consider yourself to be Black while others do not believe you to be so? The emotional oppression caused by the thoughts of outsiders affects the development of self-concept on a number of fronts. While some scholars such as Helms (1993, 1995), Cross (1991, 1995) and Atkinson, Morten, and Sue (1993) have proposed biracial identity theories and contend that the stage in the process in which one engages in "enthusiastic immersion in a minority culture" signifies his or her arrival at a level of satisfaction with the identity formation process, Poston (1990) considers this stage to be the most emotionally trying for the biracial person. Poston further notes that other theories of biracial identity development may be lacking because they assume that biracial persons eventually receive some sort of acceptance from the minority culture in which they immerse and this assumption is just not founded in any universal truth. Williams (1999) took Poston's argument further and, as a biracial woman, claimed the possibility and likelihood that moving through the process of identity development for the biracial person happens in multiple stages at a time, not a progressive stage-by-stage process. It could also be said that no individual, regardless of the race or identities to which he or she ascribes, will ever be universally accepted. While this may be true, the wholeness of the biracial person is particularly compromised when his or her racial identity is disputed by others who would deny him or her access to that personally formed identity. But power can be found in naming oneself for oneself alone and embracing wholeness without regard to the limits imposed by others as will be seen in the following section.

Is a Spirit Whole by Any Name?

Jade Cole: Exotic Biracial Butterfly

> My look is versatile. I can transform myself into all different types of ethnic backgrounds. I can kind of fit certain molds that I want to break in the industry.
> —JADE COLE, AMERICA'S NEXT TOP MODEL CYCLE 6 CONTESTANT

Throughout the reality TV modeling competition in which she participated, Jade Cole described herself as an "exotic biracial butterfly." She embraced the multiplicity of her racial background and believed the looks that were the result of that heritage were what set her apart from her competition. She capitalized on the fact that people could not readily categorize her into any one single racial box and made her phenotypic ambiguity work to her advantage. Because Cole sees herself as a biracial butterfly, that is the reality she lives. Cole's comment that she wants to break the molds that she can fit into seems initially to be oxymoronic; however, some racial theorists believe that the deconstruction of the forces that give race its power in American society will have to be initiated from within that structure. Until there is cause for enough people to pause and reconsider the validity of racially based stratification and power distribution, it will remain in place. The inability to be readily racially categorized by outsiders affords the biracial person some freedom in being able to flow in and out of a number of racial groups. It could also have the effect of causing him or her to be denied full access to any.

In suggesting that she can "transform" herself into various ethnic backgrounds, the question that arises is, where is Cole positioning her true self? In embracing her versatility, is she sacrificing a stability that allows her to be whole? In some ways, the model of self-identity Cole employs allows a biracial person to have flexibility when navigating through the spheres of race. However, the motivation behind the application of this flexibility will determine whether the act serves to inspire wholeness or to fracture a person's spirit. Whether one is truly so comfortable that he or she feels equally confident and whole in a variety of settings is one thing, but if one is forcing oneself to put on a farce in order to do so, that is another.

Blake Griffin: The Best of Both Worlds

> Having a little bit of everything—seeing what it's like from both sides, really—I think has given me a better perspective on a lot of different things.
> —BLAKE GRIFFIN, 1ST NBA DRAFT PICK 2009

Blake Griffin, born of two educators—a White mother and a Black father—has garnered public attention in response to a recent commercial in which the 2011 NBA Rookie of the Year and All-Star Dunk contest winner jumps over a car to dunk a basketball before kissing a Black girl whose image is shown on the screen of his cell phone. Many young people took to social networks in response to the advertisement, some noting that he had become more attractive or "authentic" for publicly expressing affection for his "Black side." Others shared that the commercial was the first indication they had that the light-skinned Griffin was anything but "just White" (the unstated message—a further indicator of the influence of race on American society—being that he *must* be Black to some degree if he was kissing a Black girl on the television screen). The case that Griffin not only embraces the multiplicity of his racial heritage but that he, in fact, sees it as an advantage does not account for how his racial makeup will be interpreted and his opportunities for identification limited by others. However, fortunately for him, this does not have to necessitate a change in Griffin's positive outlook on himself as a biracial person.

In the face of these and other comments that seek to categorize him, Griffin remains constant in his embracing of his whole self. He largely attributes his comfort with himself to the guidance he received from the two most influential adults in his life, his parents. He said of his mother and father, "When you look back at all the things that they've done, it makes me want to be the kind of people that they are. There's no way I'd not want to be like my parents" (in Carlson, 2009). The level of self-understanding he has reached with the encouragement of his parents allows Griffin to laugh off comments he has overheard such as that he is the highest jumping White guy a person has ever seen. The support he received from trusted adults probably has a lot to do with his assertion that he is proud of having a *biracial* president in whom he can see himself. And that type of support and encouragement is certainly behind statements such as "[Being biracial is] the best of both worlds" (in Carlson, 2009). As Griffin publicly exemplifies, with such support, it is possible to develop an identity as a biracial person founded in a wholeness that holds tight to each part that makes up that whole.

Where Does the Educator Fit In?
Lessons from Biracial Pop Culture Voices

It has already been said that race as a biologically founded distinguishing factor is a myth (Boas, 1995; Frakenberg, 1993; Omi & Winant, 1994; Takaki, 1993), so the categorical details attributed to race are thus knowingly founded in myth. However, though the biological explanations of race may be refuted, the reality of its ideological existence and its influence on American society cannot be. Race has evolved as a cultural phenomenon, a means by which we choose to categorize ourselves and others and an understanding that we cling to when making sense of the world and our places in it. As Omi and Winant (1994) explain, race cannot be thought of in a "rigid" manner; rather, it is an "unstable complex of social meanings" that have been developed as a part of a "social and historical process" (pp. 54–55). These social meanings that make up our ideas about race are sometimes subtle, sometimes obvious, sometimes divisive, sometimes uniting. Regardless of the degree to which we acknowledge the influence of race, the characteristics that society defines in terms of race are omnipresent. Choosing not to ascribe to these imposed characteristics does not indicate that one's self-perception is underdeveloped, but what does it mean when assumptions are made about character based solely on factors outside of one's control such as the racial makeup of one's parentage? Constantly having to work to erase conclusions drawn about you by matters outside of your control causes the spiritual energy that could be allocated to continual self-improvement and maintenance of self as a whole to be unduly spent. Responsibility for the efforts made to alleviate this struggle cannot be left up to the biracial person alone; those who are influential in the lives of young biracial people must be supporters of the strength necessary to continue the fight to achieve spiritual wholeness in terms of racial self-identification.

We have just gone through six examples that represent only a handful of the challenging situations in place for a biracial person seeking to achieve wholeness. Even if the list shared was exhaustive, it would still not speak in absolutes about any single biracial person striving to become or remain whole. However, using these examples as a starting point, I will identify and elaborate upon a number of lessons that we as educators must learn from our biracial students who we are hearing through these pop culture voices. We all have struggles along the path toward the goal of wholeness. Those struggles are not unique to people who are biracial, but the set of struggles they face do have general qualities that must be considered. Simple consideration cannot be the final mode of interaction, however. As educators, we have to make attempts not to eliminate those struggles, but to aid our students in overcoming them. Taking an approach described by Dei (2002, as cited in Hart, 2011) that embraces "humility, respect, compassion, and gentleness which strengthen the self and the collective human spirit of the learner" will make attainable "a journey towards wholeness and awakening of the self" (p. 39). While we cannot walk alongside our biracial students and mentees for the entirety of their journeys, we can assist in providing them with a spiritual suitcase full of those qualities Dei describes that will be needed along the way.

In the way of humility, we must put our students' needs above our own. While it is a natural human desire to categorize, we must refrain from doing so—even subconsciously—to our biracial students. As Jade Cole's self-identification as an exotic biracial butterfly tells us, we cannot assume that a student who looks a certain way self-identifies in the same manner as others who look a similar way. We must allow each student the opportunity and afford them the right to name themselves. We must be respectful of the range in decisions that are made, and furthermore, we must be respectful of our students' rights to amend aspects of their identities as they deem appropriate.

As educators, we have to be prepared to not only teach facts but to nurture souls as well. It is our duty to teach the whole student even if the student has not yet found his or her wholeness. What's more, issues surrounding coming to a happy, self-loving place with one's biracialness is only one type of transcendental challenge that the teacher will encounter. As Hart (2011) warns, "We impart our own experiences through the material we teach, bringing in assumptions and biases that are honest; yet, can be damaging to our students if they are unable to critically deconstruct the meaning in their lives" (p. 39). Every student's life will take from our teaching a different meaning and we have to ensure that we are accessible to each of them. Halle Berry shared with *Ebony* magazine, "If you're of multiple races, you have a different challenge, a unique challenge of embracing all of who you are but still finding a way to identify yourself, and I think that's often hard for us to do" (in Dubois, 2011, p. 84). At the heart of Berry's quote seems to be a request for patience and understanding on the part of the observer as the self-identification process of the biracial person is being undertaken. As educators, we must answer this call.

Spirituality—an attention to and respect of wholeness—must be the center from which our educational decisions emerge. In his book *To Know as We Are Known*, Palmer (1983) urges the teacher to adopt a foundation of spirituality as the tool used to frame his or her educational approaches. He warns against the trappings of teaching methods that neglect the spirit in favor of the mind alone. He proposes an alternative interpretation of the learner that is not the separate considerations of a mind, a body, a heart, and a spirit each, but the acknowledgment of these components together as one whole. He says, "When we consider the whole person we find more than sense and reason, more than a collection of instruments of cognition…we find all of this, but ultimately we find a self whose nature is not simply to know, but to know in relationship, as a means to relationship" (p. 53). It is through these relationships between teacher and student that we can hope to build the trust, confidence, and love that are necessary if the two are to learn from one another. Without this established relationship, as seen in Greg and Flip's scenes, a stage for learning is not set. This relationship is a necessary prerequisite if the whole student is to be nurtured and not merely stuffed full of facts. While this concept is not a novel one (see Harris Garad's chapter in this volume along with Freire, 1993, and Noddings, 2005), the deliberate infusion of a spiritual perspective pushes us as educators beyond the parameters that some have placed on our duties as the preparers of our future leaders. Through this lens, that preparation necessarily involves a cognitive, academic aspect, but it cannot thrive without an emotional, spiritual component as well.

We must embrace the limitless options for self-identification that are available. The wholeness that I am proposing we help the biracial student to attain will be the result of a widening in the range of the racial labeling messages that are available to them. In understanding that there is not necessarily a "final answer" to identity development and that it is OK to identify as Black, White, biracial, multiracial, mixed, or simply "me," biracial persons will be able to take positions of power in their personal racial identifications. Thus, understanding allows a person to embrace and enjoy, as put by Blake Griffin, the best of both worlds. At the same time, however, we must also understand and respect the more limited but equally embraced view adopted by Lenny Kravitz from his mother. The importance of the role played by the supportive, influential adult is made clear in Rebecca Walker's (2007) comment: "As long as I looked for wholeness from people who could never see me as a whole, I was imprisoned by my own self-sabotaging attractions." An inability to see a biracial person as a whole can limit that person's ability to see himself or herself as whole as well. Instead, we must encourage visions of self that are reflections of wholeness. Walker goes on to share encouragement given to her by "one of the most important people in [her] life" who told her "to connect to the part of my being that has never been broken; the part that can never be broken. He encouraged me to touch the part that is not split, torn, ambivalent, or conflicted." We must offer similar encouragements that can create settings in which biracial persons can nurture their unbroken selves.

We must be a source of stability during a process that is founded in change and exploration. Shrouded in the blanket of security that is formed as a result of supportive love and care, the biracial person can navigate a variety of contexts and remain his or her true self. A person's wholeness is not challenged by the ability to bring to the forefront different parts of his or her identity in different situations if that authenticity and trueness remains a constant. What determines one's authenticity is full commitment to one's holistic well-being. A biracial person does not have to sacrifice parts of himself or herself to navigate a variety of scenarios with enduring comfort. Part of achieving wholeness is arriving at a level of consciousness of one's wholeness. Once a biracial person sees himself or herself as a whole, entire being, he or she is always whole. He or she can move his or her whole person in and out of a variety of situations without abandoning parts of that self or sacrificing authenticity. One may enact different parts of his or her identity and wholeness, but doing so does not indicate a negation of the ever-presence of all of the parts that make up one's self.

In a best-case scenario, we are judged by the content of our character and not the color of our skin (King, 1963). As adults in professions that put us in positions of influence when considering young impressionable minds enshrined in biracial bodily temples, we cannot contribute to the fragmenting of these students' wholeness and senses of self. We can instead assist them in smoothing cracks in their spiritual foundations by not making assumptions about racial identity and by not putting categorizing terms in their mouths. We can do it by allowing time for students to get to know each other and by letting them know us as people with pride and hopes of our own and, above all, challenges and imperfections to work through just as they have. As Dillard (2006) notes, reciprocity is a component weighing with utmost importance in the supportive relationship based in spirituality shared between teacher and student. We can foster sharing that goes beyond the surface and superficial levels. We can ask hard questions while remaining ready with soft, comforting responses to offer when necessary. We can encourage all students to verse themselves well in the cultural histories that impact the state of our social affairs today in all of their varieties. We can encourage students to be reflective and to question things that do not sit right with them whether or not it is popular to do so. This reflectivity is paramount in the quest to inspire wholeness in all of our students and in biracial students in particular. When done in an honest, humble, and truth-seeking manner, this sort of reflection can serve to weed out those negative energies that serve to splinter the would-be whole.

Conclusion

Though the task of attempting to positively influence the spiritual growth of a segment of our student population who straddle two racial worlds is a great undertaking, it is happening already as you read. Some biracial persons have already achieved the wholeness that I am suggesting we encourage all students to attain. As Bob Marley, beloved reggae musician and facilitator of peace, explained about his biracial heritage, "Me don't dip on the Black man's side nor the White man's side. *Me dip on God's side, the one who create me and cause me to come from Black and White*" (as cited in Mamdouh, 2003, p. 108). Simply said, spirituality is the key to keeping the whole intact, keeping the self complete.

References

Atkinson, D. R., Morten, G., & Sue, D. W. (1993). *Counseling American minorities: A cross-cultural perspective* (4th ed.). Dubuque, IA: Brown & Benchmark.

Banks, T., Mok, K., & Barris, K. (Writers), & Barreto, L. (Director). (2006). The girl with two bad takes [Television series episode]. In D. Gabrion, L. Gervino, & J. Schneider (Producers), *America's Next Top Model: Cycle 6*. New York: 10 by 10 Entertainment.

Boas, F. (1995). *Race, language and culture*. Chicago, IL: University of Chicago Press.

Borden, B., Cannon, R., Lee, S., & Rosenbush, B. (Producers), & Lee, S. (Director). (1996). *Get on the bus* [Motion picture]. United States: 40 Acres & A Mule Filmworks.

Brown, U. M. (2001). *The interracial experience: Growing up Black/White racially mixed in the United States*. Westport, CT: Praeger.

Carlson, J. (2009). Griffins are face of Sooners, face of change in America. Retrieved from http://www.scrippsnews.com/node/41845

Cates, G., Herman, D., Seligman, M. B., & Shapiro, M. J. (Producers). (2001). *73rd Annual Academy Awards* [Television broadcast]. Burbank, CA: ABC.

Cross, W. (1991). *Shades of black: Diversity in African American identity.* Philadelphia, PA: Temple University Press.

Cross, W. E. (1995). The psychology of nigrescence: Revising the Cross model. In J. G. Ponterotto, J. M. Casas, L. A. Suzuki, & C. M. Alexander (Eds.), *Handbook of multicultural counseling* (pp. 93–122). Thousand Oaks, CA: Sage.

Dillard, C. B. (2006). *On spiritual strivings: Transforming an African American woman's academic life.* Albany, NY: SUNY.

Dubois, A. (2011, March). On the very solid fantastically full life of Halle Berry. *Ebony, 66*(5), 79–85.

Erikson, E. H. (1950). *Childhood and society.* New York: Norton.

Frankenberg, R. (1993). *The social construction of Whiteness: White women, race matters.* Minneapolis, MN: University of Minnesota Press.

Freire, P. (1993). *Pedagogy of the oppressed.* New York: Continuum Books.

Givony, J. (2009, May 22). Blake Griffin: I'm going to work to be a complete player on both ends. Retrieved from http://www.draftexpress.com/article/Blake-Griffin-Im-going-to-work-to-be-a-complete-player-on-both-ends-3223/

Hart, L. (2011). Nourishing the authentic self: Teaching with heart and soul. In N. N. Wane, E. L. Manyimo, & E. J. Ritskes (Eds.), *Spirituality, education & society: An integrated approach* (pp. 37–48). Rotterdam, The Netherlands: Sense Publishers.

Helms, J. E. (Ed.). (1993). *Black and White racial identity: Theory, research and practice.* Westport, CT: Praeger.

Helms, J. E. (1995). An update of Helms's White and people of color racial identity models. In J. G. Ponterotto, J. M. Casas, L. A. Suzuki, & C. M. Alexander (Eds.), *Handbook of multicultural counseling* (pp. 181–198). Thousand Oaks, CA: Sage.

hooks, b. (2000). *Feminist theory: From the margins to the center.* London, England: Pluto Press.

Kendall, N. (Writer), & X, J. (Director). (2011). [Television series episode]. In C. Chouinard, S. Covington, N. Kendall, C. McDonald, T. Smiley, S. Storey, & H. Williamson (Producers), *Tavis Smiley.* Los Angeles, CA: TS Media, Inc.

King, M. L. (1963). I have a dream by Martin Luther King, Jr; August 28, 1963. Retrieved from http://avalon.law.yale.edu/20th_century/mlk01.asp

Lemkov, A. F. (2005). Reflections on our common lifelong learning journey. In J. P. Miller, S. Karsten, D. Denton, D. Orr, & I. C. Kates (Eds.), *Holistic learning and spirituality in education: Breaking new ground* (pp. 17–26). Albany, NY: SUNY.

Mamdouh, A. (2003). *The loved ones: A modern Arabic novel.* Cairo: American University in Cairo Press.

Muss, R. E. H., Velder, E., & Porton, H. (1996). *Theories of adolescence* (6th ed.). New York: McGraw-Hill.

Noddings, N. (2005). *The challenge to care in schools: An alternative approach to education.* New York: Teachers College Press.

Omi, M., & Winant, H. (1994). *Racial formation in the United States: From the 1960s to the 1990s* (2nd ed.). New York: Routledge.

Palmer, P. J. (1983). *To know as we are known: Education as a spiritual journey.* San Francisco: Harper Collins.

Poston, W. S. C. (1990). The biracial identity development model: A needed addition. *Journal of Counseling and Development, 69,* 152–155.

Renn, K. A. (2004). *Mixed race students in college: The ecology of race, identity and community on campus.* Albany, NY: SUNY.

Takaki, R. (1993). *A different mirror: A history of multicultural America.* Boston, MA: Back Bay Books.

Walker, R. (2005, February 22). Ask Rebecca. Archived at http://www.rebeccawalker.com /v1/ask-answer-advice-biracial-child.htm

Walker, R. (2007, March 1). Ask Rebecca. Archived at http://www.rebeccawalker.com /v1/ask-biracial.htm

Williams, C. B. (1999). Claiming a biracial identity: Resisting social constructions of race and culture. *Journal of Counseling & Development, 77*(1), 32–35.

Biracial Identity, Spiritual Wholeness, and Black Girlhood

Bettina L. Love

As a Black feminist, I situate much of my work within the boundaries of hip-hop feminism and the study of Black girlhood. Patterson's critical examination of society's obsession with race, racial categories, and how women negotiate their biracial identity adds an important critical voice to the study of Black girlhood. Patterson's chapter highlights competing theories of racial and biracial identity, which further complicate the narratives of the lives of Black girls. According to Patterson, "for one's identity to be complete, it must include, to some degree, the issue of race" (p. 146). I completely agree with Patterson as she makes it quite clear in her chapter that one's racial identity is vital to one's search for wholeness. However, what makes Patterson's work so eye-opening and complex is her personal and theoretical exploration of biracial identity, while grappling with spiritual wholeness. For me, Patterson's work should be pedagogically unpacked and taken-up by the field of Black girlhood because it is imperative that educators, community members, and young Black girls, biracial or not, find the wholeness she describes. "Can One Ever Be Wholly Whole?" is an important addition to the field of Black girlhood and education because Black girls are searching for wholeness at the margins of society. The chapter emphasizes that a lack of identity development can be a barrier for biracial individuals' attempts to achieve a sense of spiritual wholeness. Patterson's definition of spiritual wholeness is first rooted in her concept of general wholeness, which she defines as "the ability to feel comfortable in your skin regardless of your surroundings because your true, complete self is active" (p. 149). Building on that concept, spiritual wholeness is "[a] firm belief in and understanding of oneself as an entire person allows for faith in intuition and in the 'sixth sense' that allows us to interpret things that we may not be able to see, feel, taste, touch, or hear, but that we still *know* are there" (p. 149). Understanding and developing spiritual wholeness is a vital aspect of Black girlhood because it provides a space for Black girls to deconstruct monolithic images and experiences in the pursuit of wholeness.

Brown (2009) defines Black girlhood as "the representations, memories, and lived experiences of being and becoming in a body marked as youthful, Black and female" (p. 34). Brown's definition of Black girlhood binds to Patterson's work as she expands elements of Black girlhood to biracial girlhood. Patterson's use of popular culture throughout her work raises important questions as a space to help young girls critique, while finding affirming identities in popular culture's representations of biracial men and women. Patterson illuminates the latter assertion when she discusses Jade Cole, a contestant on *America's Next Top Model*. Patterson describes Cole as someone who embraces her multiplicitous racial background, yet her lack of racial categorization by outsiders denied her access to any racial group. Thus, one could consider the biracial juggling act of race as a dance of sorts. Gaunt (2002) argues, "Blackness is often defined by one's dance card rather than one's race card. We are constantly negotiating an artificial split between the mind (supposedly the exclusive realm of the intellect) and the body (the supposed realm of impulse, rhythm, and pleasure, rather than control)" (p. 5). Patterson's work raises important questions about the dance of biracial identity and how one navigates such a space when there are multiple steps, theories, and partners in the dance of the racial self-naming process and spiritual wholeness. She also deconstructs the fluidity of one's racial identity dance. Biracial identity development can be simultaneously elusive and concrete as biracial individuals may choose a monoracial category that is not endorsed by society.

Looking for Myself: Counternarratives and Popular Culture

What Patterson does so effectively in her chapter is to clearly point out that, as educators who work with, theorize about, and teach Black girls, it is imperative that we teach pedagogically from a standpoint that acknowledges, embraces, and challenges the unparalleled struggles of biracial identity. Patterson's work theorizes and expands our understanding of the minds and hearts of biracial youth and places them in the forefront of Black life. Furthermore, Patterson's chapter provides a space for counternarratives that challenge master narratives (Denzin, 2003; Stanley, 2007). I read "Can One Ever Be Wholly Whole?" as a counternarrative interrupting our common wisdom of race and identity as she fiercely and carefully crafts her position on fostering biracial identity around one's understanding of spirituality.

The deconstruction of master narratives is critical to finding wholeness because it allows space to challenge "dominant White and often predominantly male culture that is held to be normative and authoritative" (Stanley, 2007, p. 16). At the core of Patterson's work is the art of storytelling that confronts dominant culture through popular culture examples. Patterson skillfully uses numerous popular culture vignettes to explore the complexity of biracial identity and demystify master narratives. More importantly, Patterson understands that by using popular culture she is operating in one of the most influential sites of learning for Black girls today. Black popular culture is saturated with formulaic images of Black life that reproduce messages of social inequality, sexism, racism, and classism (Love, 2012). Here again is the reason why the search for wholeness cannot be reached without examining the seductive world of popular culture that too often sends young girls self-destructive messages.

Patterson expands our thinking on how biracial youth are constantly negotiating identities within the space of popular culture. These problematic sites of learning also offer a space to critique popular culture and create experiences with practical classroom exercises and examples that are culturally relevant and rich with interpretative possibilities (Durham, 2010). Biracial identity for young Black girls today cannot and should not be discussed without including Black popular culture. Most young girls will consume images of biracial women within that context, and master narratives within Black popular culture surrounding biracial women are rooted in White male patriarchy, but portrayed as authentic thoughts. Therefore, if Black and biracial girls are ever going to find wholeness, they must first find spaces within which to reimagine their identity and culture outside the mainstream racialized categories in a quest for self-love.

Hip-Hop Feminism and the Messiness of Identity

As a hip-hop feminist, upon reading Patterson's chapter I began the process of asking myself how her work might be situated within the intellectual space of hip-hop feminism. Patterson's treatise of unpacking biracial identity through popular culture and the quest for spiritual wholeness lies within what Joan Morgan (2000) describes as "intriguing shades of gray" (p. 62). In her groundbreaking book, *When Chickenheads Come Home to Roost: A Hip-Hop Feminist Breaks It Down*, Morgan describes herself as a "daughter of feminist privilege" who has gained rights and mobility because of the struggles of feminist movements before her, but she finds herself in search of a feminism brave enough to tackle areas of gray. These in-between spaces are messy, fluid, and slippery. Moreover, within hip-hop feminism, identity is messy and unfixed. Hip-hop feminism lives and thrives in shades of gray. However, the end goal of hip-hop feminism is to question, inspire, and equip young Black girls with "empowering possibilities" (Lindsey, 2011, p. 9). Thus, the biracial identity of young Black girls complicates the already complex multilayered space of Black girlhood and hip-hop feminism. Patterson states that

> Choosing not to ascribe to these imposed characteristics does not necessarily indicate that one's self-perception is underdeveloped. That being said, it is difficult to derive meaning from assumptions made about one's character based solely on

factors outside of one's control, such as the racial makeup of one's parentage. Constantly having to work to erase conclusions drawn about you by matters outside of your control causes the spiritual energy that could be allocated to continual self-improvement and maintenance of self as a whole to be unduly spent. Responsibility for the efforts made to alleviate this struggle cannot be left to the biracial person alone. Those who are influential in the lives of young biracial people must be supporters of the strength necessary to continue the fight to achieve spiritual wholeness in terms of racial self-identification. (p. 160)

Patterson understands that the identity development of biracial individuals toward spiritual wholeness is messy because it is dependent on various factors, people, and cultural assumptions. Furthermore, most, if not all, of these factors are not easily controlled by individuals seeking to understand their racial self-identification, while attempting to achieve spiritual wholeness. Hip-hop feminism recognizes and affirms numerous facets of identity. According to Brown and Kwakye (2012), hip-hop feminists "exist with various dimensions, live fully, and we continue to exist even when we cannot be readily seen, heard, or touched" (p. 3). Patterson's chapter, similar to hip-hop feminism, merges two unlikely concepts of spiritual wholeness and biracial identity, but both theories are necessary to begin the work of "consciousness-raising" for our young girls (hooks, 2000, p. 7). As an educator, I am also concerned with marrying hip-hop and feminism to teach and learn from Black girls who come of age embodying the culture and music of hip-hop, as I once did. Hip-hop feminist pedagogy is participatory learning and teaching that addresses the ways in which youth negotiate hip-hop music and culture to form social, cultural, and political identities, while instigating social change. To me, hip-hop feminist pedagogy is important for a number of reasons, too many to discuss within the scope of this chapter. But the main reason is to eradicate the cultural mismatch or culture incongruence between educators and students, specifically Black girls.

Additionally, Black girls enter classrooms where their intergenerational knowledge, gender, oral and kinetic worldviews, and keen critical thinking skills are ignored, rarely celebrated, and never affirmed in ways that highlight their intellectual and emotional prowess. What it means to move, think, act, dream, perform, and create embodied knowledge as Black girls cannot be found in any standardized test, scripted school curriculum, or educational institution that serves to perpetuate social, gender, and racial inequalities. Moreover, the education system disregards Black girls' complicated relationship to hip-hop music and culture. Consequently, "[n]obody gives Black girls credit for being complex or for negotiating the height of those complexities" (Brown, 2009, p. xx). Hip-hop feminist pedagogy, therefore, is more than just a pedagogical tool. It is a space where Black girls can question, create, discuss, dance, perform, grapple, and negotiate identity politics. That freedom is truly invaluable as the stories of Black girls are pushed to the peripheral of everyday life.

Through the five pillars of hip-hop (DJing, Emceeing/MCing, Graffiti, Breakdancing and Knowledge of Self), hip-hop feminist pedagogy allows young girls to examine their lived experiences and multiple identities, including race and spirituality. The pedagogy embodies through different art forms a critical examination of mainstream discourses and lived experiences of folks commonly thought of as marginalized or disenfranchised. Patterson's work draws similarities to hip-hop feminism because they are both grounded in representing counternarratives and highlighting the lived experiences of Black and Brown folks, while asking questions to challenge unpacked discrepancies and contradictions that exist in the lives of young Black girls (Brown & Kwakye, 2012; Callier, 2012). Additionally, hip-hop feminist pedagogy and Patterson's treatise are spaces where negative representations of Black women and girls are called into question to inspire dialogue surrounding areas of gray. Patterson acknowledges these gray areas but also provides a space through spiritual wholeness that allows individuals some comfort to arrive at a level of consciousness of one's wholeness without abandoning parts of that self. The latter point is what makes Patterson's chapter so thought-provoking and central to ideas of hip-hop feminism and Black girlhood. "Can One Ever Be Wholly Whole?" pushes the reader to think about the possibilities and the limitations of biracial identity with and without wholeness. As hip-hop feminism is a space for life-sustaining liberation, so is finding peace with one's biracial identity. Though it is messy, complicated work, it is built with transformative self-love.

For Black girls, this space must be unapologetic and a constant evolution toward social justice. Patterson's work lays the foundation for a much-needed conversation and more thought surrounding how biracial identity is constructed, affirmed, and problematized in the space of popular culture. "Can One Ever Be Wholly Whole?" pushes the boundaries of at times two conflicting identities, biracial and spiritual, that must be reconciled to achieve wholeness. Patterson's chapter is brave and ripe for discussion.

References

Brown, R. N. (2009). *Black girlhood celebration: Toward a hip-hop feminist pedagogy.* New York: Peter Lang.

Brown, R. N., & Kwakye, C. J. (2012). *Wish to live: The hip-hop feminism pedagogy reader.* New York: Peter Lang.

Callier, D. (2012). Acting out: A performative exploration of identity, healing, and wholeness. In R. N. Brown & C. J. Kwakye (Eds.), *Wish to live: The hip-hop feminism pedagogy reader* (pp. 143–163). New York: Peter Lang.

Denzin, N. K. (2003). *Performance ethnography: Critical pedagogy and the politics of culture.* Thousand Oaks, CA: Sage.

Durham, A. (2010). Hip hop feminist media studies. *International Journal of Africana Studies, 16*(1), 117–140.

Gaunt, K. (2002). *The games Black girls play: Learning the ropes from double-dutch to hip-hop.* New York: New York University Press.

hooks, b. (2000). *Feminism is for everybody: Passionate politics.* Boston, MA: South End Press.

Lindsey, T. (2011). Black no more: Skin bleaching and the emergence of new Negro womanhood. *The Journal of Pan African Studies, 4*(4), 96–115.

Love, B. L. (2012). *Hip hop's li'l sistas speak: Negotiating identities and politics in the new south.* New York: Peter Lang.

Morgan, J. (2000). *When chickenheads come home to roost: A hip-hop feminist breaks it down.* New York: Simon & Schuster.

Stanley, C. A. (2007). When counter narratives meet master narratives in the journal editorial-review process. *Educational Researcher, 36*(1), 14–24.

Lessons in Love, Literacy, and Listening

Reflections on Learning with and from Black Female Youth

Erica Womack

Introduction

Post-Session Reflection, 10/05/10

> *Today was the first day and I think it went really well. Elzora, Amora, Kayla, Elaine, Leslie, Shey, and Elena. I prayed for at least 7 or 8 and God came thru as always . . .*
>
> *Prior to the meeting Shey shared w/ me that she had gotten into a fight w/ another girl at her group home. She had a busted blood vessel in her eye and scratches on her face....She was quiet in the group today and I'm wondering if some of the comments the girls were making made her not feel as eager to express that side I've seen or at least what she gives off as though she's proud that she cussed out the principal, teacher, and security guard last week. I wonder if being in this group will help her to channel her emotions, although I do understand that there are probably things that have happened to her that make her want to act out on these emotions.*
>
> *When we were discussing Karrine Steffans—a widely known Black video model and celebrity groupie—several of the girls were quick to suggest that it didn't matter what her background was—she didn't have to blame everything on her childhood. I had shared that on TV One she mentioned being verbally and/or physically abused by her mother. Many of them said, "So," like it didn't matter. This was before I could also mention what it might do to the female psyche if not properly treated. So going into this I'm wondering what is it going to take to increase the level of understanding and com-*

passion for the human condition? Not only that, how can we get them to move past one-sided thinking? Maybe it isn't possible. But, this is something I would like to work towards . . .

I'm also having reservations "researching" the group. Why can't I just be w/ them? Researching seems to take out the fun aspect and the good intent behind it, although, I do know what comes out of it will/might do something for them as well as for others. Me as well.

I experienced a swell of emotions on that first day—from fear, doubt, and disbelief to joy, eagerness, and optimism. Not knowing where this journey might take me, I was satisfied in *believing* that the girls would sufficiently guide me. Ironically enough, Elaine came up with our agreed-on name—African Ascension—the following week and given the importance of naming in African American/American culture (Dillard, 2006; Sium, 2011), this proved a perfect fit. The name "African Ascension" would mark our ascent (moving up) and advancement (moving forward)—that we were, indeed, on a journey to someplace together. Likewise, I hoped to benefit equally from our time together, not simply as a Black and female researcher but as a human being.

The central goals of my research were to consider how Black female adolescents conceive of self and society and how particular reading, writing, and speaking acts (or those that highlight their experiences as young Black females) helped to shape their conceptions. My interest in working with this population and in exploring this topic lies in the fact that the research on Black female youth, in general, is relatively sparse, and particularly so in the area of adolescent literacy. Additionally, several scholars (Collins, 2009; Evans-Winters, 2005; Evans-Winters & Esposito, 2010) note that if and when the lives and literacies of Black females are examined, they are frequently misrepresented as well. For these reasons, I see listening as central to the work that I do.

For two years, I had the pleasure of meeting with this group of Black girls for 90 minutes each week to read, write, and speak about their realities as young Black women—their relationships, school experiences, future goals, and identities—and to engage in critical understandings of self, other, and society. When we met there was laughter. There was crying. There was chatting. There was listening. And there was seriousness. But, most importantly, there was a show(er)ing of love.

Thus far, we (i.e., the girls, myself, and TT, one of my doctoral colleagues) have spent time analyzing texts that range from poetry to song lyrics to fiction and nonfiction literature to film to ads to music videos. Our writing activities mainly consisted of autobiographical pieces, freewrites, reader response, poetics, and journal exchanges that involved the girls and me writing and responding to one another in the pages of their notebook. Further, we opened each session with announcements of upcoming events and/or anything significant that had happened in our lives. Because I facilitated each of our activities (I often select what we read or the prompts we respond to), my goal was to ensure that all of our topics were driven by what came out of our weekly sessions and/or what the girls explicitly told me interested them.

For these reasons, I seek to address the following in this chapter: How are traditional notions of mentoring reframed through the act of listening? What do the girls teach and what do I learn? How do I listen to learn about who they are and what they know? How do the girls listen to learn about themselves and each other? And finally, why should listening to Black female adolescents matter? In this chapter, I draw upon Schultz's (2003) conception of listening as a central act of teaching, learning, and transformation that is also akin to the mentoring relationship that evolved between and among us. I also draw on Black and endarkened feminist (Collins, 2009; Dillard, 2006) frameworks as well as bell hooks's (1993, 2001) notion of compassionate listening and critical affirmation to speak to the ways in which race and gender further shaped how listening was framed within this all-Black and all-female setting.

Based on my work with the girls, I use listening here as an emotionally engaging, spiritually enriching communicative act that became a mechanism of healing for our individual and collective selves. For us, listening called up moments of hurt, healing, and resistance as well as comfort, reciprocity, and love. Thus, in exploring what it means to listen in an all-Black and all-female setting, I discovered (1) how the girls resisted dominant narratives about Black girlhood, (2) how listening became a source of both pain and pleasure, and (3) how listening functioned as an act of love between and among us. In recognizing this kind of reciprocity as a spiritual endeavor, Dillard (2006) reminds us that "This includes developing the practice as a researcher [or one can add mentor] of looking and listening deeply, not just for the often self-gratifying rewards of the research project, but so that we know what to do and what not to do in order to serve others in the process of research [or mentoring]" (p. 84).

Reframing Listening through a Learning Stance

As I listened, I learned to teach. (Schultz, 2003, p. 3)

In *Listening: A Framework for Teaching across Differences,* Schultz (2003) defines listening as "an active, relational, and interpretive process that is focused on making meaning" (p. 8) between the child/student and the adult/teacher. Schultz recognizes this process as a kind of role reversal for the child/student as speaker and the adult/teacher as audience where emphasis is also placed on the adult's desire to learn about and alongside her students. Schultz further states, "When I listen to teach, I am changed by what I hear" (p. 9). As a novice Black female researcher working with a diverse group of Black female youth, I was also transformed by what I heard. As I became more and more attuned to their experiences of growing up young, Black, and female, my role of researcher/facilitator shifted to that of mentor/friend. And, most importantly, I witnessed myself becoming a more patient, empathic human being.

Listening thus became an essential component in developing and deepening my relationships with the girls as well as in their relationships with one another. Yet, some studies indicate more emphasis is placed on telling and teaching and less on listening and learning (Meier, 2002; Schultz, 2003) when it comes to adult females' interactions with adolescent girls (Brown, 2006, 2009; Sullivan, 1996). For instance, in Rhodes, Davis, Prescott, and Spencer's (2007) study of urban female youth's relationships with adult female mentors, the effect(s) of the mentoring relationship on the adult women is never broached. The authors draw attention to its impact on the girls, instead, citing their ability to foster stronger connections with others, develop critical awareness, and garner support as positive outcomes of these mentor-mentee relationships. Nevertheless, Rhodes et al. admit more research is needed to determine the long-lasting effects of these relationships and that their effectiveness can be measured by other factors such as gender-biased programming in co-educational settings and racial and economic differences that might exist between mentors and mentees.

Brown's (2006) study of adult and adolescent female relationships in the Celebrating All Girls (CAG) program points to the significance of cross-racial (and/or cultural) awareness and dialogue between mentor and mentee in addition to the effects of this relationship on the mentor herself. To address the racial/cultural and economic distinctions between the majority White and middle-class female mentors and their mostly Black and working-class female mentees, Brown suggests mentors adopt a "femtoring [rather than a mentoring] consciousness" that "manifest through the actions of female mentors as they negotiate borders in ways that allow girls and women to see themselves in each other" (pp. 107–108). Based on Brown's findings, such actions would entail (1) a resistance to role modeling whereby CAG mentors likewise express their own desire for self-transformation, (2) the recognition of difference (e.g., race, socioeconomic status, religion, sexuality, etc.) as some of the mentors find it difficult to negotiate such borders, as well as (3) an engagement in honest dialogue that accounts for one's right to her own language.

Brown's (2006) notion of femtoring consciousness is most evident years later in her all-Black and all-female youth and adult after-school program known as Saving Our Lives Hear Our Truths (or SOLHOT) where Black girlhood is not only celebrated by both women and girls but is also treated as part of a lifelong experience (Brown, 2009). As members of SOLHOT, then, Black women and girls use reading, writing, singing, rapping, dancing, and acting to connect to one another and their histories. Rather than programming, Brown (2009) believes Black girls need power—that they do not need to be given something that they don't already possess and they do not need to be empowered as much as they need to be (re)affirmed. Most importantly, her work reminds us why it is essential that Black girls talk and Black women listen.

Rather than seeking to repair, empower, or correct the girls, I sought instead to understand them. I needed to know what the girls took away from each session, what the girls needed and/or desired from our space, as well as what they needed and/or desired to bring to it. I listened therefore I learned, yet I also recognized how critical it was for the girls to be able to do the same. hooks (2001) believes a mutual responsibility exists between speaker and listener that requires both parties to sacrifice, commit, and be attentive to one another. For hooks, these acts become expressions of love and generosity that are "healing to the spirit" (p. 165). Therefore, as *we* (i.e., the girls and I) listened, *we* loved.

Context of Study

My research took place in a reserved section of a library that is also part of a network of libraries located within a large metropolitan city in the Midwest. In this location, I have had the opportunity to recruit girls from all walks of life—those attending urban, suburban, and private high schools as well as those being home-schooled; girls living with both parents, a single parent, or in a group home without either parent; and girls who are doing extremely well in school as well as others who are routinely suspended. Potential participants were selected on the basis of three main criteria: (1) if they identified as Black and female, (2) if they were between 14–18 years of age,[1] and (3) if they were willing to participate with parental consent.

Over the course of this study, I used multiple data collection strategies that included note-taking in a research journal, videotaped recordings of meetings, videotaped interviews with participants, writings by the participants as well as any other literacy artifacts that were used or produced (e.g., readings or collaborative work) within our weekly meetings. In these interviews, I listened to learn about their lived experiences, how they engaged in various literacy practices (i.e., reading, writing, and speaking acts), and how these practices framed their perceptions of self and other and/or society.

During our meetings, we were typically seated around a large table facing one another with the digital camcorder positioned on another table behind and/or beside us to capture what was taking place in each of our discussions. Because I facilitated each of our reading, writing, and speaking activities, I wrote down everything I could recall in my journal immediately following each meeting. I recorded what happened that day, my (preliminary) analysis of what happened, and what to consider in the coming week(s) based on what took place during our meeting. I identified patterns or recurring themes that emerged within the data to highlight how listening functioned within this all-Black and female setting. Preliminary findings were culled from my researcher journal as other pieces of data were then referenced in order to explore the role of listening within our group.

Listening to Learn, Lead, and Love within an All-Black and All-Female Space

Part 1: Lessons in Literacy

> This like video actually kind of scares me…like is this how the world views Black women?
>
> —ELENA, 18

The above comment was in response to "Marriage Negotiations" and several other YouTube videos that had gone viral, each featuring distorted images of Black women as short-tempered and difficult to get along with. Elena's question struck a serious nerve by acknowledging the depths of these hegemonic readings of Black women and their broad dissemination across the globe. Given the overemphasis on these generalized views of Black females, there remains a heavy focus on what they do rather than how they think and, as a result, many young Black females' literate activities and achievements go unrecognized and unrealized. Gaining greater awareness of how Black female adolescents understand themselves and the(ir) world around them becomes especially important. Fortunately, we had the space and the time to define for ourselves what it meant to be Black and to be female each week—to trouble these images, replace them, and reinvent new ones. Recalling our frequent discussion of these topics helped me to consider how the notion of listening fit within my larger goal of understanding Black female adolescents' conceptions of self and society.

Because I did desire to understand how Black girls saw themselves and the world around them, I had to be willing to listen. The idea or act of mentoring, then, was not simply about me telling the girls what they needed to know about life, but instead what I sought to learn about who they were and what they already knew about their own lives and the lives/experiences of others. This realization also spoke to my need as facilitator/teacher/researcher to relinquish control over what occurred in every session.

For instance, in my researcher journal, I kept referring to "surface-level conversation vs. deeper a-ha moments" as I fretted over the girls' critical analysis of the texts we read, watched, and listened to while I ignored what the girls actually did say and particularly during those times when conversation strayed from the text. Though the girls were not all reading the materials I gave them to take home—such as Nikki Giovanni's *Love Poems* or Hill Harper's *Letter to a Young Sister*—I overlooked the fact that they were coming to our sessions reading themselves, one another, and society at large (Freire, 2000) in other ways. Therefore I began to listen carefully to what the girls had to say in person and on paper.

On the day of our initial meeting in October 2010, I asked the girls: "What words come to mind when you think about what it means to grow up young, Black, and female?" We then created a list based on what we have to say about ourselves and what others may have to say about us. The girls easily identified new names for old stereotypes or controlling images of the kind Patricia Hill Collins (2009) speaks about. Rather than *jezebel*, it was now *rat* or *hood rat*. Or instead of the sassy-mouthed *Sapphire*, the girls used terms such as *loud* or *ghetto* to describe commonly held views of Black female youth and women. These and other stereotypical markers (e.g., mammy, welfare queen, jezebel)—referred to by Collins (2009) as "controlling images" (p. 76)—have their roots in institutionalized racism, sexism, and economic exploitation primarily in the United States. Thus, it has largely been up to Black women *and* girls to resist such symbolic control and manipulation (see Figure 1).

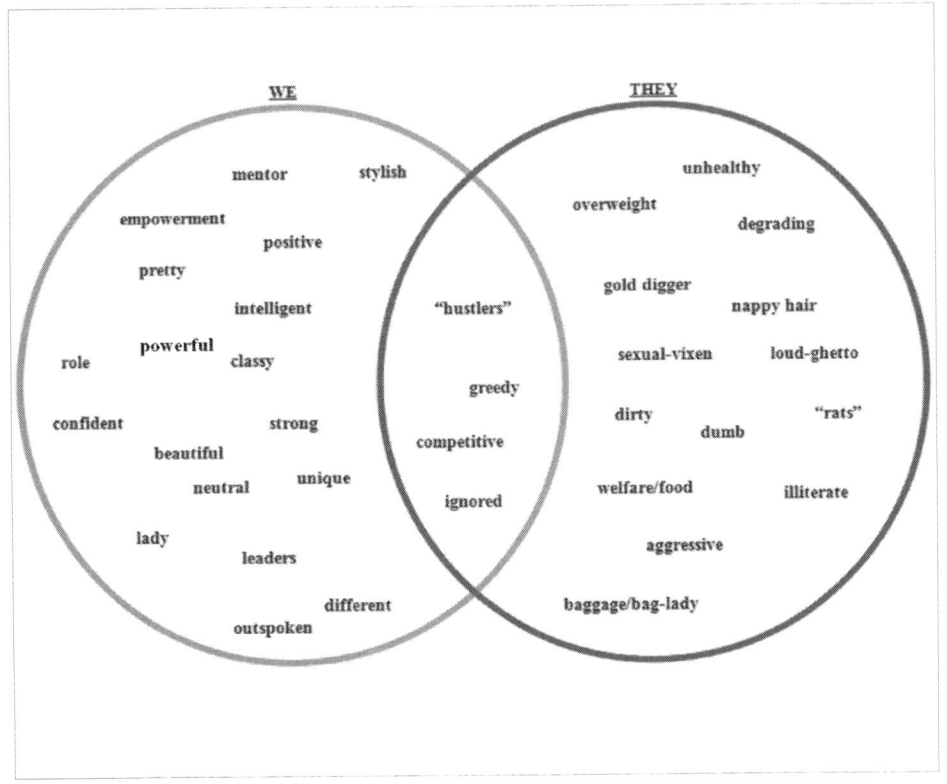

Figure 1.

I therefore asked the girls to use these words as a basis to write down what it meant to grow up young, Black, and female in the 21st century. In these reflections, I witnessed how strength, power, and love were running themes throughout each individual's journal, all of which ran counter to the common stereotypes. Shey, for instance, wrote:

My opinion of being a young black female today is we mostly feel challenge. We think of empowerment, beautifulness, our strength and weakens and challenges when we think about young black females today. We worry about our life ahead. People may think of us as gold diggers, young mother, warfare, poor, struggling, ghetto, and ubnoctious. It hard in life, droppin out, making baby's, meet men, and lost, with no help from the government!!! It's wrong! We are role models, hard working women with intelligent and confident with powerful words. We are strong leaders!

Likewise Amora wrote:

> In general we as humans many abilities. So to be categorized as a young black female, gives us opportunities in many ways. I choose empowerment, because no MATTER where any YBF comes from there is many positive things she can do. Woman are strong, being a young lady shows we are too. Yet there are females who let their weakness hit them hard, but you can't say they won't make it through. For example, abuse, failing grades, rape, money, and other bad influences. Yet all stated, makes a YBF in something strong like a rock and sweet as an apple. Which gives empowerment, breaking through the negativity.

Elaine also had this to say:

> I can speak for myself umm…To me it means being a young powerful lady. I have all of the opportunities in the world I just need to take them and progress in being beautiful, intelligent, hardworking, responsible, honest, confident young Black women. Beings black makes me feel good because I feel the reason people hate me is because they want to be me or my color. Why do people tan to get darker. I'm already dark. My skin my hair my heritage everything about me is beautiful and my Black makes me who I am.

Thereafter, I listened to how the girls regularly engaged in oppositional readings of Black female identity in efforts to create more satisfying images of their own. Whether it was the scantily clad image of Black women in hip-hop and pop videos, the controversial "Angry black woman" Pepsi ad that aired during the 2011 Super Bowl game, or the face of a prepubescent Black girl featured in an abortion ad, the girls were attuned to the misrepresentations of Black females in the broader society. In many ways, the girls *became* the alternative to those representations themselves.

Part 2: Lessons in Listening

> I don't want to talk about this. Can we talk about something else?
> (Elaine, 16)

Elaine's abrupt interjection here came after listening to another participant's, Nikayla's, story of being abused. This was Nikayla's first day joining our group so I invited her to share a little bit about herself with the rest of us. Nikayla not only revealed that she had recently moved to our area from one of Chicago's notorious housing projects, but that she had also been raped by an older male upon moving here. In that moment, I viewed Elaine's interjection as an act of silencing as she appeared unwilling to listen to Nikayla's story or empathize with her pain, so naturally I said, "No, no, no. Let her finish."

In *Listening*, Schultz (2003) discusses the idea of silencing by individuals themselves, between and among peers, teachers, and students, and through institutions overall. Therefore, she asks educators to listen for what is not being said, silencing of what someone might be getting ready to say, or of who might be getting shut out of conversation. What is not accounted for in this perspective, however, are moments like what Elaine experienced when acts of silencing become a way of alleviating pain and when listening is deemed the source of that pain. I say this because as we moved further into our discussion Elaine revealed that she, too, had been a survivor of sexual abuse. Listening for me also became difficult because of how I responded and/or failed to respond in that moment. As the adult facilitator and caretaker of the group, I became clueless as to what to do with the information and how to effectively proceed. Would only listening be enough?

bell hooks (1993) understood these tensions well for it was after witnessing the physical, spiritual, and mental anguish of many of her Black female students and colleagues that she established "Sisters of the Yam," a Black women's support group, to collectively work through their struggles. hooks found one of the best ways for Black women to be brought back to their own reality was through dialogue. She says, "It is important that black people talk to one another, that we talk with friends and allies, for the telling of our stories enables us to name our pain, our suffering, and to seek healing" (pp. 16–17). Therefore, we each had to be open to listening and to do so in a way that reflected hooks's (2001) idea of "compassionate listening," for she believes, "When we are committed to doing the work of love we listen even when it hurts" (p. 158).

Unfortunately, Elaine never returned after this session and although I was never able to learn why, I concluded and accepted that listening in our group would not always be pleasant. We would have to learn how to deal with the awkwardness and tension together and understand these moments as necessary for our individual and collective healing. Soon after I began allotting time for announcements where we adopted a listening stance to one another's stories of trauma, but also triumphs such as being accepted to college, raising one's grade from failing to passing, or being inducted into the National Honors Society.

Part 3: Lessons in Love

> We, we have fun. And we, um, we do a lot of things. We learn a lot from, um, people. You know. We learn how to like females....That's what I learned from here (laughter)....Oh, yeah. We talk about boys. (More laughter). (Shey, 17)

This comment came after I asked Shey to explain to the new girls what it is that we do in our sessions. Listening to Shey here, I am reminded of her process of recovering (hooks, 1993) from the broken relationships with other females in her family and even at school—from the principal, to the teaching staff, to even her peers. In early December 2010, she handed me a copy of one of her English assignments. It was a semiautobiographical account of the many hardships she had endured during her short time on this earth. The following is an excerpt:

> 'When you grow up...' is one of those things people ask me a lot I used to have an answer for this mysterious question but I no longer can decide. I wanted to be a writer, a successful mother with nine kids, then a medical assistant working with babies and old people, then finally a pediatric nurse for babies. But that change when my mind was change when I seen the world for what it truly is. Then I started having second thoughts because I had gone through to much and it seem like my life wasn't getting any better. I mean here I was 17 years old and my life was going down the road of destruction. My grades were already horrible they didn't have time to get up, I had been suspended at least three times, and I had the police called on me twice in one week and I just turned 17...I don't think this is a good age for fairy tales....This was the beginning of the Rain of Hell!!!

Nevertheless, Shey learned to love again through the "critically affirming" (hooks, 1993) kinds of talking and listening that took place within our group. hooks (2001) believes, "Loving friendships provide us with a space to experience the joy of community in a relationship where we learn to process all our issues, to cope with difference and conflict while staying connected" (p. 133). In those ways, Shey and others were able to begin the process of healing.

In the initial year of the study, we spent most of our time talking about our intimate relationships or about "boys" as Shey mentioned in the opening quote, yet at the same time, we were also processing how well we related to one another. Another participant, Jada, shared in one of her journals: "I have learned that I have grown in being relatable to all forms of people. I already knew that I was very opinionated, but I also discovered that I am not as abnormal as it seems sometimes, and that their are other girls who feel and have the same opinions as me." Nikayla also shared: "Well since i've been in the program i then learned how 2 be myself and not trying to impress other people i've learned how to show my girly side instead of holding everything in i learned how not 2 to be hard or mean nomore just the life style i was living in. So i've changed a lot."

For Collins (2009) Black women's friendships with other Black females constitute "safe space" (p. 111) where Black women can simply be, without apology or question. It is within these contexts that Black women can see and be seen and hear and be heard. Traditionally, the Black church and other Black organizations have served as physical representations of safe space, yet Black mothers' relationships with their Black daughters and Black women's day-to-day conversations provide security as well (Collins, 2009). The same is true of Black women's creative expression (e.g., music, art, and literature) that is often emblematic of the deep intricacies and intimacies that exist between and among Black women (Collins, 2009). Collins believes "[f]or African-American women the listener most able to pierce the invisibility created by Black women's objectification is another Black women. This process of trusting one another can seem dangerous because only Black women know what it means to be Black women. But if we will not listen to one another, who will?" (p. 114).

Being heard or listened to by not just me, but more importantly the girls themselves, allowed each of us to experience the joy of being in the kind of "loving friendships" that hooks speaks of, a bond that deepened the traditional nature of the mentor-mentee relationship.

Implications

[L]ike this is obviously a real experience, you know, and it involves different things like reading and discussion and so forth so. (interview with Elena, 02/08/11)

I think that [this group] is something that is necessary like, like we're all coming from different experiences, but sometimes we go through the same, you know, obstacles, you know, so I think it is necessary to come and talk about it whereas you may not be able to talk about it at a::ll, you know, with other people or, you know, before you come here, you know, so I think it is necessary for Black women to have things like this, you know, where they can come and kinda talk about their experiences and relate with each other, so…(interview with Elena, 02/08/11)

So what might all of this mean for researchers, educators, and anyone who works closely with youth? And why does listening to Black female youth matter, in particular? These findings suggest listening became a pathway toward collective healing (hooks, 1993) and transformation, reshaping the notion of adult and adolescent female relationships as a reciprocal, give-and-take process between and among the researcher and the researched (Dillard, 2006). My interactions with these girls offer new understandings of the mentoring relationship as more dialogic than pedagogic as the relationship serves the interests and needs of the group as opposed to any one individual, whether mentor or mentee.

Freire (2000) defines dialogue as "the encounter between men [and women], mediated by the world, in order to name the world. Hence, dialogue cannot occur between those who want to name the world and those who do not wish this naming" (p. 88). Furthermore, he contends that "Dialogue cannot exist…in the absence of a profound love for the world and for people….Love at the same time is the foundation of dialogue and dialogue itself" (p. 89). Similarly, hooks (2001) notes that love cannot exist without a willingness to listen. It is therefore necessary to view our engagement with one another—our process of giving and taking, of speaking and listening—as an act of love. Over time, we committed to being fully engaged in one another's presence—to be face-to-face, to see eye-to-eye, to speak and be spoken to, and to express our innermost feelings. And in time, we committed to honoring one another's presence through open and honest dialogue.

In the introduction to *Pedagogy of the Oppressed* (Freire, 2000), Donaldo Macedo is critical of "the transformation of dialogical teaching into a method invoking conversation that provides participants with a group-therapy space for stating their grievances" (p. 18). Yet, for Black girls who are rarely summoned to speak upon their grievances in the first place, I think this is an ideal place to begin—to begin anew in how we support and engage Black girls. These findings demonstrate how listening to and learning from Black girls becomes one way of foregrounding their lives, beliefs, and voices within academic research and within our classrooms. These findings also demonstrate the significance of listening to love in our roles as educators. Schultz (2003), too, reminds us why listening must remain at the core of our praxis:

> Central to this theory of listening is the proposition that listening necessitates action. That is, the act of listening is based on interaction rather than simply reception. . . . [T]o become a listener is to participate in . . . transformation. . . . Listening is fundamentally about being in relationship to another and through this relationship supporting change or transformation. By listening to others, the listener is called on to respond. (p. 9)

Our willingness to listen to transform was evident in Shey's comment about "learn[ing] to like females" as well as in Elena's comment about Black women needing opportunities to "come and kinda talk about their experiences and relate with each other." The same is also true of my initial fears and doubts about what our space and/or dialogue might offer, how well we would respond to one another, and how effective I might be in leading (and researching) our group. Though females in general are characterized as catty, gossipy, moody, and sneaky, these characterizations become far weightier for Black women and girls, particularly in how we are viewed both on- and off-screen. It is the way our necks roll, eyes cross, fingers point, voices raise, and tongues lash. *Sometimes.* For these reasons it became essential for us to seek transformation through dialogue, specifically in the ways we regarded ourselves and one another. It also mattered that we aimed to transcend racist, sexist, and classist stereotypes others may have cast down upon us. Additionally, it was important for us to create a space that worked against cattiness and competition and rather *toward* communion and cooperation. Indeed, being able to see ourselves in one another became our ultimate expression of transformation and love.

The girls taught me the beauty of what we (i.e., adults) can find when we take time to see them and hear them and what remains at stake when we continue to do just the opposite. Evans-Winters and Esposito (2010) note: "Traditional research in education on Black girls typically concerns itself with early pregnancy and sexuality, school dropout, drug use and abuse, and aggression" (p. 14). Thus, it is imperative that researchers and educators create more opportunities, more "real experiences" for girls to tell their stories in the ways that they wish to tell them.

The continued portrayal of Black girls as "other" fuels discourses of tragedy over triumph, lewdness over literacy, and failure over promise (Frazier, Belliston, Brower, & Knudsen, 2011). Thankfully, the Black girls I worked with have shown and will continue to show what else is possible. Their resiliency (see Evans-Winters, 2005; Frazier et al., 2011; Paul, 2003) proves they are a force to be reckoned with. I, for one, am proud to be a part of this movement and to have Black girls leading my way. For those of us teaching and learning with Black female adolescents, Brown (2009) made clear that our task is quite simple: "At the risk of romanticizing Black girls, I think we should listen more. Period. They keep telling us. Know That!" (p. 6). And I do.

Note

1. The following year I capped the age requirement at 21 in order to accommodate those who might have graduated and wished to still participate.

References

Brown, R. N. (2006). Mentoring on the borderlands: Creating empowering connections between adolescent girls and young women volunteers. *Human Architecture: Journal of the Sociology of Self Knowledge*, IV, Special Issue, 105–121.

Brown, R. N. (2009). *Black girlhood celebration: Toward a hip-hop feminist pedagogy*. New York: Peter Lang.

Collins, P. H. (2009). *Black feminist thought: Knowledge, consciousness, and the politics of empowerment*. New York: Routledge.

Dillard, C. B. (2006). *On spiritual strivings: Transforming an African American woman's academic life*. Albany: SUNY.

Evans-Winters. V. E. (2005). *Teaching Black girls: Resiliency in urban classrooms*. New York: Peter Lang.

Evans-Winters, V. E., & Esposito, J. (2010). Other people's daughters: Critical race feminism and black girls' education. *Educational Foundations, 24*(1–2), 11–24.

Frazier, F. C., Belliston, L. M., Brower, L. A., & Knudsen, K. (2011). Placing Black girls at promise: A report of the Rise Sister Rise study. *Executive Summary*. Columbus, OH: Report from the Ohio Department of Mental Health.

Freire, P. (2000). *Pedagogy of the oppressed*. New York: Continuum.

hooks, b. (1993). *Sisters of the yam: Black women and recovery*. Cambridge: South End Press.

hooks, b. (2001). *All about love: New visions*. New York: Morrow.

Meier, D. (2002). *The power of their ideas: Lessons for America from a small school in Harlem*. Boston: Beacon Press.

Paul, D. G. (2003). *Talkin' back: Raising and educating resilient black girls*. Westport, CT, Praeger Publishers.

Rhodes, J. E., Davis, A. A., Prescott, L. R., & Spencer, R. (2007). Caring connections: Mentoring relationships in the lives of urban girls. In B. J. Ross Leadbeater & N. Way (Eds.), *Urban girls: Resisting stereotypes, creating identities* (pp. 142–156). New York: New York University Press.

Schultz, K. (2003). *Listening: A framework for teaching across differences*. New York: Teachers College Press.

Sium, A. (2011). My name is "Mohamed," but please call me "John." Canadian racism, spirit injury and the renaming of the indigenous body as a rite of passage. In N. Wane, E. Manyimo, & E. Ritskes (Eds.), *Spirituality, education, and society: An integrated approach* (pp. 139–156). Rotterdam, The Netherlands: Sense Publishers.

Sullivan, A. M. (1996). From mentor to muse: Recasting the role of women in relationship with urban adolescent girls. In B. J. Ross Leadbeater & N. Way (Eds.), *Urban girls: Resisting stereotypes, creating identities* (pp. 226–249). New York: New York University Press.

Chapter 7 Visionary Response

Listening *Face-to-Face* and *Eye-to-Eye*

Seeing and Believing Black Girls and Women in Educational Practice and Research

Marcelle M. Haddix

"Hello young lady, what's your name?" I asked the Black girl sitting in front of me.

"Princess," she said, with a quiet voice with a tinge of attitude.

"Her name's not Princess, it's Amani!" corrected the White female teacher from the corner of the room.

"Yes it is! I said my name's Princess!" the Black girl demanded with full-fledged attitude at this point.

I then reassured her, "Well, guess what, how 'bout I call you Princess Amani. It's so nice to meet you, Princess Amani."

Princess Amani was a student who participated in a summer digital storytelling program I facilitated for fourth and fifth graders from our local urban school district. When I began working with the group, the teachers (both White, one male and one female) thought they would do me a favor by forewarning me that this group of students was difficult and challenging to work with, and Princess Amani was one they described as "needing to be restrained." Counter to their negative and deficit framing of this predominantly Black and working-class group of students, I observed and witnessed a group of highly energetic, curious, and motivated young people excited to create and present digital stories about the fictional characters they imagined. Not surprisingly, in her digital story, Princess Amani introduced us to a cute, little bunny named "Princess Amani" who built and ruled over a kingdom full of beautiful flowers and homes for her people.

Princess Amani reminded me of how important it is to affirm the ways that individuals represent their many selves. Princess Amani claimed her existence, despite being a young Black girl growing up in a context that marked her as bad and undesirable, as unseen and invisible. Who was I, or anyone, to deny her this existence? In the moment that we first met, we were two Black girls listening to and seeing one another, face-to-face and eye-to-eye. As Black girls, I understood what was at stake in her being able to claim and assert a positive representation of being Black and female and to have someone affirm and believe her in the process. This example is emblematic of the kinds of relationships that I aim to cultivate across my work with Black girls and women in educational contexts and in my community. In her chapter, Womack reflects on how listening is an essential component in developing and deepening love and relationships. And this resonates for me as I think about my multiple roles as researcher, teacher educator, and community member. In describing the deepening of love in the relationships between herself and the Black female youth in her research through compassionate listening, she writes:

> Over time, we committed to being fully engaged in one another's presence—to be face-to-face, to see eye-to-eye, to speak and be spoken to, and to express our innermost feelings. And in time, we committed to honoring one another's presence through open and honest dialogue. (p. 187)

Here, I will further explore this notion of "being face-to-face" and "seeing eye-to-eye" by reflecting on my work with Black female preservice teachers in practice and in educational research. Like Womack, I too confront reservations of "doing research" with and about Black girls and women, despite my affiliation and identification with this group. However, as she writes, it is important to do so because "when the lives and literacies of Black females are examined, they are frequently misrepresented as well" (p. 175). Womack highlights the act of listening as being central to the work that we must do. I too consider what it means to listen to our selves while listening to those whom we work with in our classrooms and in our research and to examine this within the context of research about Black girl/womanhood, by Black women scholars, and with Black girls and women.

Listening in Practice

Every Tuesday evening, my undergraduate seminar on teaching literacy across curriculum ends at 6:45 p.m. As the majority of the 29 students in the class hustle to pack their things and exit the classroom, a group of students of color linger and hang around. This particular semester is unusual in that out of 29 students, I have seven Black female students. In all of my years as a teacher educator, I have never had the opportunity to work with this number of women of color in the context of a teacher education course. Like most teacher education classrooms in predominantly White institutions, students of color come few and far between in my classes. So, I entered this class with amazement and excitement in having seven Black women who want to be teachers. And, like me, once a Black female student in a teacher education program at a predominantly White institution, they too are pursuing this profession as the minority in a field that remains dominated by White, middle-class, English-monolingual females.

Beyond the class, these seven women and I formed an unspoken sistahood. Though the course was about teaching literacy across content areas, our sistahood was a space to talk and listen across our different yet collective experiences of being Black women in White spaces. Just as I was amazed by their dominant presence in my class this semester, they were also shocked to walk into the class the first day and to see me standing at the front of the room. My presence too was significant to them because as Candace shared with me, "seeing you as a Black woman and a professor let me know that I could do this too." In our sistahood, our discussions span topics such as dealing with race and racism at the university to working within our communities to styling natural Black hair. What I have learned is that as much as I enjoy sharing in this space, my active, compassionate listening is important (hooks, 1993). At times, these women express being dismissed or challenged in the context of their teacher education classes when they talk about race and racism-related issues, and I can relate. When I have talked about incidents and experiences that I view as race-related and motivated by racism as a faculty member, some of my White colleagues' first inclination is to try to provide other excuses or reasons why the incident occurred. Instead of just accepting my story, they offer a counter to my story—alternative and other possibilities that distance race and racism. I have to argue, debate, and offer further explanation to be believed.

I grew up with the saying "I'll believe it when I see it." This expression meant that unless visual evidence was produced, there was legitimate doubt. For me, it was also a way to protect my hopes and dreams; there was no sense in getting my hopes up if there was no evidence to be seen. However, the degree to which this doubt lessened was also contingent upon the messenger. As a Black girl and now woman, I have to anticipate that who I am and what I have to say will not be automatically accepted or believed when I, for example, enter into a university classroom with a sea of White faces as the professor or when I assert my ideas in a faculty meeting. This speaks to the constant objectification and marked invisibility of Black girls and women in dominant White spaces. I agree with Womack when she cites Collins (2000), who writes, "[f]or African-American women the listener most able to pierce the invisibility created by Black women's objectification is another Black women. This process of trusting one another can seem dangerous because only Black women know what it means to be Black women. But if we will not listen to one another, who will?" (p. 114). It is paramount. Womack's work reminds me that, as Black women, as teachers, and as researchers, "listening is central to the work that we do" (p. 192–193). By listening to each other, we are also listening to ourselves. As the seven Black women hang around after class each week to dish about our favorite reality shows or swap hair stories, it is important for me to listen. This listening is a reciprocal act. By validating and legitimizing the experiences of other Black girls and women, I do the same for myself, for my mother, and for my grandmother.

Listening in Research

In her work, Womack discovered three specific ways that the act of listening functioned within their all-Black and all-female literacy collective: (1) as a tool to resist dominant narratives about Black girlhood, (2) as a source of both pain and pleasure, and (3) as an act of love between and among herself and her participants. This framework is useful as I reflect on my research with Black female students in teacher education (see Haddix, 2010, 2012) where prominent themes among these young Black women include feelings of isolation and notions of being "the only one"; marginalization in explorations of race and racism in the teacher education program; and their move toward hybrid enactments of culture and language in the taking on of new teacher identities. Being Black and female in teacher education is synonymous with being unseen and invisible. With the overwhelming presence of Whiteness in teacher education (Sleeter, 2001), the presence of students of color is readily overlooked. The emphasis on preparing the mostly White population of preservice teachers for today's schools mutes the needs and interests of those few students of color. Another paradoxical outcome of progressive and liberal aims of multicultural teacher education is the prevalence of colorblindness rhetoric and ideology. In honoring and celebrating diversity, the majority of White students take on a "but we're all the same" mentality. This colorblindness ideology has an unintended consequence of further alienating and marginalizing students of color. And, again, the Black female students in my work assert that being seen as Black and female is a form of respect and a way of honoring our culture, identity, and communities. As one student, Natasha, shared in an interview, "I'm Black, I'm Black...I have no problems sayin' it." Not acknowledging her Blackness and woman-ness is to disregard and disrespect her.

Through listening to the stories of my participants, I want to reclaim and redefine the personal and community experiences of Black girls and women as forms of knowledge production. This knowledge production is realized through language, and in particular, the stories that are told, retold, and not told. This storytelling has been studied as part of Black rhetorical traditions (Smitherman, 2006), and in my own work, I examine storytelling as a discursive feature of Black female language to represent a collective "voice" that privileges multiple, varied, and complex perspectives. As a Black woman researcher, I intently listen for their stories and the ways that we craft and co-create these stories. As Black women, we make language do what we want it and need it to do. As Black women, we style our stories, and we have fun with language. We perform language. In African American verbal arts and rhetorical traditions, there is as much meaning communicated in the way the story is told as in the actually content of the story.

Many of the Black female students in my research identify as speakers of African American Language (AAL; Smitherman, 1999) and African American female language practices (Fordham, 1993; Lanehart, 2002; Richardson, 2003) as ways of representing. Richardson (2003) defines the concept of African American female languages and literacies as "ways of knowing and acting and the development of skills, vernacular expressive arts and crafts that help females to advance and protect themselves and their loved ones in society" (p. 77). Black females represent their identities linguistically through the genres of storytellin,' steppin'/ rhymin,' singin,' dancin,' preachin,' and stylin' (Smitherman, 2006). Topics of conversation, from men to hair to popular culture, are all understood from our social locations as Black women. We give "attitude" with neck rollin,' hand gesturin,' and talkin' loud (Richardson, 2003; Smitherman, 2006). African American females' language practices "reflect their socialization in a racialized, genderized, sexualized, and classed world in which they employ their language [and literacy] practices to advance and protect themselves" (Richardson, 2003, p. 77). But, our awareness of our affiliation to AAL differs when we are among our sistas and when we are in White spaces. As Natasha shared about speaking out in predominantly White classes,

> I can remember, like, being in the classroom and like, thinking through everything I was going to say before I said it. I can remember doing things like that and just making sure like, Did I use the word correctly? Am I, you know, nervous to say anything? But I would still say it if I felt like it.

This is significant given that "being silenced" remains a prevalent theme in the research literature on students of color in education.

However, in my work, Black female students in teacher education use silence deliberately to protect their voices and their identities. There is a distinct difference in "being silenced" and choosing to "be silent." Silence was not a state imposed on them by the dominant culture: It was the way they resisted and subverted such power and dominance. In fact, not intimately engaging in conversations about race, for example, in a classroom full of their White counterparts was a deliberate choice. Yet, their deliberate silences serve as ways to protect our Black female discourse practices. As a Black woman and speaker of a nonstandard dialect who was once an English education major in a predominantly White teacher education program, I often felt insecurities about how my native tongue of AAL would affect my ability to teach. Currently, as an English and literacy teacher educator working with students at a predominantly White institution, I confront similar instances where students of color retreat from pursuing teaching because they fear that their racial and/or linguistic identities mark them as inadequate or underprepared to be effective classroom teachers.

What I have learned through my research with Black female students is that when we have students in our teacher education classes who are silent, we must still listen. These women made decisions about what to say and when to say it as a larger indication of how they position themselves in any given context. To be "believed" by others and to represent an authentic self in any given context, Black female students are constantly resisting notions of how to be and what to say that are dictated by others and by larger dominant narratives about what it means to be Black and female. Listening to Black female students represent their identities through the use of AAL is another way that who they are is seen, believed, and affirmed. What is said, unsaid, and how is heard and understood. By listening through the silence, I witnessed both the pain and pleasure of my participants in recalling experiences being Black and female in teaching and teacher education: As Womack suggested, listening served as a reciprocal act of love. Through my work with Black female students with whom I share cultural and linguistic norms, I too am affirmed. I learned to be confident and proud of who I am, as a Black woman and speaker of AAL, and as a university professor and scholar, and to represent my self as a form of subverting and resisting the dominant definitions of who

I am. I am not afraid to proclaim loudly that I love being a Black woman, that I love Black women, and that I love our language. As Natasha exclaimed, "This is me and this is how I talk and I don't feel the need to turn it on and off." When we listen among Black sistas, we protect Natasha's prerogative to declare "this is me" and to challenge racist and sexist ideologies that ignore and negate such acceptance.

Listening in Love

In her chapter, Womack posed important questions for individuals committed to and engaged in humanizing research to address, including "What do the girls teach and what do I learn? How do I listen to learn about who they are and what they know? How do the girls listen to learn about themselves and each other? And finally, why should listening to Black female adolescents matter?" (p. 176). By centering the act of listening in our teaching, research, and community work, we redefine and transform relationships between ourselves and those we serve. I want to underscore Womack's argument that the act of listening has reciprocal benefits: I can see and believe the young Black girls and women I work with, like Princess Amani, Candace, and Natasha, while at the same time, I can see and better understand *myself*.

I opened my response by reflecting on my work as a teacher educator and researcher concerned with the experiences of disenfranchised and marginalized students in teaching and teacher education. Similar to Womack, I entered into this work not knowing what to expect, yet aware of my own experiences and wanting to know about theirs. I entered into research saying that I wanted to privilege the voices of preservice teachers of color. I constantly question, though, who am I to represent their voices and their stories? Am I worthy of listening to their stories? Why do I seek out their stories? By drawing on authoethnographic methods in my own work, I too have come to understand that I learn about myself when I listen intently to the voiced experiences of others, and I count being in a position to listen as a privilege. The fact that the Black women find me worthy to listen to their stories suggests that I am being constructed and understood in a particular way. They too affirm and validate who I am: face-to-face and eye-to-eye.

In her essay "The Transformation of Silence into Language and Action," Audre Lorde (1984) wrote: "And where the words of women are crying to be heard, we must each of us recognize our responsibility to seek those words out, to read them and share them and examine them in their pertinence to our lives" (p. 43). This is the spirit of Womack's work: She does not shy away from this responsibility, despite the ongoing struggles and challenges inherent in doing the work that requires us, as Black women scholars and teachers, to simultaneously look inward. Through her example, I am affirmed in my resolve to continue to do this work. By listening to Black girls and women, we acknowledge and affirm Black girls and women as producers of knowledge. By the mere act of inquiring about the lived experiences of Black girls, we validate and legitimate their existence. My doing so is in the spirit of saying "I see you" and "I believe you." Maybe most importantly, it also says "I love you" and "I love my self."

References

Collins, P. H. (2000). *Black feminist thought: Knowledge, consciousness, and the politics of empowerment* (2nd ed.). New York: Routledge.

Fordham, S. (1993). "Those loud Black girls": (Black) women, silence, and gender "passing" in the academy. *Anthropology and Education Quarterly, 24*(1), 3–32.

Haddix, M. (2010). No longer on the margins: Researching the hybrid literate identities of Black and Latina preservice teachers. *Research in the Teaching of English, 45*(2), 97–123.

Haddix, M. (2012). Talkin in the company of sistas: The counterlanguages and deliberate silences of Black female students in teacher education. *Linguistics and Education, 23*(2), 169–181.

hooks, b. (1993). *Sisters of the yam: Black women and recovery*. Cambridge, MA: South End Press.

Lanehart, S. L. (2002). *Sista, speak! Black women kinfolk talk about language and literacy*. Austin, TX: University of Texas Press.

Lorde, A. (1984). The transformation of silence into language and action. In *Sister outsider: Essays and speeches by Audre Lorde* (pp. 40–44). Berkeley, CA: The Crossing Press.

Richardson, E. (2003). *African American literacies*. New York: Routledge.

Sleeter, C. E. (2001). Preparing teachers for culturally diverse schools: Research and the overwhelming presence of Whiteness. *Journal of Teacher Education, 52*(2), 94–106.

Smitherman, G. (1999). *Talkin that talk: Language, culture, and education in African America*. New York: Routledge.

Smitherman, G. (2006). *Word from the mother: Language and African Americans*. New York: Routledge.

Course Syllabus for *Spirit, Race, and Dialogue in Education: A Doctoral Seminar*

Instructors

Cynthia B. Dillard, PhD (Nana Mansa II of Mpeasem, Ghana, West Africa), Professor, and Chinwe L. Ezueh Okpalaoka, PhD, Director, College of Arts and Sciences, Undergraduate Recruitment and Diversity

Course Description*

This course, Spirit, Race, and Dialogue, is designed to provide a space for dialogue and explorations about the pervasive individual, epistemological, structural, systemic, and institutional dimensions and complexities of "race" and identity from a spiritual perspective. A major goal of this course is to move beyond "surface" level discussions of race to ones that both examine and embody the ways that we live and experience the phenomenon of race and identity(ies) as living spiritualities. So a major goal is to also learn to "be" within discourses and theories of spirituality and to marshal those to speak back to our academic lives and work. Part of this work is continually posing a different set of questions both to our inner lives but also to the outward structures in education and society. In the end, Spirit, Race, and Dialogue is about developing new responses to our "struggles" with race and identities, our discussions of them in the research, and moving toward the creation of new sites of possibilities, discourses, and understandings about race and the human condition, informed by the foundations and theories of spirituality.

This course is framed by four questions that undergird the dialogue that you will engage personally, but that also undergird the very essence of our collective work together:

- Why are we here?
- Why do so many feel a sense of angst and limit, especially in our dialogues around race in our work of teaching and research?
- Is it possible to heal ourselves, our work, our understandings of each other, our research, particularly around race?
- How do we make a space in our academic lives to do that?

Any student with a documented disability who may require special accommodation should notify the instructor as early as possible in the course to receive effective and timely accommodation.

Required Books

1. Carson, Clayborne, & Shepard, Kris. (2001). A call to conscience: The landmark speeches of Dr. Martin Luther King, Jr. New York: Warner Books.
2. Dillard, C. B. (2006). On spiritual strivings: Transforming an African American woman's academic life. Albany, NY: SUNY.
3. Hanh, Thich Nhat. (1998). Teachings on love. Berkeley, CA: Parallax Press.
4. hooks, bell. (2000). All about love: New visions. New York: William Morrow.
5. Miller, John P., Karsten, Selia, Denton, Diana, Orr, Deborah, & Kates, Isabella Colalillo. (Eds.). (2005). Holistic learning and spirituality in education. Albany, NY: SUNY.

6. Palmer, Parker. (1983/1993). To know as we are known: Education as a spiritual journey. New York: HarperCollins.
7. Paris, Peter. (1995). The spirituality of African peoples: The search for a common moral discourse. Minneapolis, MN: Augsberg Fortress.
8. Rodriguez, Jeanette, & Fortier, Ted. (2007). Cultural memory: Resistance, faith, and identity. Austin: University of Texas Press.
9. Walker, Alice. (2006). We are the ones we have been waiting for: Inner light in a time of darkness. New York: World Press.
10. Wane, Njoki N., Manyimo, Energy L., & Ritskes, Eric J. (2011). *Spirituality, education & society: An integrated approach.* Rotterdam, Netherlands: Sense Publishers.

General Course Information

The emphasis in this course is on **dialogue and creative interaction** around the core topics of spirituality and race (identity). In other words, our individual and collective responsibility is to assist one another in understanding and extending what we know about race and spirituality in our lives and in our work in teaching and learning. Further, we have the responsibility to share and be present to the ways our particular understandings and perceptions of spirituality and race influence our work in community with others.

I believe it is fair to assume that you have come to this class with questions (however vague or "fuzzy") about spirituality, race, and dialogue and about how all three can influence (and maybe *should* influence) the varied educational settings in which you live and work (or desire to live and work!).

In addition to the inner questions that undergird this course, there are three outward structures that will shape the environment within which we will engage, individually ("solo" work) and collectively, in SRD:

> *The Dialogue*—An explicit focus on talking to one another through discussions, weekly journaling, etc.

Living Ground—An explicit attention to experiencing and living "race" (identity) in/with body, mind, and spirit and an ongoing examination of "unchained" memories/experiences with/in race.

Re-membering, Bearing Witness, and Creating Anew—An explicit creation of new ways of being in our scholarship, teaching, lives, and work.

Given these structures, you will be expected to engage in the following course "assignments":

"Solo" Work

1. Creative Autobiography of Spirit, Race, and Dialogue

In this autobiography (which will be prepared and presented to the class next Wednesday), you should focus on an examination of your inner and outer life with relation to spirit, race, and dialogue, especially in relation to your own education and teaching. Some possible questions for reflection:

- What were the primary influences related to the development of a racial/cultural identity?
- What were your educational experiences with spirit, race, and dialogue?
- How do you describe your "race" and who and/or what contributed to your understanding of it?
- How have those understandings limited or widened possibilities for your engagements in terms of teaching, research, your life?

Your autobiographical presentation should focus on language "art(s)" outside of written narrative. Some possibilities for this introductory autobiography might include poetry, art, music, dance, and the like.

2. Weekly Journal Writing and Responding

You will be responsible for writing a journal in which you commit to paper thoughts, musings, feelings, or other information related to the class discussions, or other related activities or issues. You need to prepare **three typed copies** of your journal to bring to class on Wednesdays: one to share with another student of your choosing and one with me. By the following session, each writer will receive a thoughtful written response from that student and from me. The purpose of the journal is to generate a dialogue between the class participants that will assist in extending/broadening our individual and collective understandings of spirit, race, and dialogue. You will respond in writing to three journal entries each week: one to a peer and one to each of your instructors. It is important to respond to the **substance** of the journal entry. Simply writing "good idea" or "I don't agree" gives little for the writer to really think about. As an active participant with the writer and an engaged professional, you need to provide the writer with true *feedback*. If you agree (or disagree), provide supporting information as to why. If you can, suggest other readings or ways that the writer can further explore the issue. If you are somehow moved by the writing, let the writer know. This kind of authentic responding to writing is important to the development of language and thinking for all of us, as both teachers and learners.

3. Final Paper (25–30 pages)

This final paper provides a forum for you to "talk back," using spirit, race, and dialogue as a radical intervention in your field of study. While it may be in draft form, this will be moving toward submission for publication by the end of the quarter.

Collaborative Work

4. Discussion Leader(s)

You will lead one of the weekly book discussions. Each pair/leader will have +-1½ hours, within which you will share your interpretations of the text in relation to spirit, race, and dialogue. You should plan to lead the discussions in a way that actively and creatively engages all of us with/in the text and helps us to ask new questions as a result of our engagements. Please keep in mind the outward structures of SRD.

5. *Course Syllabus*

You will create either an undergraduate or graduate level syllabus for a course in your field that is influenced by y/our work in SRD. More on this later.

6. *A Digital Documentary of Spirit, Race, and Dialogue*

As a final project, you will develop a 10–15 minute digital story that represents some aspect or element of engagements with/in race and spirituality. **The story will not exceed 15 minutes**. The purpose of this "mini-documentary" is for you to develop a story or representation of some aspect of spirit, race, and dialogue that can educate others about something learned or made clearer through marshaling the discourses and theories of spirituality to examine an "educational" issue. This story might also help us to very clearly see your understanding of new visions of race, informed by spirituality. The only requirement is that your voice(s) will provide narration. Additional information will be provided in class for support.

You will share your documentaries during the last session of class. The documentary, saved on a CD/DVD/flash drive, is all that is to be turned in on the due date.

Weekly Session Outline

Session #1: 9/28/11
Welcome and introductions. Overview of course

Session #2: 10/5/11
Presentations of creative autobiographies

Session #3: 10/12/11
Finish autobiographies. Overview of definitions and spirit, race, and dialogue (Dillard/Okpalaoka). Texts: Palmer and Wane

Session #4: 10/19/11
Text: Paris

Session #5: 10/26/11
Text: Dillard

Session #6: 11/2/11
Text: Miller et al.

Session #7: 11/9/11
Texts: Hooks & Hanh

Session #8: 11/16/11
Text: Rodriguez & Fortier

Session #9: NO CLASS

Session #10: 11/30/11
Text: Carson (MLKing)

Session #11: 12/7/11
Presentation of digital documentaries. Final Celebration Dinner

Contributors

Cynthia B. Dillard (Nana Mansa II of Mpeasem, Ghana) is the Mary Frances Early Endowed Professor in Teacher Education at the University of Georgia (UGA). She is the author of numerous articles and two books, *On Spiritual Strivings: Transforming an African American Woman's Academic Life* and *Learning to (Re)member the Things We've Learned to Forget: Endarkened Feminisms, Spirituality, and the Sacred Nature of Teaching and Research.* She has won numerous awards for teaching and research and is the Director of the Ghana Study Abroad in Education! Program at UGA. Dr. Dillard holds the honored position of Nkosua Ohemaa or Queen Mother of Development in the village of Mpeasem, Ghana, West Africa, where she has established an early childhood program and is currently building an elementary school.

Chinwe L. Ezueh Okpalaoka is Director of Undergraduate Recruitment and Diversity Services in the College of Arts and Sciences at The Ohio State University. In this role, she oversees the recruitment and retention of underrepresented undergraduate students. Her research interests include immigrant education, immigrant ethnic identity development, and African/African American feminist studies. Her first book, *(Im)migrations, Relations, and Identities: Negotiating Cultural Memory* will be published later this year.

Tami A. Augustine is a doctoral candidate in the School of Teaching and Learning at The Ohio State University, as well as the School's Program Manager for the Master of Education (MEd) Middle Childhood Education Program. Her research interests include spirituality in teaching and learning, social studies teacher education, and critical global education.

Robin M. Boylorn is Assistant Professor of Interpersonal and Intercultural Communication at the University of Alabama. Her research focuses on issues of diversity and social identity with an emphasis on the lived experiences of Black women. Her first book, *Sweetwater: Black Women and Narratives of Resilience* (2013), offers an intergenerational account of growing up Black and female in the South. She is also coeditor, alongside Mark P. Orbe, of the forthcoming *Critical Autoethnography: Intersecting Cultural Identities in Everyday Life.*

Barbara Dray is Assistant Professor in Special Education and Linguistically Diverse Education in the School of Education and Human Development at the University of Colorado Denver. Dr. Dray teaches cross-listed courses that include both bilingual/ESL content and special education. Her research interests include transformative learning, culturally and linguistically responsive special education, and teacher education. Her most recent publication, "Mindful Reflection as a Process for Developing Culturally Responsive Practices," appeared in *TEACHING Exceptional Children.*

Eyatta Fischer is a doctoral student in Adolescent, Post-Secondary, and Community Literacies in the School of Teaching and Learning at The Ohio State University. Her research interests include teacher education, urban education, digital literacies, narrative composition, and facilitating democratic engagements through communities of practice.

Marcelle M. Haddix is Assistant Professor and Program Director of English Education in the School of Education at Syracuse University. Her scholarship focuses on how to best prepare all teachers working in culturally and linguistically diverse settings. She also studies the experiences of students of color in literacy and English teacher education. Her work is featured in *Research in the Teaching of English, English Education, Linguistics and Education,* and *Journal of Adolescent and Adult Literacy.* She also directs the Writing Our Lives Program, designed to support the writing practices of urban youth within and beyond school contexts.

Brooke Harris Garad is a doctoral student studying Global and Multicultural Education in the Department of Teaching and Learning at The Ohio State University. Her research interests include postcolonial philosophy, teaching about the world (particularly Africa and the African diaspora), and the role of empathy and care in cultivating global and multicultural perspectives.

Gilbert Kaburu is a doctoral student in The School of Teaching and Learning at The Ohio State University. His current role as a graduate associate with the Mathematics Coaching Program includes working with coaches on teaching mathematics for equity and social justice. His research interests include critical pedagogy, social justice education in sub-Saharan African countries, and post-conflict reconciliation.

Khosi Kubeka is a Junior Research Fellow in the Department of Social Development at the University of Cape Town, South Africa. Her research and teaching interests focus on youth developmental well-being (with special focus on identity formation and transition to adulthood) and the interface between work and family as experienced by women. She teaches courses on youth development within the context of community development, social work assessment and intervention at the community level, and social research methodology.

Chris Landauer is a doctoral student in Social Studies and Global Education at The Ohio State University. In addition to his studies, he works as a transition coordinator within the Columbus City School District, where he supports students with special needs in coordinating plans for their transition from high school into postsecondary education, employment, and independent living.

Bettina L. Love is Assistant Professor in the Department of Elementary and Social Studies at the University of Georgia. Her research focuses on the ways in which urban youth negotiate hip-hop music and culture to form social, cultural, and political identities. A continuing thread of her scholarship involves exploring new ways of thinking about urban education and culturally relevant pedagogical approaches for urban learners. Her work has appeared in numerous books and journals. She is the author of *Hip Hop's Li'l Sistas Speak: Negotiating Hip Hop Identities and Politics in the New South.*

Angela Cartwright Lynskey Angela Cartwright Lynskey is an Assistant Professor in the West College of Education at Midwestern State University. While completing her graduate studies, she enjoyed a ten-year career as an Ohio public high school teacher. Her research interests include multicultural and equity issues in education, the intersection of religion and politics in education, spirituality in education, and teacher education.

Samara D. Madrid is Assistant Professor in the Department of Elementary and Early Childhood Education at the University of Wyoming. Her research examines the social and cultural aspects of teacher and child emotion within the school and peer cultures of classrooms. She is coeditor of the 2011 Hampton Press volume *From Toddlers to Teachers: Learning to See and Understand the School and Peer Cultures of Classrooms*. She also has a forthcoming coedited volume with Routledge titled *Reframing the Emotional Worlds of Early Childhood Classrooms.*

Carmen L. Medina is Associate Professor in the Literacy, Culture and Language Education Department at Indiana University. Her research and teaching focuses on literacy as social and critical practices, critical performance/drama pedagogies, biliteracy education, and Latino/a children's literature. Recently she has been working on a research project examining Puerto Rican children engagement and interpretive practices at the intersections of global/local landscapes and networks. She has a book in press (with colleague Karen Wohlwend) titled *Literacy, Play and Globalization: Converging Imaginaries in Children's Critical and Cultural Performances* for the Routledge Research Series.

Ashley N. Patterson is a doctoral student in the Multicultural and Equity Studies in Education Program in the School of Teaching and Learning at The Ohio State University. She examines racial identities through an intersectional lens to understand how those identities show up in and influence academic settings. She will continue to study biraciality and the interactions between popular culture and identity development as she continues to develop as a researcher.

Erica Womack is a recent Doctor of Philosophy graduate from The Ohio State University. Her current research explores the ways in which Black female adolescents conceive of self and society and how particular reading, writing, and speaking acts help to shape their conceptions. Her other research interests include African American language and literacies, Black/endarkened/womanist feminisms, critical pedagogy, culturally relevant pedagogy, and urban education.

Deborah Justice Zurmehly is a doctoral candidate at The Ohio State University in the School of Teaching and Learning. She is also faculty in Early Childhood Development and Education at Columbus State Community College. In her advocacy work for young children and families, she has served on the Board of Directors of the Ohio Association for the Education of Young Children and currently serves as president of the organization. Her research interests include spirituality in teaching and learning, and diversity and equity studies in teacher education.

Studies in the Postmodern Theory of Education

General Editor
Shirley R. Steinberg

Counterpoints publishes the most compelling and imaginative books being written in education today. Grounded on the theoretical advances in criticalism, feminism, and postmodernism in the last two decades of the twentieth century, Counterpoints engages the meaning of these innovations in various forms of educational expression. Committed to the proposition that theoretical literature should be accessible to a variety of audiences, the series insists that its authors avoid esoteric and jargonistic languages that transform educational scholarship into an elite discourse for the initiated. Scholarly work matters only to the degree it affects consciousness and practice at multiple sites. Counterpoints' editorial policy is based on these principles and the ability of scholars to break new ground, to open new conversations, to go where educators have never gone before.

For additional information about this series or for the submission of manuscripts, please contact:

Shirley R. Steinberg
c/o Peter Lang Publishing, Inc.
29 Broadway, 18th floor
New York, New York 10006

To order other books in this series, please contact our Customer Service Department:

(800) 770-LANG (within the U.S.)
(212) 647-7706 (outside the U.S.)
(212) 647-7707 FAX

Or browse online by series:
www.peterlang.com